Moving Beyond Capitalism

The book speaks to the widespread quest for concrete alternative ways forward 'beyond capitalism' in the face of the prevailing corporatocracy and a capitalist system in crisis. It examines a number of institutions and practices now being built in the nooks and crannies of present societies and that point beyond capitalism toward a more equal, participatory, and democratic society – institutions such as cooperatives, public banks, the commons, economic democracy. This seminal collection of critical essays draws on academic and activist voices from the U.S. and Canada, Mexico, Cuba, and Argentina, and from a variety of theoretical-political perspectives – Marxism, anarchism, feminism, and Zapatismo.

Cliff DuRand is a lifelong political activist and retired Philosophy professor. He is a founder of the Radical Philosophy Association in the U.S. and of the Center for Global Justice in Mexico.

'Intelligent, diverse and provocative, *Moving Beyond Capitalism* analyses the fascinating landscape of the evolving institutions of economic democracy in the context of global capitalism's crisis. DuRand and his collaborators will inspire readers with their vision and inform them with their sober evaluation of the task ahead. This is a much-needed book for those who want to build a better future.'

Jeff Faux, founder and distinguished fellow of the
Economic Policy Institute, USA

'This book is the perfect vehicle for launching Routledge's new Critical Development Studies series. It entails a range of theoretical and analytical probes into a system in crisis, and provides readers with an illuminating set of reflections on the way forward – how to move towards a more just society, a world beyond capitalism. A must read for any and all of us concerned about the current course of world capitalism which is pushing the world deeper and deeper into crisis. A world system in which wealth and power is concentrated in the hands and banks of an exceedingly small group of superbillionaires, less than a tenth of 1 percent of the population, cannot last. But the question is how to bring down this system before it brings everyone and the entire planet down.

This book explores this important issue and provides some compelling answers.'

Henry Veltmeyer, co-editor of the Routledge Critical Development
Studies series and Professor of Sociology and International
Development Studies at Saint Mary's University, Canada

'Drawing on the experiences of cooperatives worldwide and the progressive initiatives of the people of Chiapas, Cuba and Venezuela, this volume is a major contribution to the theory and practice of twenty-first century socialism in the struggle to build a new society out of the ashes of the old.'

Harry Targ, Department of Political Science, Purdue University, USA

Routledge Critical Development Studies

Series Editors

Henry Veltmeyer is co-chair of the Critical Development Studies (CDS) network, Research Professor at Universidad Autónoma de Zacatecas, Mexico, and Professor Emeritus at Saint Mary's University, Canada.

Paul Bowles is Professor of Economics and International Studies at UNBC, Canada.

Elisa van Wayenberge is Lecturer in Economics at SOAS University of London, UK.

The global crisis, coming at the end of three decades of uneven capitalist development and neoliberal globalization that have devastated the economies and societies of people across the world, especially in the developing societies of the global south, cries out for a more critical, proactive approach to the study of international development. The challenge of creating and disseminating such an approach, to provide the study of international development with a critical edge, is the project of a global network of activist development scholars concerned and engaged in using their research and writings to help effect transformative social change that might lead to a better world.

This series will provide a forum and outlet for the publication of books in the broad interdisciplinary field of critical development studies—to generate new knowledge that can be used to promote transformative change and alternative development.

The editors of the series welcome the submission of original manuscripts that focus on issues of concern to the growing worldwide community of activist scholars in this field.

To submit proposals, please contact the Development Studies Editor, Helena Hurd (Helena.Hurd@tandf.co.uk).

1. Moving Beyond Capitalism
Edited by Cliff DuRand

Moving Beyond Capitalism

Edited by Cliff DuRand

Routledge
Taylor & Francis Group

LONDON AND NEW YORK

First published 2016
by Routledge
2 Park Square, Milton Park, Abingdon, Oxon OX14 4RN

and by Routledge
711 Third Avenue, New York, NY 10017

Routledge is an imprint of the Taylor & Francis Group, an informa business

British Library Cataloguing in Publication Data
A catalogue record for this book is available from the British Library

Library of Congress Cataloguing in Publication Data
A catalog record for this book is available from the Library of Congress

ISBN: 9781472475947 (hbk)
ISBN: 9781138202948 (pbk)
ISBN: 9781315596167 (ebk)

Typeset in Times New Roman
by Out of House Publishing

Contents

Figures and table

Figures

Table

Contributors

Dario Azzellini is Assistant Professor at the Institute for Sociology at the Johannes Kepler University (Linz, Austria), writer and documentary director. His research and writing focuses on social transformation, movements, participative democracy, workers' control and co-management, privatization of military services, migration and racism, and extensive case studies in Latin America. He is Associate Editor for 'WorkingUSA' for *Cuadernos de Marte* (war sociology, University of Buenos Aires) and the web site workerscontrol.net. He has published several books, essays and documentaries about social movements, privatization of military services, migration and racism, workers' control, Italy, Mexico, Nicaragua, Colombia and Venezuela. Together with Oliver Ressler he is producing 'Occupy, Resist, Produce', a series of documentaries on recuperated factories under workers' control in Europe. And together with Marina Sitrin he is co-author of *They Can't Represent Us: Reinventing Democracy from Greece to Occupy* (2014). His latest book is *An Alternative Labour History: Worker Control and Workplace Democracy* (2015).

Ellen Brown is an attorney, founder of the Public Banking Institute and author of 12 books, including the best-selling *Web of Debt*. In *The Public Bank Solution*, her latest book, she explores successful public banking models historically and globally. Her 200+ blog articles are at EllenBrown.com.

George Caffentzis is a philosopher of money. He is also co-founder of the Midnight Notes Collective and the Committee for Academic Freedom in Africa. He has taught and lectured in colleges and universities throughout the world and his work has been translated into many languages. His books include: *Clipped Coins, Abused Words and Civil Government, Exciting the Industry of Mankind, No Blood for Oil!* (an e-book accessed at www.radicalpolytics.org) and *In Letters of Blood and Fire: Work, Machines and the Crisis of Capitalism*. His co-edited books include: *Midnight Oil: Work Energy War 1973–1992, Auroras of the Zapatistas: Local and Global Struggles in the Fourth World War* and *A Thousand Flowers: Social Struggles against Structural Adjustment in African Universities*.

Gregory Diamant has been involved in progressive politics since his early teens working and organizing in civil rights and anti-war campaigns, and on social and environmental justice issues and labour rights. He is a retired businessperson and has taught in NYC schools with disadvantaged children. For the past ten years he has also been lecturing in Mexico on subjects in European history and culture and social and environmental justice matters.

Cliff DuRand is a lifelong political activist and retired philosophy professor. In 1982 he founded the Progressive Action Center as a home for the left in Baltimore and was also a founder of the Radical Philosophy Association. Since 1990 DuRand has organized and led annual educational trips to Cuba, for which he was named Profesor Invitado at the Universidad de la Habana. In 2004 he helped found the Center for Global Justice in Mexico. He is co-author and co-editor of *Recreating Democracy in a Globalized State* (2013) and a popular public speaker and essayist. His articles have been published on Truthout.org, in *Z Magazine* and *Monthly Review* as well as at www.globaljusticecenter.org.

Gustavo Esteva is an independent writer and grassroots activist. He works with grassroots organizations and communities. He is an active voice within the de-professionalized segment of the intellectual community of the global South. He collaborates with Universidad de la Tierra in Oaxaca and the Centro de Encuentros y Diálogos Interculturales. He writes a column for *La Jornada* in Mexico, and occasionally in *The Guardian*. He is a prolific author, he has published more than 40 books and hundreds of essays and articles. He lives in a small Zapotec village in Oaxaca, in Southern Mexico.

Olga Fernández Ríos is a Researcher at the Instituto de Filosofia in Havana, Cuba and its Director from 1988 to 1999. She was Professor of Marxist Studies and Sociopolitical Theory at the Central University in Villaclara and at the University of Havana. She has held diplomatic postings, first in the Cuban Mission at the UN in New York and for the last ten years in the Cuban Interest Section in Washington, DC and in the Cuban Embassy in Chile, in both places in charge of Academic Exchanges. She is a member of the Cuban Academy of Sciences. Her research interests focus on the theory and practice of democracy, state and political systems. Her publications include: *Formación y desarrollo del estado socialista en Cuba* (1988) and *Dilemas sociopolíticos de la transición socialista en Cuba* (2016) and many articles on democracy, socialism and values in Cuba.

Margaret Flowers is co-director of It's Our Economy, an organizer of PopularResistance.org, co-hosts Clearing the FOG radio and is published regularly in *TruthOut*, *AlterNet*, *CounterPunch* and *Al Jazeera* (English). Flowers is a Maryland paediatrician. She serves as Secretary of Health in the Green Shadow Cabinet. Flowers views the struggle for health care as part of a broader social, economic and environmental justice movement.

Jerry Harris is National Secretary of the Global Studies Association of North America and a member of the International Executive Board of the Network for the Critical Study of Global Capitalism. He teaches at DeVry University in Chicago where he was Chair of the Faculty Association for ten years. He is currently Board Chair of the Hothouse, a cultural performance and advocacy organization. Harris' political activities have included anti-war organizing, and labour organizing in the oil refineries of southern California, tobacco industry in Kentucky and steel mills of Chicago. He has authored *The Dialectics of Globalization: Economic and Political Conflict in a Transnational World* and numerous articles on transnational capitalism and globalization in *Science & Society* (New York), *Race & Class* (London), *Das Argument* (Berlin) and *International Critical Thought* (Beijing).

Rebecca Hollender lived in Bolivia for six years, where she was the facilitator of the Working Group on Climate Change and Justice, a social collective consisting of 50 Bolivian NGOs who work on the topic of climate change from a perspective of ecological and ethical justice. She also represented Bolivia as a member of the official government delegation at the UN Framework Convention on Climate Change, 17th Conference of the Parties (COP 17), Durban, South Africa (November–December 2011) and UN Conference on Sustainable Development (Rio+20), Rio, Brazil (June 2012). She is currently a Doctoral Student at The New School for Public Engagement in Public and Urban Policy. Her research interest is alternatives to development.

Cynthia Kaufman is the Director of the Institute of Community and Civic Engagement at De Anza College where she also teaches philosophy. She is the author of two books on social change: *Getting Past Capitalism: History, Vision, Hope* (2012) and *Ideas for Action: Relevant Theory for Radical Change* (2003). She is a lifelong social change activist, having worked on issues such as tenants' rights, police abuse, union organizing, international politics and most recently climate change.

Len Krimerman taught for more than four decades on anarchism and democratizing democracy as Professor of Philosophy at the University of Connecticut, where he also helped create and coordinate degree-granting programmes in learner-centred education, community engagement and creative community building. He was a founder of the ICA, the first technical assistance organization for worker co-ops in the USA, and of the International Institute for Self-Management, a board member of the northeast USA's Cooperative Development Institute, and assists the development of consumer, artisan, food sovereignty and worker owned co-ops in eastern Connecticut. He co-founded *Changing Work* magazine, now known as GEO, Grassroots Economic Organizing, www.geo.coop. He is co-founder of the Windham Hour Exchange, a time bank with about 200 members, which has a mission to help start and support social and cooperative enterprises through the exchange of labour, and outside commercial markets.

Michael McCabe is Director, Logos Public Sphere Project, *Logos, A Critical Journal of Modern Society & Culture*. He previously served as co-chair of a statewide anti-austerity coalition that he founded in 2010 after serving as National Youth Co-Chair of the Democratic Socialists of America. He is Outreach Coordinator of The Left Forum, Outreach Coordinator of Fight Back USA and Founder and Co-Chair of The Take Back Trenton Coalition. McCabe is pursuing graduate study in Urban and Regional Planning at the Bloustein School, Rutgers University. He has authored *A Left in Crisis: An Appeal for Critical Self-Reflection in an Age of Economic and Ecological Crisis* (Forthcoming, *Logos Journal*, 2014) and co-authored with David Van Arsdale, et al. 'Manifesto for Economic Democracy and Ecological Sanity', in *Occupy the Economy: Challenging Capitalism* (2012).

Camila Piñeiro Harnecker is a Professor and Researcher in the Center for the Study of the Cuban Economy at the University of Havana. She is editor of *Cooperatives and Socialism: A View from Cuba* (2012) and author of *Rethinking Cuban Socialism: Proposals for a Democratic and Cooperative Economy* (2013). She has been a consultant to the Union of Local Industry (UNIL), a group of state enterprises in Havana, the Office of the Havana City Historian and the Ministry of Light Industry. She is a member of the editorial board of *Otra economía* (RILESS) and *Observatorio iberoamericano del desarrollo local y la economía social* (OIDLES) and *WorkingUSA*.

Andrés Ruggeri is a social anthropologist at the University of Buenos Aires and is the director of the Programa Facultad Abierta that is dedicated to researching, supporting and advising worker-recuperated enterprises. He is author or co-author of various books on recuperated enterprises and has lectured on the subject in countries throughout Latin America, Europe and Asia. He has authored *¿Qué son las empresas recuperadas?: autogestión de la clase trabajadora* (2014), translated into Italian, Greek and French. He is also the author of *Del Plata a La Habana*. He helped create the Documentation Center for recuperated enterprises that operates inside the Chilavert Printers Cooperative. He coordinates the International Gathering of the 'The Workers' Economy', held twice in Argentina, once in Mexico, and again in Brazil, along with a European gathering in France.

David Schweickart is the author of *After Capitalism* (2011), *Against Capitalism* (1996) and *Market Socialism: The Debate among Socialists* (1998). His works have been translated into Chinese, Spanish, French, Slovak, Catalan and Farsi. He has delivered lectures in Cuba, Spain, Italy and El Salvador among other countries. He has PhDs in both mathematics and philosophy. He is professor of philosophy at Loyola University in Chicago, where he was named faculty member of the year in 1999.

Marcelo Vieta is Professor in Workplace and Organizational Learning for Social Change at the University of Toronto, Program in Adult Education and Community Development and the Centre for Learning, Social Economy and Work (CLSEW), Ontario Institute for Studies in Education. Forthcoming book: *There's No Stopping the Workers: Crisis, Autogestión, and Argentina's Worker-Recuperated Enterprises* (2015).

Kevin Zeese, JD co-directs Its Our Economy where he advocates for economic democracy, and is an organizer of PopularResistance.org. He co-hosts Clearing the FOG radio, is co-founder of Come Home America which brings people from across the political spectrum together to work against war and militarism, and serves on the steering committees of the Private Manning Support Network. Zeese was an organizer of the Occupation of Freedom Plaza in Washington, DC. He serves as president of Common Sense for Drug Policy and is a co-founder of the Drug Policy Foundation, now known as Drug Policy Alliance. Zeese serves as Attorney General in the Green Shadow Cabinet and has worked to improve election integrity in the United States.

Foreword

This book, like all books, is a product of its time, overdetermined by the myriad influences shaping its authors and their projects. Unlike most books, this one is self-consciously and assertively critical. Its premise is that the economic systems dominating the last century – chiefly private capitalism and secondarily what it calls 'state socialism' – failed. The latter system's multiple implosions in the 1980s revealed deep, cumulative discontent with many aspects of actually existing socialism and the received socialist tradition. The discontent boiled over into system dissolution. It also stimulated important new departures in that tradition's thought and strategies for social change. The global capitalist crisis since 2008 has likewise provoked and revealed rising discontent with that system while also revitalizing traditions critical of capitalism. Once again huge new audiences with little or no direct connection to anti-capitalism's past are discovering and engaging with those critical traditions (including socialism).

This book responds to the crises of both state socialism and private capitalism and develops further the critical responses to them. The book's authors explore alternative ways now being pursued to build different, better systems than either private capitalism or state socialism. The authors' central concerns and goals are designated by words like community, collectivity, communism, cooperative and the commons. They want to move away from what hampers or undermines community, especially (but not only) in the economic dimensions of social life. Thus capitalism's conflict-ridden, exploitative structure is the problem for which they propose a variety of communitarian solutions or steps forward. Similarly, state socialism's paternalistic government is the problem for which cooperative, micro-level enterprises and residential groupings hold important solutions.

Beyond the many interesting, different specifics of the collected articles, their unifying theme is the centrality finally of taking democracy and solidarity seriously as fundamental social foundations. Capitalism, they show, never could do that and it eluded state socialism as well. So the task is to find and explore the possibilities in contemporary social spaces (particular institutions, historical moments, etc.) for genuine social movements beyond private capitalism and state socialism. In this task of critical imagination as well as in its social analyses, *Moving Beyond Capitalism* provides important contributions.

Readers can work with and from the articles in this book to pose and answer important analytical as well as strategic questions fast becoming urgent. Community versus individual can apply, in economics, to property owner-ship, enterprise management, enterprise direction (e.g. corporate boards of directors), task responsibility and so on. Are *all* such dimensions of new and better economic systems to be communal versus individual, or are only some dimensions to be transformed, and then which ones? Will the community of owners, for example, be identical to the communities, respectively, of directors and managers, and if not, how will such different work-defined communities collaborate? How are we to organize the interactions and interdependencies between, on the one hand, democratically organized workplaces/enterprises and, on the other hand, residential communities? Since households are usu-ally sites of production, how are their production systems to be democratized and integrated within a larger system of democratized enterprises and resi-dential communities?

Marx's ghost looms over all efforts to criticize and move beyond capitalism. That is the legacy of Marxism's remarkable rise and spread to become the pre-eminent tradition, since the 1870s, of both theoretical critiques and practical struggles to move beyond capitalism. That spread generated a multiplicity of tendencies, theories, perspectives within the tradition. For many interpreters, Marx's *Capital* presents a capitalism riven by the core conflicts between and among employees and employers. It shows that there is always more than the war between surplus producers and the employers who take that surplus (partly as 'their' profits). Thus, workers who produce surplus have complex differences from and struggles with, as well as affinities to, those workers who do not. Likewise, those capitalists who appropriate surplus from workers collaborate *and* conflict with those capitalists who don't. Multiple classes in complex struggles over the production and distribution of surpluses is Marx's 'tableau economique' in *Capital*; those complex class struggles frame his criti-cal social analyses. To move beyond capitalism requires engaging the Marxian tradition (including critically) as many of this book's chapters do.

Other traditions of social criticism are at play in the book's chapters as well (strands of anarchism, radical democracy, feminism, environmentalism, among others). The book's scope, goals and achievements draw on a rich background of others' efforts to think and move beyond the limits of the last century's economic systems.

Let me conclude by commending the book's focus (not exclusive) on economics. Critical social movements since 1945, especially in the US but beyond as well, have often shied away from direct confrontation with the capitalist economic system. Many thought that was strategically necessary given Cold War conditions. One could embrace anti-racism, feminism, environmentalism, civil rights for gays and immigrants, and so on but was very often advised to steer clear of attacking capitalism. That would split the social movement, dilute its message, invite popular aversion, draw down government persecution and so on. The relatively few who nonetheless did criticize capitalism frequently found themselves immediately and simplistically equated with (and denounced for) advocating the actually existing state socialism. From there it was a short step to having such critics' loyalty questioned.

Not surprisingly, then, over time critical approaches to capitalist economies and the mainstream ('neoclassical' was its academic name) economics that celebrated capitalism faded from its citizens' consciousness. Politicians, mass media, business leaders and academics functioned increasingly as if debate over capitalism between its celebrants and the critics was finished, over, no longer pertinent to modern life. The idea that modern society could and should do better than capitalism simply stopped occurring in most public discussions in capitalist countries. What criticism of capitalism survived morphed into criticism of *one kind* of capitalism (private) and its economics (the neoclassical mainstream) from the standpoint of advocates of *another kind* of capitalism (limitedly state-interventionist) and their economics (Keynesian economics). 'The' debate in economics became focused substantively, whatever its language, on more versus less state intervention rather than capitalism versus any fundamentally alternative system. Social movements increasingly avoided dealing with economics or, when they did, tended to do so within the narrow limits of the debates over government intervention.

Almost no-one debated, for example, the virtues and flaws of capitalism's top-down, hierarchical, corporate structure (major shareholders selecting boards of directors, etc.) in comparison to democratically organized workers' self-directed enterprises. Despite the long existence of worker cooperatives of varying sorts and an accumulated literature on them, theoretical as well as empirical, and despite the remarkable contemporary success story of the Mondragon Cooperative Corporation based in Spain, economic debates almost totally ignored the specifics and implications of such non-capitalist enterprise organizations.

The Occupy Wall Street movement of 2011/12 broke with most of the social movements since 1945 in the US when it (very successfully) foregrounded economic issues with its special emphasis on inequality (the 1 per cent against the 99 per cent). From its beginnings, Occupy explicitly confronted capitalism per se as the problem. Building on those beginnings, this book similarly foregrounds capitalism – and pointedly *not* in terms of more versus less state interventions. That economic system – understood in terms of its particular organization of production and distribution of goods and services – is the problem that must be thought and moved beyond as a central struggle of this historical moment.

Richard D. Wolff

Acknowledgements

This volume grew out of a week-long conference in the summer of 2014 in San Miguel de Allende, Mexico. It brought together nearly 200 activists and scholars under the auspices of the Center for Global Justice. Many of the thought-provoking presentations are now in this book. I want to thank members of the Editorial Review Committee for their careful evaluations of the papers proposed for publication: Bob Stone, Margaret McLaren, Olga Fernández, Elisa Servin and especially Cynthia Kaufman. They helped shape what went into this book. I am responsible for what was left out. Indeed, there were many fine papers that there just wasn't room for. Many of them can be found in the Moving Beyond Capitalism conference archives at www.globaljusticecenter.org.

The conference marked the tenth anniversary of the Center for Global Justice, a research and learning centre founded by myself and two additional academics: Bob Stone and Betsy Bowman. The Moving Beyond Capitalism conference was made possible by the tireless labour of a team of dedicated volunteers. Among them were Susan Goldman, Jim Carey, Olivia Canales, Gregory Diamant, Peter Weisberg, Chris Kellogg, Liz Mestres and many others. They helped lay the foundation for this book.

We also owe thanks to Lydia Carey for her fine translations from Spanish of several of the chapters and to Mark Rushton for his careful work preparing the manuscript for publication. Special thanks goes to Henry Veltmeyer for his editorial skill shepherding this book through to press and making it the inaugural volume in the Critical Development Studies series. But above all else we must acknowledge the contributions of all those who struggle for a just world. They inspire us all to build a better world beyond capitalism.

¡Venceremos!
Cliff DuRand

Abbreviations

A2D	Alternatives to Development
ALBA	Bolivarian Alliance for the Peoples of Our America (Alianza Bolivariana para los Pueblos de Nuestra América)
ANAP	Asociación Nacional de Agricultores Pequeños
ANEC	National Association of Cuba Economists
BANPAZ	Autonomous Zapatista People's Bank
BRICs	Brazil, Russia, India and China
CAP	Community Action Program
CEEC	Center for the Study of the Cuban Economy
CELAC	Community of Latin American and Caribbean States (Comunidad de Estados Latinoamericanos y Caribeños)
CEO	Chief Executive Officer
CIA	Central Intelligence Agency
CST	Socialist Workers Councils
CTC	Cuba Workers' Union (Central de Trabajadores de Cuba)
CWCF	Canadian Worker Co-operative Federation
DAWN	Democracy at Work Network
EPSC	Enterprises of Communal Social Property
EZLN	Zapatista Army of National Liberation (Ejército Zapatista de Liberación Nacional)
FDR	Franklin Delano Roosevelt
FEMA	Federal Emergency Management Agency
GDE	Grassroots Democratic Economy
GDP	Gross Domestic Product
GEO	Grassroots Economic Organizing
GHG	Greenhouse gas emissions
ICA	International Cooperative Alliance
IMF	International Monetary Fund
IPCC	Intergovernmental Panel on Climate Change
NAFTA	North American Free Trade Agreement
NGOs	Non-Governmental Organizations
ONEI	National Office of Statistics and Information
OWS	Occupy Wall Street
PACA	Philadelphia Cooperative Alliance
PCC	Cuban Communist Party (Partido Comunista de Cuba)

PD	Post-development
PRI	Institutional Revolutionary Party
PSUV	United Socialist Party of Venezuela
RIPESS	Intercontinental Network for the Promotion of Social Solidarity Economy
SGEP	Southern Grassroots Economies Project
TCPs	Self-employed Workers (Trabajador por Cuenta Propia)
TPP	Trans-Pacific Partnership
TTIP	Trans-Atlantic Trade and Investment Partnership
UBPCs	Basic Units of Cooperative Production
UK	United Kingdom
UN	United Nations
UNASUR	Union of South American Nations (Unión de Naciones Suramericanas)
US / USA	United States
USAID	United States Agency for International Development
USDA	United States Department of Agriculture
USFWC	US Federation of Worker Cooperatives
USSR	Union of Soviet Socialist Republics
USW	United Steelworkers
WORCs	Worker-Owned Rockaway Cooperatives
WTO	World Trade Organization

Introduction

Cliff DuRand

We live in one of those pivotal moments of history: poised between a social order in crisis and a new world yearning to be born. The crisis is both economic and political. The economic system we know as capitalism is in a serious crisis that has become evident since the financial collapse of 2008 and is still unresolved. And the political system that we call democracy is likewise in crisis, dysfunctional and unable to steer us through troubled waters.

As a result of this impasse – an economic system causing deep pain for so many but great wealth for a few and a political system unable to address those felt needs – there is a widespread sense of powerlessness and helplessness among our people. The problems are so large, and the changes that are needed are so deep, that we feel unable to fix them. Our nation's institutions are failing us and despair grows among the people.

But, at the same time that there is hopelessness on the national scene, on a local level there is much to give us hope. People are building alternative institutions to meet some of their needs in the communities where they live. People are building financial institutions that are democratically accountable and more fiscally responsible than the Wall Street banks. People are creating worker-owned cooperatives that give them job security rather than having to work at low wages for a big corporation. Community gardens and farmers markets bring local growers and consumers together for healthy food and conviviality, independent of the corporate dominated food system that is making us obese and ill. In many ways, in the nooks and crannies of the failing existing system, people are finding little free spaces to create alternative institutions and nurture different practices that point in a new direction, that operate by a different logic, that embody different social relations from the capitalism of the larger society. They are moving beyond capitalism. Ordinary people are building the cells of a new society at the grassroots level. This is local democracy at work.

Capitalist crisis

The financial crisis of 2008 was a moment of truth that laid bare some of the realities of corporate capitalism. Its own internal contradictions led to the collapse of its financial sector, with grave consequences to the system as a whole. It took a strong, decisive intervention by the state to save capitalism from itself. US Treasury Department Secretary Hank Paulson went to Congress with a three-page plan to bail out the bankrupt Wall Street banks by infusing the financial system with trillions of taxpayer dollars (more was to come later). A *Los Angeles Times/Bloomberg* poll in September 2008 found that 31 per cent favoured using taxpayer money to bail out the banks; 55 per cent opposed it (McManus 2008). The public reaction was swift. Congressional offices were swamped with the demand from constituents: Vote NO! 'The banks caused the problem, let them pay the price'. And for once, the people's elected representatives listened to the people and voted against the bailout. But the political elite, tied so closely to Wall Street firms, did not accept 'no' as an answer. Paulson, Bernecke, et al., the politburo of the financial elite, went back to the Congressional leaders and said, 'Look, these banks are too big to fail. They could bring down the entire economy of the US and the global economy too'. They conferred with Congressional leaders and showed them how the entire economy would collapse if the banks were not saved. And so Congress voted again on the Paulson plan and approved the bailout against the wishes of their constituents. We, the taxpayers, are still living with the consequences years later, as our grandchildren will as well.

What does this episode show us? It shows us that in so far as we are all dependent on (or believe we are dependent on) the health of financial capital, our representatives and the citizens themselves will protect their interests even at our own expense. The big banks and other large corporations rule politically because they rule economically. Wealth produces the political power of the wealthy over the dependent classes. That is the fundamental secret of corporate power. Their power rests on our dependency.

This is what Cynthia Kaufman (Chapter 13) calls the economic dependency trap of capitalism. We have all become so dependent on the corporate system of capitalism that we feel there is no alternative but to save it when it collapses. The popular will was to abandon it, but most people went along with the rescue of a system that had lost its legitimacy in their eyes. The banks are too big to fail and we were not able to envision an alternative to actually existing capitalism, odious though it be.

Declare independence from Wall Street

Our response to this dilemma should be to DECLARE INDEPENDENCE FROM WALL STREET. What I mean by this is not just to issue a proclamation, but to begin to actually detach our lives from the corporate institutions by building alternatives in our local communities. We need to build resilient institutions where we live, institutions like public banks, local currencies, community-based agriculture, consumer cooperatives, participatory budgeting, worker-owned cooperatives, alternative media and more. In fact, these institutions are already being built in many communities across the country. Building this new economy is the challenge before us. Then the next time the system collapses (and it will) we will be able to see a way to survive without it.

Public banks are a case in point. There was one state that was little affected by the banking crisis of 2008. That was North Dakota. It fared well largely because it has the country's only public bank. Established in 1919, the Bank of North Dakota is held by the state government, which deposits all of the tax revenues in it. Those funds are then used to make loans for agriculture, students, small businesses, etc., partnering with local banks around the state, functioning as a central bank for the state. Unlike most state and local governments elsewhere, North Dakota does not send its revenue to Wall Street by depositing it in the Bank of America or CitiCorp. As a result North Dakota had the lowest rate of mortgage defaults, the lowest unemployment rate, and it has a healthy state budget since the profits from bank loans go back into the state treasury – all because it declared independence from Wall Street long ago.

How can such a semi-socialist institution exist in a politically conservative state like North Dakota? Answer: the state bank has a proven record of benefiting the people of the state. When public institutions meet the concrete needs of people in their daily lives, ideological labels lose their importance.

There is an important lesson in this for all of us who seek a better world.

Some 20 states are now considering establishing public banks on the North Dakota example. Municipal governments and large hospitals and universities can also create their own public banks. There is something of a social movement growing with groups across the country proposing public banks in their localities. Ellen Brown's (Chapter 1) Public Banking Institute provides organizing and technical assistance. These local, democratically controlled financial institutions can augment public monies in financing infrastructure projects by not having to pay interest on bonds. They can finance local development efforts and loan startup capital to local businesses such as cooperatives. By keeping banking close to home, public banks can strengthen communities, rather than distant corporations. And if they are run democratically for the common good, they can bring communities together across class, race and ideological lines. In fact, in 2014 the public Bank of North Dakota outperformed the Wall Street banks (Brown 2014).

Own your own job

Worker-owned, self-managed cooperatives are another institution that can strengthen communities and offer working people a measure of independence from the corporate world. Co-ops bridge the divide between employees and employers since their members are both workers and owners. And since they are democratically run, co-ops can operate without a managerial/supervisory stratum. The members supervise one another. They share a common interest that makes a co-op a more agreeable place to work and the collective work more productive. And unlike a capitalist business, more of the wealth generated circulates in the local community and the business itself will not relocate elsewhere in search of lower-wage workers.

Beyond these benefits, cooperatives nurture a democratic personality. One's daily worklife is based on cooperative social relations and an ethic of solidarity. Participation in collective decision-making promotes a sense of shared responsibility. Individual interest is linked to a collective interest. I prosper only if we prosper. Daily worklife re-educates members away from individualism into a broader self-identity based on awareness of interconnectedness with others. It thus develops one's social being; it engenders a new human being and prepares the way toward a new society beyond capitalism.

But, you might object, to move beyond capitalism we need to confront it directly, not just hide from it in the nooks and crannies of society. Public banks and cooperatives will not overthrow capitalism. At best they only provide a limited escape from it. I agree. If we were to succeed in building an alternative strong enough to threaten capital, they will find us and seek to stamp out our institutions. But by then we will have awakened in people's consciousness, an awareness that there is a better way, that a different world is possible. And now we will respond with the power of a popular front struggling to defend the alternatives we have come to know and value. Or it might not even come to that if the crisis of capitalism leads to its collapse. In that case, we will be there with our alternative already in place, firm in the knowledge that we don't need Wall Street any longer.

How does the ruling class rule?

This brings me to a fundamental question. How does a ruling class rule? I'm not just talking about the governing elite. I'm talking about those great concentrations of wealth in the big corporations and banks, like General Motors and Goldman Sachs. It's not just a matter of buying influence with political decision makers. Wall Street has long occupied Washington, long before its agents infiltrated the administration and its lobbyists occupied Congress and its money flooded political campaigns.

Fundamentally, the ruling class rules because the interests of the ruling class rule over the society as a whole. It's because the interests of the subject classes are dependent on them. They rule because we are all dependent on them, workers and consumers alike. The system works only if their interests are served. When there is a crisis, as in 2007–2008, they must be rescued lest the whole system collapses. It is because we are all dependent on them that they have the power to hold the rest of society, the 99 per cent, hostage. That's what it means to be a ruling class. We are ruled by their interests.

Thus the solution to the political dominance by 'big moneyed interests' does not lie in campaign finance reform, although that would certainly be a step forward. But even if there were complete public financing of elections, the responsibility of the governing class is to maintain the social order. And in a class-divided society that means protecting the interests of the ruling class upon which we all depend, thereby maintaining that division.

In times of high political mobilization of the dominated classes, governability may require making concessions to those popular classes even though that may limit the benefits to the ruling class. That is the price they have to pay in order to have an effective political instrument that maintains that class division. But as the popular classes demobilize, the state reverts to its default position.

What then is the solution? The beginning lies in step-by-step overcoming that dependence on the ruling class. As I have argued, that can be done even in a class-divided society by building alternative institutions that empower people in their lives. That is most easily done at the local level with public banks, cooperatives, communal councils, participatory budgeting, local currencies, eminent domain, etc.

The US has a tradition of local governance in a federal system. While the powers of local and state governments are limited, they have not been fully utilized. They have the potential to carve out spheres of empowerment that are less closely tied to the interests of the ruling class. With them we can begin to declare our independence from Wall Street.

In so doing we also are developing schools of democracy, educating people in the virtues and skills of citizenship. This was Jefferson's vision: the little republics would ensure the health of the larger republic.

This strategy of localization does not directly confront the ruling class. It does not storm the barricades. But given correct leadership it can be transformative. It begins by just quietly planting the seeds of a new order in the little free spaces remaining in society. But it is not a reformist strategy that simply makes the present system a little more tolerable. Because among the seeds planted is the vision of an alternative, more democratic society, a participatory democracy. And at some point that may become too threatening a vision for the ruling class and they will have to strike back. Yes, the time will come when we will have to take to the barricades. But then the people will respond to the call to defend their institutions. So it can lead to a systemic change.

That in sum is my long-term strategy for moving beyond capitalism even when we do not have state power and there is no immediately foreseeable prospect of revolutionary insurrection.

Twenty-first-century socialism

Let me now shift our attention from the US to those countries in the global South where popular forces do hold state power. I refer to Venezuela and Cuba and those liberated areas in the Mexican state of Chiapas held by the Zapatistas. Here we will see many of the same principles in operation although under very different circumstances.

Twenty-first-century socialism is usually associated with the Bolivarian Revolution in Venezuela. There, the state led by Hugo Chávez and supported by the popular classes has been fashioning an alternative to the failed state socialism that prevailed elsewhere in the twentieth century. Socialism is a transition toward a more equal society without exploitation guided by a participatory democratic solidarity. The construction of institutions to realize this vision is the historical challenge of our epoch. In the socialist projects that prevailed in the twentieth century, state power was used to construct economic institutions that were to operate according to an overall plan designed to develop forces of production and meet the material needs of the population. While this state socialism had some impressive successes, we now know that neither was it able to sustain itself nor did it lead toward the kind of society envisioned.

The Bolivarian Revolution seeks to reinvent a socialism truer to the original vision. This is a model in which the state – rather than acting for society in a paternalistic way – plays a facilitating role to develop the capacities of civil society to direct the common affairs of the people. In Venezuela, the state provides resources at local levels to facilitate cooperatives and communal councils. It is planting the seeds of an alternative economy and an alternative government alongside capitalist society. In effect, the state is creating a situation of dual power. Following the principle of subsidiarity, it empowers ordinary people collectively in their daily lives. In so doing it is nurturing the seeds of a non-capitalist society within what is still a capitalist one. But equally important, it is developing non-capitalist sensibilities within civil society. These are crucial for energizing a democratic movement beyond capitalism.

In Cuba we see a similar effort to build a twenty-first-century socialism, only not within a capitalist society but within existing state socialism. The renovation of Cuba's socialism that has been under way for the last few years and is projected to take 15 years, seeks to transform a state-directed society into one in which other social entities play a more participatory role. This involves a devolving of state powers to lower levels of government and a strengthening and diversification of civil society in a different relation to the state than previously. Significant areas of economic activity are being turned over to small private businesses and cooperatives that operate in market relations with each other, the public and the state.

The development of new urban cooperatives is especially important in this. In the last year, their members have established hundreds of co-ops in urban services that are independent and self-governing. In a large measure their success or failure will depend on the existing political culture and its transformation. A half-century of the Revolution has engendered an ethic of solidarity common among the Cuban people. They are not afflicted by the atomistic individualism common in the US. There is a high level of social consciousness. There is also a long-established habit of participation in public affairs. However, under state socialism this tended to be a passive participation that accepted the directions that came from above. A paternalistic state provided for the well-being of its subjects who in turn gave it their loyalty. There were ample opportunities for participation, but little for initiative. That is the feature of the political culture that will have to change if a socialist civil society is to emerge from the reforms now under way.

Cooperatives provide the space for both initiative and participation in promoting a common good. They hold promise of nurturing the New Man, the New Human Being, that Che Guevara called for in socialism. If values of cooperation, solidarity and democratic participation can be built into the daily lives of Cubans, that can make socialism irreversible because it comes not from the state but from the character of the people themselves.

Here, as in the Bolivarian Revolution, a revolutionary state is supporting the building of a *cooperative civil society*. The *buen gobierno* in Zapatista territory is also building cooperative alternatives to nurture the human development of men and women. As Gustavo Esteva so eloquently points out in Chapter 16, it is understood that it is in civil society that real social change has to be rooted if we are to see an alternative to hierarchical domination, whether it be from a paternalistic state or private corporations. It is this understanding of the central importance of a vibrant civil society, or constituent power, that links the New Economy movement in the North with twenty-first-century socialism in the South.

Conclusion for the US left

As we have seen in the US, local efforts to build a degree of independence from corporate capitalism point toward a society that is more participatory, more cooperative and more democratic. This is the same direction that twenty-first-century socialism points in the global South. In both cases, institutions that move beyond capitalism point toward a kind of socialism, that is, a society in which associated producers are empowered to democratically found anew a society that is more equal and in which all may flourish.

Whether this is called socialist, it is an alternative that is more humane and nurturing of our human capacities. As capitalism collapses around us we will invent that new future. Indeed, we must in order to survive.

Philosopher Slavoj Žižek has written recently of

> the recurrent story of the contemporary left. A leader or party is elected with universal enthusiasm, promising a 'new world' – but, then, sooner or later, they stumble upon the key dilemma: does one dare to touch the capitalist mechanisms, or does one decide to 'play the game'? If one disturbs these mechanisms, one is very swiftly 'punished' by market perturbations, economic chaos, and the rest. [At the moment of triumph,] at this precise conjuncture, radical emancipatory politics faces its greatest challenge: how to push things further after the first enthusiastic stage is over.
>
> (Žižek 2015)

Žižek raises a crucial question here. What do we do after we have toppled the old regime, after we have the levers of state power in our hands? I suggest the reason we face the dilemma of either encountering chaos or having to go along with the still dominant capitalist relations is because we have failed to build an alternative to them before coming to power. We failed to realize that the revolution had to begin long before this moment of triumph. If we had built alternative institutions in the nooks and crannies of capitalist society, then they could sustain us while serving as a platform from which we construct a new society while dismantling the old. If we had made the long march through the institutions of society, then we would be ready to found society anew once the old system collapses. That is what this book is about.

Part I

Economic democracy /
The social economy

1 Beyond capitalism to sustainability

The public bank solution

Ellen Brown

Thomas Picketty's paradigm-shattering 2013 book *Capital in the Twenty-First Century* pierced the capitalist mantra that greed is good. Left to its own devices, the 'free market' will not smooth out inequalities and preserve freedom, democracy and economic opportunity for all. Rather, wealth accumulates at the top, with the top one per cent of the population now having nearly 40 per cent of all US wealth, while the bottom 70 per cent is chained to a precarious existence living paycheque-to-paycheque, if they have paycheques at all. In *The Economics of Revolution*, David DeGraw (2014) writes:

> Having that much wealth consolidated within a mere 1% of the population, while a record number of people toil in poverty and debt, is a *crime against humanity*. For example, it would only cost 0.5% of the 1%'s wealth to *eliminate poverty nationwide*. Also consider that at least 40% of the 1%'s *accounted* for wealth is *sitting idle*. That's an astonishing $13 trillion in wealth hoarded away, *unused*.

Today, the economy has been destabilized to the point of imploding. Warnings are heard daily that the market, the dollar and the economy itself are about to crash. The *Titanic* is on the rocks, and where are the lifeboats? The burning questions today are what a more sustainable system might look like, and how we can transition to it without massive collateral damage.

Wall Street's ability to control both the creation and distribution of money and credit are key reasons why the finance industry has become so powerful – and why the rich are getting richer while so many are treading water or getting poorer. To create a sustainable economy where wealth is enjoyed broadly, not only by the 1 per cent, we must address and transform our system of money creation and distribution.

The benefits of bank credit can be maintained while eliminating these flaws, through a system of banks operated as public utilities, serving the public interest and returning their profits to the public. Examples from around the world and through history show that it works admirably well, providing the key to sustained high performance for the economy and well-being for the people.

What Wall Street doesn't want you to know is:

- it alone controls the creation and distribution of money and credit;
- this is the basis of Wall Street's stranglehold on our economy (and our government); and
- there is an alternative to this system, one that actually creates enduring prosperity for the many, rather than bubble cycles of wealth for the few.

The secret Wall Street would rather you not know is that publicly owned banks are a powerful and historically proven way to create long-term, broadly shared wealth and prosperity, in contrast to our current private banking system which is largely focused on speculation, short-term profit, and preys on – rather than serves – the real economy.

In his June 2015 encyclical 'Praised Be', Pope Francis added his moral voice to the widening call to rethink our banking system.

> Today, in view of the common good, there is urgent need for politics and economics to enter into a frank dialogue in the service of life, especially human life. Saving banks at any cost, making the public pay the price, forgoing a firm commitment to reviewing and reforming the entire system, only reaffirms the absolute power of a financial system, a power which has no future and will only give rise to new crises after a slow, costly and only apparent recovery. The financial crisis of 2007–2008 provided an opportunity to develop a new economy, more attentive to ethical principles, and new ways of regulating speculative financial practices and virtual wealth. But the response to the crisis did not include rethinking the outdated criteria which continue to rule the world.
> [...]
> A strategy for real change calls for rethinking processes in their entirety, for it is not enough to include a few superficial ecological considerations while failing to question the logic which underlies present-day culture.
>
> (Pope Francis 2015)

'Rethinking the outdated criteria which continue to rule the world' is a call to revolution, one that is necessary if the planet and its people are to survive and thrive. Beyond a change in our thinking, we need a strategy for eliminating the financial parasite that is keeping us trapped in a prison of scarcity and debt.

Interestingly, the model for that strategy may have been created by the Order of the Saint from whom the Pope took his name. Medieval Franciscan monks, defying their conservative rival orders, evolved an alternative public banking model to serve the poor at a time when they were being exploited with exorbitant interest rates.

The Franciscan alternative: banking for the people

To remedy the situation, Franciscan monks, defying the prohibitions of the Dominicans and Augustinians, formed charitable pawnshops called *montes pietatus* (pious or non-speculative collections of funds). These shops lent at low or no interest on the security of valuables left with the institution.

They did not seek to make a profit on their loans. But they faced bitter opposition, not only from their banking competitors but *from other theologians*. It was not until 1515 that the *montes* were officially declared to be meritorious.

After that, they spread rapidly in Italy and other European countries. They soon evolved into banks, which were public in nature and served public and charitable purposes. This public bank tradition became the modern European tradition of public, cooperative and savings banks. It is *particularly strong today* in the municipal banks of Germany called *Sparkassen*.

The public banking concept at the heart of the *Sparkassen* was explored in the eighteenth century by the Irish philosopher Bishop George Berkeley, in a treatise called *The Plan of a National Bank*. Berkeley visited America and his work was studied by Benjamin Franklin, who popularized the public banking model in colonial Pennsylvania. In the US today, the model is exemplified in the state-owned Bank of North Dakota.

Our evolving monetary scheme

Fortunately, changing the rules of the game need not mean the end of life as we know it. Governments routinely change the rules when all else fails. In fact, the rules have changed every 20 or 30 years for the last three centuries. Here is an outline of the trial-and-error evolution of the US monetary scheme, dating back to the seventeenth century:

- In the late 1600s, money consisted of precious metal coins, along with paper promissory notes redeemable in coins. The London goldsmith-bankers expanded the money supply when they started issuing more of these banknotes than they had gold, called 'fractional reserve' lending.
- In 1691, the American colonies broke away from the precious metal system and began issuing their own paper scrip as an advance against future tax revenues. The colonies flourished as a result; but it was easier to issue the scrip than to collect it back in taxes, and some colonies wound up overprinting and devaluing their currencies.
- In the early 1700s, the colony of Pennsylvania refined this new system by forming its own bank, which made loans of publicly issued money collateralized by land. This paper money returned to the government on repayment, eliminating the inflationary component and making the system sustainable. Interest on the loans funded the government without taxes, price inflation or government debt.
- In 1751, King George II banned the issue of paper scrip in the New England colonies; and in 1764, King George III banned it in all the

colonies. When Benjamin Franklin went to England to try to dissuade Parliament, he made the tactical mistake of expounding on how the scrip allowed the colonies to flourish without debt – including debt to the Bank of England – which came out strongly against lifting the ban.

- Cutting the colonies off from their source of financial liquidity precipitated a depression and a revolution; and in 1791, the First US Bank was established. Although it wound up being privately owned, it was chartered by Congress to perform several central bank functions, including the issuance of paper banknotes supposedly backed by gold. Many more notes were issued than there was gold to back them, expanding the money supply on the 'fractional reserve' system.

- The First US Bank was followed by the Second US Bank, which was shut down by Andrew Jackson in 1836. From then until the Civil War, the country went through a period of 'free banking'. There was no national currency, and private banks had the power to issue money in the form of their own banknotes. Again, these notes were supposedly backed by gold; but far more notes were issued than there was gold, expanding the money supply. The system was unstable and was plagued by bank runs.

- In 1863, President Lincoln revived the colonial system by issuing unbacked US Notes or Greenbacks to help fund the Civil War.

- In 1863 and 1864, the National Banking Act establishing the national banking system and created a single national currency. Federally chartered national banks could issue this currency as banknotes bearing their own names. State and local banknotes were eliminated by taxation.

- Lincoln was subsequently assassinated; the Greenbacks were recalled; and in 1876, silver was demonetized (no longer accepted as legal tender), shrinking the money supply and plummeting the country into depression.

- In the latter half of the nineteenth century, the money supply was reflated through a new form of money called 'checkbook money'. Banks created money in the form of deposits entered on their books when they made loans.

- Following a particularly bad bank panic, the Federal Reserve was established in 1913 ostensibly to backstop bank runs. No longer were banks allowed to create money simply by issuing their own banknotes. They had to balance credits with debits and run their accounts through the Federal Reserve, which alone could issue the national currency.

- Despite this backstop, in 1929 the country suffered the worst bank run in history. Franklin Roosevelt responded by taking the dollar off the gold standard domestically in 1933. Among other banking reforms, the Glass-Steagall Act was passed, preventing bankers from speculating with their depositors' money.

- In 1944 the Bretton Woods system was agreed to internationally. Gold and US dollars redeemable in gold were made the international reserve currency.

- In 1971 Richard Nixon took the dollar off the gold standard internationally, after runs on US gold reserves caused the Treasury to run dangerously low.

- In 1974 Henry Kissinger made a secret deal with the OPEC countries to sell oil only in US dollars, effectively 'backing' the dollar with oil.
- In 1999 the Glass-Steagall Act was repealed; and in 2005, the Bankruptcy Reform Act gave derivatives 'super-priority' in bankruptcy. The result was the massive expansion of the 'near-monies' of the shadow banking system, including derivatives and repos.
- In 2008 the rules were changed again when the shadow banking system collapsed. The US government bailed out the banks, blatantly defying the capitalist model by socializing the banks' losses while privatizing their profits.
- In 2010, the Dodd-Frank Act effectively said 'no more government bail-outs'. Banks were to recapitalize themselves instead with 'bail ins' – confiscating the money of their creditors, including their depositors.

When in the course of human events ...

Confiscating customer deposits may keep the zombie banks alive, but one good Cyprus-style bail-in is liable to be enough to trigger a second US revolution. In *The Economics of Revolution*, David DeGraw (2014) quotes from the Declaration of Independence and names these grounds for breaking with the existing regime:

> An extensive analysis of economic conditions and government policy reveals that the need for significant systemic change is now a mathematical fact. Corruption, greed and economic inequality have reached a peak tipping point. Due to the consolidation of wealth, the majority of the population cannot generate enough income to keep up the cost of living. In the present economy, under current government policy, 70 percent of the population is now sentenced to an impoverished existence.

The question, then, is what should replace the current system? In America, the monetary system of Benjamin Franklin's Pennsylvania has been described as our most sustainable model. In 1938, Richard A. Lester, an economist at Princeton University, wrote: 'The price level during the 52 years prior to the American Revolution and while Pennsylvania was on a paper standard was more stable than the American price level has been during any succeeding fifty-year period' (Lester 1938).

In the private banking model, profits are largely re-invested in money-making-money schemes, where they continue growing exponentially in a way that dangerously unbalances the system. Public banks are financially sustainable because they return their profits to the government, which recycles them back to the economy to be spent on infrastructure and social services. Bank profits feed the economy rather than feeding off it.

The only contemporary example in the US of a state-owned depository bank is in North Dakota, which is also the only state to have escaped the credit crisis. Other countries having strong public banking systems that also escaped the credit crisis include the BRICs (Brazil, Russia, India and China), Germany and Korea (cf. *The Public Bank Solution*, Brown 2013).

Besides a network of public banks, promising monetary reforms that have been proposed include preventing currency wars with a new Bretton Woods-style international accord, devising private systems of exchange involving mutual credit clearing systems of some sort, and stimulating demand with a national dividend issued by the central bank directly to the people.

Nearly half the US state legislatures explored over the last four years the possibility of creating public banks to responsibly leverage state assets and establish public credit for sustainable economic development, just as the Bank of North Dakota has been doing for almost a century. Predictably, the big banks and other entrenched and powerful economic interests opposed these initiatives vehemently – and none of the initiatives made it into law.

Wall Street fought these initiatives so hard because publicly owned banks threaten their entire business model as public banks enable governments to:

- save up to 50 per cent of the lifetime cost of public works projects (for example, California could have saved $6 billion in long-term interest on its recently completed Bay Bridge, which cost $6 billion to build);
- save hundreds of billions on management fees for public funds (a study released earlier this year showed that the City of Los Angeles loses over $200 million per year on fees and other unnecessary expenses by banking with the big banks);
- create strategic, reasonable interest loans to key segments of the economy such as students, homeowners and small businesses;
- enjoy another key benefit of public banks: backstopping smaller banks, enabling them to take on larger deals, leading to a more diverse and vibrant financial sector not dominated by the biggest banks (North Dakota enjoys the most diverse banking sector per capita in the US).

To guarantee freedom, democracy and opportunity for all, we need more than just the right to vote and to compete in the market. We need to restore strongly progressive income taxes that rein in the overreaching power of the 1 per cent, and especially of the .001 per cent. We need to enforce anti-trust laws to rein in the mega-banks and mega-corporations. And we need an economic bill of rights that guarantees a secure standard of living for all. We can have all that without drowning the government in debt, with a twenty-first-century economic model that returns the power to create money and credit to the people.

2 Building a grassroots democratic economy

The rising tide of local self-reliance, workplace democracy and social justice

Len Krimerman

> We need to begin to actually detach our lives from the corporate institutions by building alternatives in our local communities. We need to build resilient institutions where we live, institutions like public banks, local currencies, community-based agriculture, consumer cooperatives, participatory budgeting, worker-owned cooperatives, alternative media and more.
>
> (Cliff DuRand, Introduction to this volume)

Detaching from capitalism is happening

The strategy of detaching from capitalism by building resilient local and democratically controlled enterprises is, at the least, a realistic one. In fact, considerable progress is already being made by it.

What I term a 'Grassroots Democratic Economy' (GDE) is taking shape here in the belly of the beast (and elsewhere, but I shall focus on the USA). There is evidence of a rising tide of democratically and locally run initiatives, a tide that appeals to and is increasingly directed not by governments or corporations, but by the people who live and work within the enterprises they have created.

The above quote identifies some of the many forms of GDE that have recently come to life; others would include shareable cities network,[1] transition town network,[2] resilient communities,[3] and community commons initiatives.[4] In what follows, I will concentrate mainly on the worker cooperative and democratic workplace component of this rising tide, but almost all of the evidence I'll provide of that one movement is mirrored by similar developments in other parts of the emergent GDE.

Some of this evidence has surfaced in a number of informative and readable articles published over the past two years. In these you will find such good news as:

*   'New York City's newly approved budget allocates $1.2-million for developing and supporting worker-owned cooperative businesses' (Flanders 2014).

- 'The Southern Grassroots Economies Project (SGEP) ... is building networks across the US South to promote and launch sustainable cooperative economies. Our work is inspired by the rich history of social justice struggle in the South and looks to the example of the worker-owned cooperatives of Mondragon, Spain and Emilia Romagna, Italy for guidance .... The individuals and organizations within the SGEP are working to create a culture of [democratic] community-based ownership in the South – a culture that will fundamentally alter our relationship with business, work, and community wealth'.[5]
- ' "Too often we have seen Wall Street hollow out companies by draining their cash and assets and hollow out communities by shedding jobs and shuttering plants," said United Steelworkers (USW) President Leo Gerard in 2009. "We need a new business model that invests in workers and invests in communities." Gerard [announced] a formal partnership between his 1.2 million-member union and Mondragon, a cluster of cooperatives in the Basque region of Spain' (Dean 2013).
- 'Workers in Maine Buy Out Their Jobs, Set an Example for the Nation' (Brown *et al.* 2014).
- 'On remote Deer Isle, Maine, the movement for a more just and democratic economy won a major victory this summer. More than 60 employees of three retail businesses – Burnt Cove Market, V&S Variety and Pharmacy, and The Galley – banded together to buy the stores and create the largest worker cooperative in Maine and the second largest in New England'.[6]
- 'The Highlander Center, a training centre for social movements with deep roots in the South, just launched its Appalachian Transition Fellowship – a program to mentor and support 14 young Appalachians as they work on economic development projects throughout the region. Their goal is to accelerate the creation of a diverse economy by working on projects that create jobs and livelihoods in the wake of coal's decline' (Solomon 2014).
- 'The worker cooperative movement has hit a new stride. Re-emerging in the 1960s, cooperatives tend to elicit thoughts of natural food stores and specialty bookshops but the movement has grown to include tech companies, co-working spaces, international businesses, large factories and much more'.[7]

But is it sustainable?

All of these good stories certainly bring welcome news, especially if one compares them with the relatively dormant situation only a few years ago, when unions were by and large dismissive if not hostile to worker-owned businesses, and only a few relatively isolated co-ops could be found throughout the southern states.

However, the question naturally arises as to what actual meaning these new initiatives carry for the rise of a GDE. Workplace democracy, community-based ownership, local time banks, shareable cities initiatives and the like might be part of a passing fad, without much staying power, or may have hit their limit, offering no real challenge to Wall Street and the now-dominant world capitalist economy.

Some four decades ago, a movement in many ways similar to GDE came to life in the USA, and elsewhere. It challenged the conventional and dominant way learners were treated and learning organized. Calling for detachment from both the public and private systems of (mis-)education, it offered a wide spectrum of grassroots democratic 'free schools', 'learning communities', 'experimental colleges'; by some accounts close to a thousand of these formed in the late 1960s and early 1970s. Most of these were started by groups of parents and their children, and most kept their expenses minimal, so as to reach out to low-income families. But the movement was not sustainable; it died as quickly as it arose, and by 1975, it became hard to find even a hundred of them, and those remaining tended to be extremely expensive.

Will something like this be the fate of the now-emerging GDE? I don't think so. But to see why, we'll need to go quite a bit below the surface of the preceding quotes. One way to do this is to ask just how the current GDE differs from the free school movement.

First, free schools were all on their own, isolated, unable to draw support from one another. This is far from the case within today's GDE: it has formed large-scale regional associations (such as the Eastern Conference for Workplace Democracy and the Western Worker Cooperative Conference), as well as more local regional hubs (in Austin, the Pioneer Valley in Massachusetts, Philadelphia, the San Francisco Bay Area, Madison, Portland, Oregon, New York City, western North Carolina and others). And, of course, there is the national organization, the US Federation of Worker Cooperatives (USFWC), now in its tenth year. All of these provide their members with collective and welcoming environments in which they can learn and collaborate together, share lessons and resources, and begin to develop a culture of cooperation.

Each has its own vision and constituency, but all would endorse something like this vision statement from the Philadelphia Area Cooperative Alliance:

> *We envision a vibrant and growing network of cooperative enterprises that operate in all* sectors of the economy to build a better world – providing essential services, strengthening democratic organizations, creating quality jobs, building community wealth, reducing poverty, strengthening our local economy, protecting the environment and increasing community engagement.[8]

Second, a 'secondary' support network, specifically designed to assist start-ups as well as providing guidance to established enterprises, was entirely missing from the free school phenomenon. GDE, however, has created numerous sources of such support. Here is a partial list:

- The Democracy at Work Network (DAWN) of the USFWC; national focus
- Cooperation Texas in Austin
- Colors Coop Academy of Detroit
- Green Worker Coops of New York City
- Cooperation Jackson of Jackson, MS
- Worcester We Own It in Worcester, MA
- SELC Worker Coop Academy, WAGES, Arizmendi and NoBAWC of the San Francisco Bay Area
- Ohio Employee Ownership Center and Cooperative Development Center at Kent State in Ohio
- Center for Workplace Democracy in Chicago
- New Orleans Cooperative Development Project in New Orleans
- Portland Project for Cooperative Innovation in Portland, OR
- Philadelphia Cooperative Alliance (PACA) in Philadelphia
- NYC NoWC of New York City
- The Working World[9] in New York City, but with a cross-border focus as well
- Center for Participatory Change[10] in western North Carolina
- Valley Alliance of Worker Co-operative[11] in western Massachusetts and southern Vermont.

First, for me, what is especially remarkable about this list is not just that these secondary or support organizations have formed across the nation, and are providing the educational, technical, marketing and other assistance needed to start and maintain successful enterprises. This *is* indeed amazing, given that only a decade ago, most of these had yet to be formed.

Second, what strikes me most about them is that they are run, in the main, by the same sorts of folks that they serve. That is, *cooperative practitioners*, rather than researchers, lawyers, or people trained entirely in business schools, but lacking hands-on expertise or wisdom. DAWN, the first on this list, is an especially good example here, as its assistance is offered by people who have worked for years as co-op members, and have received many months of training to become 'peer advisors' skilled in how to cope with the distinctive issues facing other co-ops.

Third, free schools most often were not very diverse; most served middle-class, white families. The opposite holds for the GDE: marginalized groups are well represented, in terms not only of membership, but also of leadership. In addition, workshops given at conferences within the GDE are increasingly held in both Spanish and English, and occasionally in Portuguese. And workshops on developing sensitivity to alternative cultures have become common in these conferences.

Fourth, free schools erupted almost spontaneously, blooming with little or no prior preparation, and few predecessors. Yes, A.S. Neill's learner-driven Summerhill school had been running for four decades in the UK, but this was a singular story, and one that was too remote to offer much direct practical guidance to North American free schools.

Just the opposite is true of the current blooming of our GDE: since 1975, efforts to build such an economy have been quietly but resolutely undertaken. Those who were involved decades ago are still involved, and their long-haul practical wisdom has been influential in enabling the current rising tide, e.g. in creating the USFWC and many of the support organizations mentioned above.

To put this point differently: if you had visited a free school back in the late 1960s, you would have found – on the whole – lots of children, from toddlers to teenagers (or of college age), and a few teachers a decade or so older than their oldest students. But if you visit a contemporary democratized workplace, or time bank, or any other GDE enterprise, you'd be dazzled by the age range in most of them. The founders of these enterprises, on the whole, are sticking around, to everyone's benefit.

Finally, with the marginal exception of teachers, free schools did not in general generate much if any income for themselves. On the contrary, parents had to pay for places in them, though far less than for private schools. But workers in a cooperative, on the contrary, receive wages for being part of that enterprise, and share in the overall profits or surplus the enterprise produces.

Aside from this comparison with free schools, there are additional reasons for thinking that the GDE is here to stay. For one, *it is pragmatic, rather than ideological*. Years ago, when I helped found a chicken-processing cooperative in Willimantic, CT, my anarchist comrades chastised me as a 'traitor' for accepting funds from a government agency and a Catholic charity. Today, the USFWC accepts quite substantial funding from the USDA to support its new Democracy at Work Institute – so long as the money can be used to meet its mission.[12] But at the same time, the Federation also supports local or regional groups who reject such external sources of funding as undermining the self-directed capabilities of cooperative practitioners. This pragmatic position creates a 'big tent' or large network of support, in which opposing strategies are tolerated and even combined. And it helps keep everyone distanced from ideological disputes.

One last reason for viewing the GDE as more than a fugitive phenomenon involves its amenability to important changes. For example, not only are worker cooperatives, in many different locales, working together and with co-ops in other regions, but they are beginning to see the importance of collaborating outside the co-op box.

In 2006, to begin a workshop at a USFWC conference in New York City, I suggested that we examine a disturbing question: 'If worker cooperatives are such a good thing, why are there so few of them?' My own answer to this question was that, unintentionally, worker co-ops were themselves part of this problem, in that their vision and missions remained narrow and self-regarding. That is, they were behaving as if cooperatively owned and managed enterprises – by themselves – could turn around our exploitive, anti-democratic, soul- and planet-crushing undemocratic economy.

Cooperative or self-managed enterprises may be organized democratically and may become allied with one another; they may even make charitable donations or provide discounted prices to neighbouring non-profits. But, I argued, they typically have no incentive or support to go beyond their self-imposed walls or to merge cooperative loyalty with any wider or more transformative forms of solidarity. They will thus feel no responsibility to collaborate, coalition, partner, or organize in mutually beneficial ways with e.g. labour, immigrant, social justice, participatory budget, time bank/community currency, restorative justice and other groups or constituencies other than those within the cooperative community.

At that 2006 USFWC gathering, this notion of cross-organizational collaboration outside the co-op family got a very mixed reception. (In contrast, it was very well received a month later at the CWCF conference in Edmonton.[13]) Many were the objections: e.g. 'It asks too much of us', 'It violates the need for co-ops to be politically neutral', 'How can we tell which other groups or organizations to collaborate with?', 'It's too confrontational'.

But that was then. Today a very different story is emerging. At the 2014 USFWC conference in Chicago, you could find this workshop description:

> Building Grassroots Coalitions Around Worker Ownership / Desarrollo de coaliciones de base en torno a la propiedad de los trabajadores.
> A critical element in the growth of large-scale worker cooperative movements around the world is their alliances with other grassroots movements, running the gamut from organized labour to communities of faith to movements for economic, racial and language justice.
> This session looks at possibilities for building such coalitions in the U.S., looking at models for organizing and already existing coalitions. Exploring how faith-labour immigrants' rights, and racial justice coalitions have begun to connect with worker cooperatives, we will discuss how to build coalitions to increase our scale and power.[14]

In short, there is now enthusiasm for, rather than resistance to, cross-organizational collaboration, for 'moving movements together'. Elements within the GDE no longer see themselves as the sole or primary initiative to bring about transformative change. This, for me, is a definite sign of a mature movement, and a further reason to see this new economy as sustainable.

In conclusion

Let's start with what I'm not claiming. My point is *not* that a full-blown GDE has come to life, or that the road ahead will now be smooth or without extremely difficult challenges. My claim, rather, is only that this emerging economy has made an excellent start, in several crucial directions, and has the capacity and willingness to keep itself alive, well and growing.

Specifically, it has created local, regional and national associations to overcome isolation and spark collaboration, as well as practitioner-directed support networks to assist start-ups and established enterprises. It is diverse and culture-sensitive in many ways; based on decades of preparation and hands-on experience; provides a living wage income for many of those who are most engaged; is pragmatic, open to conflicting approaches and non-ideological; and is willing to build cross-organizational coalitions with a variety of grassroots and social justice movements.

Nor have I characterized this GDE as 'problem-free' or without flaws or gaps. As I don't need to argue, we all have clay feet, and our share of moderate if not major imperfections. For example, my friends and comrades in the GDE are exuberant and love to dance, but I am still waiting for the first collective rousing song to be written by and for this movement.

More seriously, the issue of cooperatives and other democratic workplaces being 'growth aversive', keeping employment and the number, as well as size, of enterprises relatively small, has not yet been addressed in any depth.

Way back in the 1990s, Tim Huet of the San Francisco Bay Area's Arizmendi Association of Cooperatives raised this issue in an article published by GEO. Here's a small part of what he wrote:

> worker cooperatives tend to stop growing once members feel their business has reached a healthy and productive size. Unlike capitalist cancers which grow for their own sake and destroy their host environment, cooperatives aim for homeostasis, a healthy balance. Unfortunately this pro-social characteristic of cooperatives can be a fatal weakness in economic competition with capitalist businesses. The cooperative grocer, bookstore, etc. enjoying its homeostasis can be devoured by a malignant capitalist growth (chain, mega-wholesaler, etc.) ….
>
> And even if a worker cooperative wishes to grow, perhaps spurred by the realization of a growing capitalist threat, it will encounter special obstacles. It is true that all small businesses, capitalist or otherwise, are threatened by the growing scale of economic competition, but cooperatives face particular challenges of capitalization and acculturation when trying to rapidly expand into a market or 'catch up'.
>
> Acculturation is always a challenge for democratic workplaces as they must re-shape the behavioral/thought patterns incoming workers have acquired from autocratic employers and schools. This process of democratic cultural development works best through a slow process of absorption; culture transfer may be very difficult if the workforce is suddenly doubled by an influx of workers ignorant of democratic management. It is a singular challenge to develop a democratic culture from scratch, which a cooperative might have to if it needs to develop branches remote from its base.[15]

In 2006, Tim presented a version of his 'growth aversive' thesis at a USFWC Conference. Covering that Conference for GEO, I wrote a critique of this presentation, but other than that, the issue Tim raised – a crucial one for the future of any GDE – seems to have been ignored.[16]

But in any case I have not attempted to provide a full-scale assessment of the current GDE; that's a question for a much longer research project. Rather, my aim has been to showcase and appreciate the substantial distance already travelled by the tenacious shapers of this grassroots democratic work, and to offer evidence that they are providing the resources, opportunities, lessons and human capital to build and sustain a great deal more grassroots democratic growth.

Some have contended that it will take 'several generations' to develop a well-rooted GDE. Michael Johnson, for example, claims:

> [t]his shared vision of abundance and solidarity at the core of these emerging local and regional dynamics will probably take about a generation to root firmly, *if it does*. In three or four generations these changes could possibly become a substantial part of the political economics in the US. *Possibly* .... So we are talking about a process that will take a long time. A long, long time beyond our lifetimes.[17]

His discouraging speculation might be true or it might not; but believing it will only tend to make it self-fulfilling. So also is the apparently opposed view of Kevin Zeese, echoing Tom Paine: 'We are at a critical convergence in history, where ... we have it in our power to begin the world over again'.[18]

My own view differs from both of these. I see the future of GDE as *fundamentally unpredictable*: who would have predicted, even ten years ago, where we now stand? Nor do I know how to assess claims about 'critical historical convergences'. It is better, I'd suggest, to set aside speculative predictions, and instead celebrate what we have already done and commit ourselves to doing ever more of it. The point is to stay on the path, and enjoy the journey for its own sake, rather than attempting to identify if, when, or how some pre-fixed destination, or worldwide transformation, will be reached. As Vaclav Havel, the Czech playwright and dissident, put it, 'Hope is definitely not the same thing as optimism. It is not the conviction that something will turn out well, but the certainty that something makes sense, regardless of how it turns out' (2011).

I have that sort of hope and certainty about detaching ourselves from capitalism by continuing to support and build today's GDE.

But what about the immense power and brutal militaristic force of the dominant capitalist regime? Yes, detachment from it to a GDE will likely not be sufficient to overthrow that evil regime; for that we will also need protest, resistance, opposition – on a scale even larger than the recent marches against climate change. Still, neither will resistance by itself suffice; something new, different, much better – and alive – will need to be available and welcoming. Resistance and reconstruction, indignant rage and constructive creativity, need to be seen as allies, rather than enemies. Neither alone will get us far; both are essential.

And both can be and are being combined. A recent article by Judy Rebick, entitled 'Long Live Occupy: Occupy Three Years Later' (2014), reveals that this sort of collaboration has already begun. The author quotes Toronto Occupy organizer Sakura Saunders:

> I believe that Occupy, Idle No More and Quebec's student movement showed us that there are hundreds of thousands of people, if not millions of people, who want dramatic change but are on the sidelines waiting for a movement that inspires them to hope, and this is what I hold onto in continuing to organize past these moments of heightened activity.

Rebick then concludes:

> In my view, Occupy as a movement continues in the particular forms of activism we are seeing emerging around the world. Whether Occupy Gezi in Turkey or Occupy Hong Kong, all these actions have similar qualities. While they include big marches, their focus is on building alternative communities, however short-lived, that are providing the necessities of life, political debate and cultural activities, as well as protests. They are all organized collectively with relatively flat structures, participatory democracy like the general assemblies and a valuing of whatever skills and ability people bring into the community.

Moreover, stories of alliances like this one between resistance and reconstruction/detachment are far from uncommon. For example:

> Begun in the spring of 2013, WORCs (Worker-Owned Rockaway Cooperatives) is an initiative to rebuild after Sandy in a way that addresses both the storm's impact and the long-term systemic issues in the neighborhood. The program's goal is to equip Far Rockaway residents with the skills and financing to launch small, worker-owned businesses that fill a need in their community. More than 40 residents have already joined the weekly, three-month training program – people who now work for others as babysitters, house cleaners, exterminators and upholsterers but dream of being their own bosses and keeping wealth inside their neighborhood. So far, the group has developed plans to launch five worker-owned businesses: a construction company, a bakery, a health food store, an entertainment collective and a pupuseria.
>
> (The Working World n.d.)

They are now in the process of turning these plans into realities. WORCs is a joint initiative between The Working World (cf. above) and Occupy Sandy.

Occupy Sandy organizers approached members of The Working World, who they knew through Occupy Wall Street, and together they came up with the idea.

Let's make them more and more uncommon!

Let's make them less and less uncommon.

Notes

1 www.shareable.net/sharing-cities [accessed 6 March 2016].
2 www.transitionnetwork.org [accessed 6 March 2016].
3 http://waldenlabs.com/category/resilience/ [accessed 6 March 2016].
4 http://communitycommons.org [accessed 6 March 2016].
5 http://sgeproject.org/about/; see also www.geo.coop/content/southern-cooperative-movement-0 [both accessed 5 March 2016].
6 www.geo.coop/content/island-employee-cooperative-buyout [accessed 4 March 2016].
7 www.shareable.net/blog/16-worker-co-ops-redefining-the-cooperative-movement [accessed 6 March 2016].
8 www.philadelphia.coop/about-us/ [accessed 6 March 2016].
9 www.theworkingworld.org/us/ [accessed 6 March 2016].
10 www.cpcwnc.org/ [accessed 6 March 2016].
11 http://valleyworker.org [accessed 6 March 2016].
12 http://institute.usworker.coop/about-dawi/mission-vision [accessed 6 March 2016].
13 www.geo.coop/node/57 [accessed 6 March 2016].
14 http://conference.coop/schedule/building-grassroots-coalitions-around-worker-ownership-desarrollo-de-coaliciones-de-base-en-torno-la-propiedad-de-los-trabajadores/ [accessed 2014].
15 http://geo.coop/archives/huet.htm [accessed 6 March 2016].
16 For my reply to Tim, see www.geo.coop/node/57 [accessed 6 March 2016].
17 http://geo.coop/story/another-world-emerging-well-maybe [accessed 6 March 2016].
18 http://truth-out.org/news/item/14076 [accessed 6 March 2016].

3   Workers' economy in Argentina

Self-management, cooperatives and recovered enterprises in a time of global crisis[1]

Andrés Ruggeri

In December 2001, when the implosion of the neoliberal model in Argentina turned the world's gaze to the great emerging social movements or those fostered by the country's enormous crisis, activists and academics in many countries looked on with interest at one of the most intriguing and hopeful movements – factories occupied by their workers, or more accurately, recovered enterprises. Even though cases of worker self-management of bankrupt enterprises or factories, emptied and abandoned by their owners does not lack historical precedent, in Argentina as well as other parts of the world, this was the first time, at least in the past few decades, when a movement, with its own characteristics and identity, came out of these circumstances.

The recovered enterprises emerged in a country that, throughout the 1990s, had been the 'poster child' of the IMF and World Bank, had followed the Washington Consensus instructions to the letter and, therefore, exemplified the high social cost of complete submission to the global neoliberal hegemony. The existence of these enterprises also provided hope for the possibility of creating alternatives to a seemingly unstoppable globalization after the fall of the Soviet Union and its centralized and authoritarian economic model. Intellectual critics of the so-called developed nations thought that the cases of worker self-management in a country like Argentina could serve to demonstrate the viability of an alternative to neoliberal globalization.

How many of those activists that came to the southern hemisphere to observe the rare phenomenon of worker self-management up close seriously considered that the very core of global capitalism would enter into a profound crisis less than ten years later, while Argentina, and South America in general, would begin to transition into an unorthodox path to development that, even despite not superseding the capitalist system, has allowed these countries to recover their most important social indicators and look toward the future with new hope? The cases of worker self-management that were once seen as exotic and only possible within the context of a weak state and a fragile economy in a Third World country became a powerful reality in the prosperous European Union and even in the United States, and the recovered enterprises began to be studied from a different perspective. Curiosity was replaced with genuine interest in something that could happen at home.

Crisis and self-management in Latin America

In Argentina and other Latin American countries, the employee recuperation of enterprises is a process that has gained notoriety despite its still relatively low quantitative level. Recovered enterprises exist in almost all South American countries and in Mexico, even though they have only constituted a relatively important movement in Uruguay, Brazil and Argentina. In contrast, in Venezuela, the process of occupation and self-management has transpired thanks to joint management resulting from the Bolivarian government's policies that in the last few years have broadened the range of public participation in collectives to extend to the communities where the factories reside, through the coordination of worker and community councils (Azzellini 2012a).

In countries such as Mexico[2] the phenomenon is far from unknown, but despite the fact that there exist many large cooperatives originating from trade union conflicts, they have not acquired their own identity, differentiating themselves from traditional cooperatives, causing the process to become diluted within cooperativism and the solidarity economy in general. In Brazil, the first cases were in the 1980s and the 1990s, with fewer in the past years. Uruguay and Argentina are part of a more homogeneous reality and it is in Argentina where the 2001 crisis provided the necessary mixture for occupied enterprises and factories, transformed into self-managed businesses to form a unique identity and a movement that got the world's attention through its symbolic power to question private property and the capitalist management of economic units.

Without rehashing the case of Argentina, which we have detailed in other papers, we highlight one of its particular characteristics: the development process of worker self-management that emerged under very difficult conditions and as a purely defensive action, as a resistance to job loss within a general crisis, without the support or significant opposition of political parties, unions or state programmes. These are self-management processes that are not a result of a revolutionary or anti-capitalist spirit, but stem from necessity and the abandonment experienced by the workers.

This situation, that brought about conflict and in turn the occupation of these businesses, resulted in – at a loss for other solutions – the formation of worker cooperatives that, instead of as was predicted, were successful, not only in overcoming the first and most important obstacles of the reactivation of the ruined and bankrupt plants and establishments, but also in carrying out collective management, without models or state instruction and, most importantly, without previous knowledge of this kind of development. Which is to say that this was an authentic worker experience carried out within an overwhelming crisis, but simultaneously subject to the creativity of its protagonists in their ability to overcome a situation without a common solution.

It should also be noted that the path to self-management was possible thanks to the support of strong social solidarity networks, that offered not only traditional militant support, but also innovative ideas and outreach initiatives including activities that were not strictly economic, and at the very least dissimilar and in conflict with the company's capitalist concept. Simultaneously, these businesses had to confront their inability to overcome something that was nevertheless out of their hands – the capitalist trade relationships that they continued to be subject to as productive units that continued to function as formal enterprises within the bosom of the capitalist market. This, of course, brought on an entire series of restrictions and pressures that affected the self-management rationale and the internal solidarity to the process.

Within this context, the recovered enterprises have been growing in number, in number of workers and in economic activity in the last 12 years, as is documented by the research of the Open Faculty programme team, including around 360 cases and 16,000 workers today (Ruggeri 2005, 2011, 2014). However, if we consider that most recovered enterprises are registered as cooperatives, why do we insist on identifying these cases as separate and different and what political and economic implications might this have?

In my opinion, what is interesting about recovered enterprises is not only the process of self-management that, for whatever reason, results in a cooperative, but the combined process in which a private, capitalist enterprise, that exploits wage labour, converts to collective management by former payroll employees and the problems and solutions that result – problems, in some cases, similar to cooperatives in general, but in many other ways similar to those historical periods and processes that twentieth-century Marxism called 'workers control' and the anarcho-syndical movement prefer to call collectivization or socialization (Mandel 1973; PCP 2011).

We insist that the process by which a recovered enterprise is formed differs from that of cooperatives in general and from the various forms of the so-called social and solidarity economy in certain fundamental ways. The first is, as we have said, how a capitalist economic unit, with a hierarchical and vertical structure, characterized by its accumulation of capital through the exploitation of wage work (whether its activity is production or service-oriented), is converted into a business collectively managed by its workers.

Even if this process can be identified in the origins of many cooperatives historically, including the very beginning of cooperativism as a movement, it differs from other cooperative enterprises in its collectivization of the ownership of means of production. Even though this signifies a generalization in the socialization or collectivization process, it carries with it the same profound questioning of the fundamentals of capitalist management, economically or socially.

The second important reason that recovered enterprises are different from other cases of cooperatives is the clear affiliation with the experience of the working-class struggle. We could argue that in all or in the majority of cooperatives and solidarity economy undertakings the main actors are the workers, but we see a substantial difference between the majority of these cases and the difficult process that arises at the heart of the conflict between capital and work (management's abandonment and the uncontrolled conflict stemming from that abandonment or forced closing).

This difference forms a part of the self-perception of the recovered enterprises' main actors as workers instead of cooperativists or 'outsiders', concepts that lack a connection to the working class (Trinchero 2009). The recuperation of enterprises and factories by workers as an extreme method of defending their jobs, and later as a self affirmation of their own identity as independent workers, also questions organizational structure and traditional tools of the workers' struggle, meaning, the role of unions, class-based political parties and cooperatives themselves, the majority currently removed from the historical, common origins of grassroots movements.

This means returning to the cooperative movement's origins as a movement of workers' organization based on non-capitalist economic models, which must not only respect the principles of solidarity and self-management, but also must be clearly opposed to the capitalist exploitation of wage labour.

Crisis within crisis

For Argentinians and South Americans that have repeatedly lived through crisis in the last few generations, the situation in countries like Spain and Greece seems like a rerun. A crisis brought on by finance capital that is worsened – using the argument that it is the only way to confront it – by following the well-known and outdated recipes of 'austerity' that leave millions of workers unemployed: cut funding designated for social protections, force the state to do away with public enterprises and cut expenses that frame the welfare state (the welfare state) that has been hard-fought for decades.

Meanwhile, on the other side of the coin, they designate extensive funding for the strengthening of tools of repression to counter the inevitable social protest, facilitate the intense mobility of capital in the search for best conditions for the exploitation and precarization of work and the maximum capability for accumulating capital, designate amounts never before seen from public funds for the 'rescue' of the banking sector responsible for the crisis and then punish those that try to respond differently. The difference between a crisis with these characteristics happening in the periphery of the capitalist system and one in the countries in the centre of global capitalism is, precisely, the centrality of the economies affected, the strength of institutions and financial tools in play, the strength of the hegemonic ideology and capitalist culture and the institutional and repressive force of the states and their ability to respond as guardians of capital's strongest interests.

Paradoxically, worker and grassroots movements in these countries seem to have a weaker ability to resist, due to the multiple mechanisms of social protection that they have been able to achieve in generations past, weakening their antibodies for workers' struggle and organization, allowing a quick and expensive reply by governing capitalists. The conformism and resignation to what changes are possible, even in the most reformist of the social democratic parties that make up the largest part of Europe's left, handicapped in adapting and becoming the 'human' version of global neoliberal capitalism, are no small factor in the defencelessness and disappointment of their base.

Over the past two or three years there have been many labour conflicts and the closing of many enterprises and productive establishments in most European countries and also in the United States. The case of the Republic windows and doors factory in Chicago was one of the most well known in North America. Nevertheless, Southern Europe's process of recuperation, in countries much more affected by the crisis, is more important. Cases such as Vio.Me in Thessaloniki, Greece, are taking on similar roles to the recovered enterprises in Argentina in December 2001. There are other lesser known examples, including within militancy of the radical left of these countries, such as various cooperatives that we could categorize as recovered enterprises in Spain, especially in Catalonia and certain places in France, some of them already functioning for several years.

In Italy laws have allowed for the formation of cooperatives from the very beginning of the collapse. But in Italy as well, as is the norm when collapse is sudden and there is a high rate of fraud, the actual difficulties that workers face in taking over enterprises are large and torturous, and there are distinct perspectives about the process' dimensions and identity. Some researchers claim the existence of dozens of recovered enterprises, but the cases in which these businesses self-identify as recovered enterprises has been, up until now, very rare, such as the Roma-based Officine Zero and the Milan-based Rimaflow.[3] Both of these cases were factories which closed with very few possibilities of restarting production in their previous line of work, and that were occupied by a group of their former workers that together with a group of social and political activists tended to recreate the Argentine model of the 'open factory' as the location of various activities and solidarity, cultural and labour projects, without much chance of achieving recuperation as an industrial unit.

Narrowing our gaze somewhat we can see some particularities in these still unknown cases of European enterprises recovered by their workers. The first is that, in contrast to Latin America, the Europeans seem to have greater difficulty building the solidarity networks to sustain and support these businesses (even though the aforementioned cases owe a large part of their survival to the existence of these same networks). The social security institutions that still exist create a situation where the closing of factories is not permanent for workers, which is what usually occurs in Argentina and Latin America in general. Unemployment insurance allows workers to continue receiving regular income for a certain time, delaying the moment when they are confronted with the situation of having no income at all, and discourages the emergence of radical struggle methods in order to stave off unemployment.

The perceived extent of the crisis and the gravity of chronic unemployment is also different, especially at the beginning of the crisis, and the idea that economic deterioration is just a passing phenomenon is, whether consciously or unconsciously, behind the lack of response from workers at the moment when they lose their jobs. The complicity or lack of vision by the majority of unions also adds (in this case similarly in Latin America) to the passivity of the workers' movement, which has weakened in the past several decades and left them helpless to react, in part due to the loyalty policies of the social democratic parties in some governments. By the time unemployment payments run out, not only are the establishments definitively closed, but the work groups are also completely dissolved, pulling each worker down their own individual paths.

But there is another characteristic that differentiates the European cases from those of South America, related to the nature of the crisis. In several more well-known examples, such as the French company Fralib, a tea factory near Marseille, or Italy's Rimaflow, the closings are not due to genuine bankruptcy but to the business owner's decision to take advantage of lower labour costs in other parts of the world, in particular Eastern Europe.

The closing of both plants was not due, as was the case in the majority of the Argentinian and Brazilian cases, to a decision to stop company production because of an inability to move the business forward or the convenience of moving shares over to the financial market, but because of an outsourcing of production to (in this case) Poland, where the same level of production could be performed with lower taxes and, particularly, lower labour costs, which makes up for the increase in distribution costs for that same product in the same markets in which they were sold before. In the case of Fralib, the plant belonged to the multinational Unilever, especially pertinent in this discussion, in which we can see 'the crisis' was not necessarily the problem, but instead a good pretext to increase the mobility of capital in the search for the highest possible profitability and wealth accumulation at the expense of workers' rights and by surpassing historical national regulations. The transnationalization of the regulatory framework does away with an important quantity of the legislation achieved by the workers' movement in decades past, replaced by European and international norms that lack a framework for the reaction of the worker class, that has lost all its ability to act on the international stage, while capital, through investment, gains mobility and the ability to legislate in its favour at the global level.

These kinds of problems, that in countries like Argentina are still expressed in terms of the centre–periphery conflict (by which national production is replaced by imported products, coming from transnationals that operate in countries with very low labour costs, and the imposition of policies by global finance organizations through mechanisms like deregulation/international regulation and the management of credit and external debt), in the European example demonstrate the formation of a supranational government of finance capital. This is expressed by a triumvirate (the European Central Bank, the IMF and the European Commission) that imposes adjustment plans, cuts to wages and public investment that only a short time ago were unthinkable, the dismantling of social security and the deterioration of work conditions, which are the causes of the programmed shutting down of production based on the search for greater profitability and not the impossibility of competing or producing due to the crisis.

To the contrary, the crisis is the ideal context for transnational corporations that have no productivity or financial problems, nor difficulties in placing their production in local markets, to close plants in the countries that not only have the best labour laws, but also the best salaries and that have unions with a certain level of power, and relocate them to regions that offer better conditions for wealth accumulation at the cost of their workers. In this way the crisis is an opportunity for the large European bourgeoisie, under the command of financial interests disguised as the central banks with the greatest economic potential, to quickly take apart the mechanisms, regulations and framework of the State of Well-Being.

The recovery of enterprises by workers in these countries becomes a process that is quite possibly more arduous than in South American economies or others in the Third World in general, because governments don't currently have the slightest interest – nor do they see the need – to give in to the workers that are demonstrating as they have yet to get to the point where the social cost of their policies matters to them that much. There is also the scarce cooperation of support networks, the incomprehension of the majority of union members and the still nonexistent self-management movement (that simultaneously contributes to the force and the indifference of the traditional cooperative organizations), making it significantly more difficult.

On the other hand, the benefit of having living examples in other parts of the world and the existence of broad social sectors that are not only not accustomed to crisis (to living miserably), but that also can potentially see very clearly what risks they are exposed to by continuing to advance in the dismantling of the achievements of past generations, could be an important factor in mobilization and organization. Along with that, the greater possibility of an economic response and the reorientation of support networks mainly constructed for internal solidarity towards society itself (only and always when volunteerism is transformed into militancy) could create an organizational framework that could strengthen experience and advance the interplay between self-management theory and practice.

To understand the logic by which capitalists decide to abandon efficient, productive establishments, sometimes the most cutting-edge in technology, in places where the market for these products has not only not disappeared, but in some cases has expanded, is fundamental to understanding the dynamic of international capitalist exploitation of labour and the increasing mobility of the transnationalization of capital. This logic continues to function as long as workers in these companies' countries of origin do not resist closings, on one hand (and worker self-management is not only a way to maintain a labour source and advance a different concept of production, but also a form of resistance to the abuses of capital), and while the workers of the Third World can improve their work conditions and raise their wages, on the other. In the best possible scenario, workers fight for the self-management of their factories, in this way restricting the unpunished flow of capital.

The case of Argentina, despite low numbers, demonstrates that when workers take control of abandoned enterprises as a tool of simultaneous defensive and offensive struggle, it improves the labour conditions of everyone, the self-managed and the wage earners, and owners begin to feel, for the first time in decades, that someone is restricting them. And if it is no longer the state, with its inter-class commitment (the so-called welfare state), that sets these limits, it is going to have to be the workers.

These issues make the South American experience – and particularly that of Argentina, due to its number and that a specific self-management movement was constructed (beyond the organizational and political fragmentation that keep it from demonstrating as an organic whole) – a touchstone that allows the re-insertion of the debate of self-management into the global left. The hegemonic economic theory and the political practice of the communists and social democrats in the twentieth century, especially after the Russian Revolution and the fall of the Spanish anarchists in the 1930s, left the option of self-management almost completely out of the political discussion, except for a few rare cases.[4]

The conclusive failure of the Soviet brand of socialism (including in countries in which communist parties retook power after the fall of the USSR), especially economically where it should have proven (according to the theory and widespread belief in the nineteenth and beginning of the twentieth centuries) its superiority to capitalism – meaning its capacity to provide more or less satisfactorily and equally for the needs of the whole of society – opened up an era where these hegemonic theories of the left confronted their own limits.

This new era caused the social movements of the working class in the last two decades to begin to consider, generally through practice, the self-management alternative. That was how, first through practice and later in theory, the experiences of recovered enterprises, autonomous communes, non-monetary trade networks and alternatives started to gain weight in the reconstruction of new anti-capitalist thought. It is in the area of economics where capitalism demonstrates its strength and its weakness all at the same time, and it is in this area that we are still very much theoretic orphans, which is unforgivable given that there exist concrete examples with a certain level of development to study, analyse and extract conclusions from.

In this way, recovered and self-managed enterprises fulfil a role that goes much further than a valiant defence and recuperation of jobs: they provide the initial push for the reformulation, reconstruction or direct constitution of a new economic theory and practice where workers are able to overcome traditional schemes (or one imposed scheme as more or less the only path throughout the twentieth century) and question self-management in a way that up until now they have been unable, or only marginally able to do.

In this sense, the degree to which recovered enterprises and self-management stop being a particular phenomenon in specific countries and historical moments and become an international strategy of working-class struggle (as international as the predatory movement of capital), the possibility of reconstructing the project of a post-capitalist society and economy that reinvents the old socialist project, that recognizes what the diverse traditions of the left and the grassroots movements of the nineteenth and twentieth centuries in distinct parts of the world had to offer, will be possible.

Notes

1 Translation by Lydia Carey.
2 Mexico has a strong tradition of autonomy and self-management in rural collectives, especially in indigenous areas, and fewer in urban areas.
3 Even though there is still no published research about this issue, we can cite work by researchers such as Vieta that makes reference to about 100 recovered enterprises in the Italian territory, and Carrano who mentions 30. For information about Rimaflow, see Magnani and Semenzin (2013).
4 After the Second World War, the May strikes in France, the independent workers' movement in Italy, the Yugoslavia experience and the industrial areas of Chile during Allende's administration were the most important moments when the self-management debate and worker control regained an important role.

4 Cooperative Cuba

Cliff DuRand

Cuba is poised to be the first country in the world to have cooperatives make up a major part of its economy. It is a laboratory for a new society.

(Cliff DuRand, below)

Cuba is engaged in a fundamental reshaping of its society. Calling it a renovation of socialism or a renewal of socialism, the country is re-forming the economic system away from the state socialist model adopted in the 1970s toward something quite new. This is not the first time Cuba has undertaken significant changes, but this promises to be deeper than previous efforts, moving away from that statist model. Fidel confessed in 2005 that 'among the many errors that we committed, the most serious error was believing that someone knew how to build socialism'. That someone, of course, was the Soviet Union. So, Cuba is still trying to figure out for itself how to build socialism.

To understand the current renovation it is important to distinguish between ownership and possession of property. The productive resources of society are to remain under state ownership in the name of all the people. Reforms do not change the ownership system. Reforms are changing the management system, bringing managerial control closer to those who actually possess property. So while the state will continue to own, greater autonomy will be given to those who possess that property. In effect, Cuba is embracing the principle of subsidiarity, which holds that decisions should be made at the lowest level feasible and higher levels should give support to the local. This means more enterprise autonomy in state enterprises and it means cooperatives outside of the state.

It is expected that in the next couple of years the non-state sector will provide 40 per cent of the employment. Along with foreign and joint ventures, the non-state sector as a whole will contribute an estimated 45 per cent of the gross domestic product (GDP). It is hoped that co-ops will become a dominant part of that non-state sector.

Cooperatives

Already 83 per cent of agricultural land is in co-ops. Much of that has been in the UBPCs (Basic Units of Cooperative Production) formed in the 1990s out of the former state farms. But these were not true cooperatives since they still came under the control of state entities. Now they are being given the autonomy to become true co-ops.

Even more significantly, new urban cooperatives are being established in services and industry. As of May 2015 there are 498 authorized urban cooperatives, mainly in commerce, restaurants, personal services, construction and industry. Another 205 are awaiting papers.

In December 2012 the National Assembly passed an urban co-op law that established the legal basis for these new co-ops. These are some of its main provisions (Peters 2012):

- A co-op must have at least three members, but can have as many as 60 or more. One vote per *socio*. As self-governing enterprises, co-ops are to set up their own internal democratic decision-making structures.
- Co-ops are independent of the state. They are to respond to the market. This is to overcome the limits that hampered some agricultural co-ops in the past.
- Co-ops can do business with state and private enterprises. They will set their own prices in most cases, except where there are prices established by the state.
- Some co-ops will be conversions of state enterprises, e.g. restaurants. They can have ten-year renewable leases for use of the premises, paying no rent in the first year if improvements are made.
- Others will be start-up co-ops.
- There will be second-degree co-ops, which are associations of other co-ops.
- Capitalization will come from bank loans, a new Finance Ministry fund for co-ops and member contributions. Member contributions are treated as loans (not equity) and do not give additional votes. Loans are to be repaid from profits.
- Co-ops are to pay taxes on profits and social security for member *socios*.
- Distribution of profits is to be decided by *socios* after setting aside a reserve fund.
- Co-ops may hire wage labour on a temporary basis (up to 90 days). After 90 days a temporary worker must be offered membership or let go. This has since been lengthened to one year. Total temporary worker time cannot exceed 10 per cent of the total workdays for the year. This gives co-ops flexibility to hire extra workers seasonally or in response to increased market demands, but prevents significant collective exploitation of wage labour.

This is a big step forward for Cuba. Since 1968 the state has sought to run everything from restaurants to barber shops and taxis. Some were done well, many were not. One problem was worker motivation. Decisions were made higher up and as state employees, workers enjoyed job security even with poor performance. However, their pay was low. Now as *socios* in cooperatives they will have incentives to make the business a success. The co-op is on its own to either prosper or go under. Each member's income and security depends on the collective. And each has the same voting right in the General Assembly where co-op policy is to be made. Co-ops combine material and moral incentives, linking individual interest with a collective interest. Each *socio* prospers only if all prosper.

Remittances

Much of the start-up capital from members is likely to come from remittances sent by relatives living abroad. This is a good way to harness for the social good some of the $2.455 billion of remittance money (2012 figures) that comes into Cuba. Although 62.4 per cent of the population receive remittances, the bulk of this money is likely to come to whiter Cubans. As a result, black Cubans will end up being underrepresented in this sector of the economy. In the long run, this presents social dangers.

Recommendation

Preferential bank lending policies can avoid this problem. Cuba does not need to adopt race-based affirmative action policies to correct this imbalance. Banks can give preference in their lending policies to those co-ops that lack funding from remittances. To each according to their need.

State plan

If co-ops are truly autonomous, how can this sector of the economy be articulated with planning? Guideline #1 says the socialist planning system is to remain 'the principal means to direct the national economy'. How can market and plan work together? In addition to responding to the market, co-ops are also charged (by charter?) with a 'social object'. In addition, local entities can also request that they assist in specific social projects. Their participation is voluntary. This applies to individual co-ops.

But beyond this, the investment function can be used to direct the development of this sector. Bank lending priorities can be based on state development plans. The model for economic democracy developed by David Schweickart shows how this can operate. In *After Capitalism* (2011) Schweickart envisions a society made up of democratically managed cooperatives exchanging goods and services in a free market. But the allocation of investment capital is made by government bodies at national, regional and local levels based on social criteria democratically decided upon. Something like this would seem to fit well the new economy developing in Cuba today.

Co-ops are recognized as a socialist form of organization in the Guidelines or *lineamientos*. In part, this is because they foster a social consciousness. By bringing people together in their daily work life in democratically self-managed organizations, co-ops nurture the democratic personality and the human being is more fully developed. This point has been strongly advocated by Cuban economist Camila Piñeiro Harnecker (2011a). She argues that co-ops 'promote the advancement of democratic values, attitudes and habits (equality, responsibility, solidarity, tolerance for different opinions, communication, consensus building)'. Co-ops are little schools of democracy in which the new socialist person can thrive, more so than was possible under state socialism (Lebowitz 2012). Thus co-ops spontaneously generate at the base of society momentum toward that society of associated producers that is the aim of socialism. Co-ops are the kind of institution that can make socialism irreversible by embedding its practices in daily life.

Private businesses

The other component of the non-state sector is made up of private businesses. These small and medium-sized private businesses are called self-employment or *cuentapropistas*. While limited areas of self-employment were opened up in the 1990s (*paladares* or home restaurants), this was expanded to 178 occupations in 2011. In part, this was designed to quickly absorb the large number of redundant state employees that were to be dismissed. It also allowed underground activities that had flourished since the Special Period[1] to come out into the open and operate legally where they could be licensed, regulated and taxed.

The acceptance of small private businesses signifies that the leadership recognizes that a petty bourgeoisie is compatible with socialism. As it is often said, the state cannot do everything. Contrary to a common claim in the US media, this is not the beginning of capitalism. The Guidelines say that accumulation of wealth is to be avoided. This means the petty bourgeoisie will not be allowed to grow into a big bourgeoisie, a capitalist class.

Unlike co-ops that nurture a social consciousness, private businesses foster individualism. Self-interest becomes the primary concern of private businesses. For that reason the petty bourgeoisie is a decidedly non-socialist class. While its existence is allowed, its growth should not be encouraged where co-ops can do the job instead. Unlike the *paladares* that could employ only family members, these private businesses can hire others as well. While this is also called self-employment, in reality it is wage labour. While the private exploitation of wage labour is widely understood to be incompatible with socialism (as well as in violation of the Cuban constitution), it is accepted as necessary to quickly absorb surplus workers.

In recent years, small private businesses have been the fastest growing element in the Cuban economy. If they were to come to make up a sizable portion of the non-state sector, they could easily acquire significant political influence, moving Cuba away from socialism. This is because class power is fundamentally rooted in the weight a class has in the economy as a whole and thus the dependence other classes and groups have on its success.

For that reason, the continued development of socialism requires that co-ops rather than private businesses come to make up the bulk of the non-state sector. This is likely to be the case for several reasons:

1   Co-ops are favoured by the state in terms of tax policy and loan policies.
2   In direct competition between co-ops and private businesses co-ops often are in more advantageous positions. For example, state restaurants that convert to co-op restaurants generally have better locations than private restaurants.
3   Labour efficiency and productivity is high in co-ops due to the greater incentives for *socios*.

Recommendation

In the long run it would be desirable to convert many private businesses into co-ops so all who are employed there can enjoy the benefits equally (no exploitation) and participate in decision-making (democracy). This could be done by restrictions on the size of private businesses, tax incentives for conversion, and political organizing of their wage-labour force.

> Cuba could adapt a kind of Meidner Plan whereby a percentage of prof-its would go into a workers fund representing equity in the business. In a matter of years the workers could thus become owners and the business become a cooperative.
>
> Wright 2010: 230–4

Role of the CTC (*Central de Trabajadores de Cuba*)

In view of the new and growing diversity among Cuba's workers, the role of its labour movement needs to be rethought. Under state socialism the CTC represented the interest of the working class as a whole in the councils of government. Unlike unions in a capitalist society that represent workers in an industry or particular workplaces in an adversarial relationship with capital, in state socialism the state and the working class are considered to be united in their interests. It is for this reason that the CTC has been given a central position in the political structure. Its role is not to represent workers in negotiations with their employers, but to be their voice in making public policy in a socialist society.

Previously only 9 per cent of employment was in the non-state sector. Now it is 22 per cent and is expected to grow to 40 per cent. This raises new ques-tions for the labour movement. Reportedly, 80 per cent of *cuentapropistas* have joined unions. How can the CTC represent the interests of those *cuen-tapropistas* who are private business owners? The petty bourgeoisie has inter-ests different from the working class (even though they do work in their own businesses). How can the CTC at the same time represent the interests of the *cuentapropistas* who are in fact the wage labourers they employ (and exploit)?

Furthermore, how can the CTC represent the interests of cooperative *socios* given the fact that they are at once both owners and workers? While the CTC could advance socialism by advocating for the cooperative sector as a whole as opposed to the private business sector, it might be more suitable to have a separate federation of cooperatives to carry out this role. It might also take on an entrepreneurial role for cooperatives, doing market research, organizing workers for new start-up co-ops, providing training in self-management, and even monitoring co-ops to ensure compliance with their own self-governance processes.

Twenty-first-century socialism

The project called twenty-first-century socialism has been associated primarily with the Bolivarian Revolution in Venezuela. It is an attempt to reinvent socialism after the collapse of the state socialism that characterized the twentieth century. In Venezuela this has involved using state power to promote cooperatives and communal councils at the base of society as seeds of a future socialism. Social transformation is constructed both from above and from below (Azzellini 2013: 25–30). In Venezuela this is taking place in what is still overwhelmingly a capitalist society. In Cuba we see a very similar process in the context of a state socialist society. Here the state is also promoting cooperatives, relaxing administrative control over enterprises and decentralizing governmental power to the local level. Both see the empowerment of associations at the base of society and the active participation of working people in directing their affairs as key to building the new socialism. As Azzellini points out in Chapter 17, in the Venezuelan case this is seen as eventually replacing the existing bourgeois state with a new communal state, the beginnings of which are being constructed by associations of communal councils.

In the case of Cuba, resistance to this dispersal of power away from the state is reportedly coming from the state bureaucracy itself. Some see this as motivated by the self-interest of an entrenched bureaucratic class that will block Cuba's reforms. Others see the resistance as due to bureaucratic habits that are slow to change. In that case it can be overcome by a change of mentality (Fernández Ríos 2014). There is also bureaucratic resistance in Venezuela. That is why power and resources are being sent directly to communal councils, effectively bypassing traditional channels. Something like that same strategy is being used in Cuba as some taxes are being collected at the local level rather than nationally to be distributed downward. This then shifts the capacity to initiate action to the local level, a far cry from the vertical structure of state socialism.

Democratically self-governing cooperatives are an essential feature of twenty-first-century socialism. They empower the associated producers in their daily work, giving them some control over their lives. At the same time these little schools of democracy are the soil in which the new socialist person will thrive, more so than was possible under state socialism. And with that it becomes possible to envision the state eventually withering away as society comes more and more under the direction of a truly civil society, or what Marx called the associated producers.

Conclusion

Cuba is poised to be the first country in the world to have cooperatives make up a major part of its economy. It is a laboratory for a new society. Those who are implementing the Guidelines are aware that they are redesigning society and approach the challenge in an experimental way. The new urban co-ops are being set up as experiments. As difficulties emerge lessons are to be learned so as to improve the process as it goes along.

One difficulty is already evident. That is the need for education in cooperativism (Diaz forthcoming). Previous experience in the UBPC agricultural co-ops showed that workers were not practised in democratic decision-making. Nor did the co-ops have the autonomy necessary for them to feel they were really in control. The UBPCs were actually under the control of state enterprises, such as the sugar *centrals*. Now for the first time they are being given real autonomy.

Likewise, the workers in urban state enterprises now being cooperativized have deeply established habits of compliance with higher authority. Under state socialism decisions came from higher up. It was a structure that bred passivity. That is part of the 'change in consciousness' so often talked about these days that needs to take place.

Many years ago Cuban philosopher Olga Fernández pointed out to me that under the model of socialism Cuba had adopted, rather than the state withering away, it was civil society that was withering away. Today's renovation of socialism is an effort to rejuvenate civil society, to construct a socialist civil society. Cooperatives may be a key link in that rejuvenation that can sustain Cuba on its way to a society run by the associated producers. If it can succeed, it will be of world historical importance.

Note

1 The Special Period refers to the period following the 1990 collapse of Cuba's trade relations with the Soviet Union and Eastern Europe that ushered in years of severe economic depression.

Part II
The commons

5   Commoning together

Cliff DuRand

We often are not aware of how extensive the commons are in society today and how much they enrich our lives. There are public spaces available for all to use, such as streets and sidewalks, parks and squares, as well as public institutions like fire departments and public libraries. The commons of libraries has been vastly expanded by the Internet, which has created an immense knowledge commons containing the whole of accumulated human knowledge that is virtually free to all. Air and water are also held in common for our mutual benefit.

Like all commons, customs, laws and regulations govern use. Ideally these are set by a participatory governance process among the commoners. But in practice these are not always set by nor enforced by the community. Governments control many commons and sometimes they are not managed for the good of all. For example, in the autumn of 2011 in many cities in the US police forcibly evicted Occupy protesters from public parks and squares, thereby denying them effective exercise of constitutional rights to peaceful assembly and to free speech. Nevertheless these public spaces are generally common at least in the sense they are not private property.

There are other commons besides these public spaces. There are open grassy areas and even common facilities on most college campuses often called 'the commons'. Similarly, there are the corridors and plazas in shopping malls that are private property, but available to the public under rules established by management – rules like 'no political demonstrations allowed'. The same restrictions often also apply to college campuses. But then there are other commons freely available to all in private spaces open to the public such as drinking fountains and rest rooms. Drinking fountains are an interesting example of a communist sector within a capitalist economy. Potable water is available to all based on need with no payment necessary. 'To each according to their need'. Capital is not very happy with such free goods and seeks to commodify them for sale in a market for profit. So now they sell drinking water in plastic bottles for more than you pay for a comparable volume of gasoline. There is something about a commons that capitalism does not like.

Indeed, historically the privatization of common land (enclosures) was crucial in the development of capitalism. As Karl Marx pointed out, when peasants were denied access to the traditional commons where they had collected firewood and grazed their animals, they were often no longer able to eke out a living on their land and had to sell their labour power to capitalists. The enclosure of commons is a process still going on in advanced capitalism. David Harvey calls it accumulation by dispossession. Water is extracted by Coca-Cola to fill those little plastic bottles, frequently depleting aquifers that were an essential commons for local communities. Similarly, mining extracts resources from the commons, despoiling the land and destroying the livelihood of peoples. The practice of mountaintop removal to extract coal or minerals involves not only the removal of the overburden of rock and forest, but also the human overburden of communities that have long used this commons.

These examples suggest several features of commons. They are shared resources available to all commoners for their benefit without being the property of individuals. They provide benefits to individuals, but they are not exclusionary. Commons stand outside market relations, being governed by common consent. Thus they are democratically controlled. Those advocating for extension of the commons argue for democratic processes to manage them. There is frequently a tension between commons and the capitalist market (as private property for individual enrichment) as well as between commons and the capitalist state (with its hierarchical control). Nevertheless, some commons can exist alongside capitalism if the predatory tendencies of the latter can be contained. By expanding commons and creating new ones, commoners are empowered and their freedom is secured and expanded.

These points can be illustrated with the Mexican *ejido* system of land tenure. Based on the culture of pre-conquest communal society, *ejidos* were established as a result of Mexico's 1910 Revolution for land and liberty. The large private land holdings of the *haciendas* were recuperated by the peasantry and re-established as commons. The 1917 constitution gave legal control of specified land to communities to be used and governed in common. Typically each family was given the use of a piece of the common land but did not own it (i.e. they could not sell it or commit it as collateral for loans). *Ejidos* were not usually cooperatives since each family worked their 'own' land and enjoyed its benefits. The associated commoners or *ejidatorios* did collectively decide on the governance of the common land in order to protect and sustain it. It is this system that gave stability to the rural communities of Mexico for decades.

A central feature of the North American Free Trade Agreement (NAFTA) was to provide for the dissolving of the *ejidos* by the privatization of the land. *Ejidatorios* could decide to take individual ownership of their portion of the commons. The state promoted this privatization that opened up a market for land as a commodity. This has led to the increasing concentration of land ownership by the wealthy and foreign investors and the displacement of large numbers of *campesinos* that have become wage labourers migrating to the cities or *El Norte*. The Zapatista dream of *Tierra y Libertad* (Land and Liberty) has been replaced by Wage Labour and Servitude.

The commons was a key basis for most societies throughout history. The territory of a tribe was the common resource to sustain its livelihood. And it was governed by the commoners so as to be sustainable. They were the stewards of their territory. This is a point that is sometimes misunderstood by modern thinkers. For instance, in his last book, anthropologist Jared Diamond focuses on territoriality in traditional societies and restrictions on movement across their borders. He goes on to claim that 'no traditional society tolerated the relatively open access enjoyed by modern Americans or European Union citizens, most of whom can travel anywhere within the U.S. or the European Union' (Diamond 2012: 49).

Diamond asserts this is unlike traditional societies in which there are borders between the territories of different tribes that restrict access to outsiders. What this fails to understand is that within these modern nation-states there is not open access to most of the territory since it is private property. Access is tightly controlled by individual owners who build walls around their territory and control access with locks and guards. Whereas within traditional societies there is very open access since the territory is common to members of the community. The absence of private property gives people freer access and movement.

Today the struggle to preserve and expand commons is a struggle to protect and expand human freedom in community – not just freedom of movement but also freedom from capital. That is exactly what public banks are about. In the US, the supply of money and credit is presently controlled by private banks in the interest of capital accumulation. As we have seen in Chapter 1, public banks give that control to communities to serve the common good of people. The establishment of public banks is a commoning of money and credit.

One way to move beyond capitalism is to expand the commons. While commons are not necessarily anti-capitalist, they are non-capitalist and do deprive capital of opportunities for accumulation while also building resources that give people a measure of independence from capital. The commons empower people in democratic communities.

6 Building the commons as an antidote to the predatory market economy

Margaret Flowers and Kevin Zeese

These are times of radical change. We are in the midst of an evolution. As David Bollier writes in *The Wealth of the Commons*:

> We are poised between an old world that no longer works and a new one struggling to be born. Surrounded by centralized hierarchies on the one hand and predatory markets on the other, people around the world are searching for alternatives.

> (Bollier and Helfrich 2012)

The old world is one of concentrated economic power that hoards wealth, that creates corrupted and hierarchical governance to serve and further concentrate wealth through exploitation of people and the planet. People are experiencing the ravages of this global neoliberal economy in which the market reigns supreme and everything is a profit centre, no matter the human and environmental costs.

We are at a crossroads in the global economic order. If not stopped, the two massive 'trade' agreements under negotiation at present, the Trans-Pacific Partnership (TPP) and the Trans-Atlantic Trade and Investment Partnership (TTIP), will cement this globalized neoliberal market economy through greater deregulation, profit protection and an extra-judicial trade tribunal in which corporations can sue sovereign nations if their laws interfere with profits.

There is another way. We've reached a tipping point in awareness of the effects of the current global economy that has erupted in a worldwide revolt as we can see in the Occupy, Arab Spring, Idle No More and Indignado movements. People are searching for alternative ways of structuring the economy and society that are empowering and more just and sustainable. Part of this work includes understanding and building the 'commons', which is the opposite of the predatory market economy.

As we will describe below, concentrated wealth is derived by taking from the commons for personal gain in an undemocratic way. We can reverse the current trend toward privatization and wealth inequality by claiming the commons and using it for mutual prosperity. The commons cannot exist without a participatory governance structure. Therefore, building the commons is a fundamental step toward real democracy.

Bollier makes the case that there is 'enormous potential of the commons in conceptualizing and building a better future' (Bollier and Helfrich 2012). Understanding the commons gives us a vocabulary, vision and practical opportunities to create a new world in which governance builds from the bottom up and connects us from the local to the global level.

What are the commons?

What is considered a commons is defined by a particular community and includes more than the physical spaces we usually think of. A commons is something that is a community's entitlement and for which the community shares responsibility to protect, sustain and grow. A commons cannot exist without human involvement through a participatory governance structure.

As David Bollier says,

> a commons arises whenever a community wants to manage a resource in a collective manner, with a special regard for equitable access, use and sustainability. It is a social form that has long lived in the shadows, but which is now on the rise.
>
> (Bollier and Helfrich 2012)

Roman law actually declared certain things intrinsically common property, notably air, wildlife and navigable waters. The term 'commons' dates back to medieval England where it was found in the Charter of the Forest, a companion document to the Magna Carta, created in 1217. It referred to certain rights that everyone had, even on land owned by the aristocracy, for example, to graze their animals or gather wood.

When we declare something a commons, it gives us a new understanding and new vocabulary to reclaim it. For example, the initial view of the broadcast media was that they aired on 'public airwaves'. The airwaves were something we all shared and were a resource for the public good. However, public airwaves were gradually transformed into 'commercial airwaves', in which content is controlled by advertisers and wealth owners. They do not have a public responsibility to share information but view the airwaves as a private opportunity to build wealth. When we understand the airwaves to be a public commons, they can be transformed to serve the public, for example, requiring free airtime for all candidates to reduce the influence of money in elections.

In this era of transformation, the concept of the commons is rising up, often without much attention by the media or government. People are developing tools to create commons. One of the most underappreciated parts of the commons is our collective knowledge. People are building on this collective knowledge with new tools like open-source software, which can be shared without the monopolistic practices of corporations such as Microsoft, or the sharing of information through Creative Commons copyrights rather than restrictive for-profit copyrights. People also are working to build information through 'wikis' that allow crowd sourcing of information to create a shared, deep pool of knowledge. Indeed, the Internet has created a momentum for commons culture because it has made incredible amounts of information widely available for free.

Political economist Gar Alperovitz writes about the commons in *Unjust Deserts: How the Rich Are Taking Our Common Inheritance and Why We Should Take It Back*. He describes how 'Every new breakthrough starts from a plateau of knowledge created by others and preserved and passed on by society' (Alperovitz and Daly 2009). The wealthiest people in the world today would not have attained their wealth without the 'plateau' of knowledge created by the many generations that came before them. Often this knowledge is paid for out of our commonwealth, that is, taxes paid by everyone to provide funds for research like pharmaceuticals or to create the Internet; or by using public land to provide the space to build railroads and roads or to acquire minerals and other natural resources.

Alperovitz points out that Bill Gates, who made his fortune from computers, software and the Internet, could not have been a multibillionaire if it had not been for the commonwealth that created the infrastructure and knowledge on which he built his fortune. Or, as Warren Buffett said:

> Take me as an example. I happen to have a talent for allocating capital. But my ability to use that talent is completely dependent on the society I was born into. If I'd been born into a tribe of hunters, this talent of mine would be pretty worthless. I can't run very fast. I'm not particularly strong. I'd probably end up as some wild animal's dinner.
>
> (Obama 2006: 191)

These are realities for everyone who has gained tremendous wealth. In other words, it is the commons – our common knowledge, infrastructure and technology – that allows people to advance and create individual wealth. Once this is understood, it allows for new thinking about equitable allocation of wealth and replenishment of our commons through progressive taxation and it provides a moral foundation for shared prosperity. It also raises questions and moral doubts about the siphoning off of the commons, depleting it rather than enriching it for all and sustaining it for future generations.

There can be a very positive role for government in legally recognizing and structuring the commons to share the wealth that comes from it. One example is the Alaska Permanent Fund,[1] which was created to share more equitably the wealth created from public lands. When oil is taken from public lands, a percentage of the profit goes into the Alaska Permanent Fund, which manages the money and then distributes a yearly cheque to every person in Alaska from birth to death. These cheques usually range from $1,000 to $2,000 per person and can provide a family of five with income of $5,000 to $10,000 every year.

What would have happened if the investment we all made by providing lands for railroads and highways or inventing the Internet or pharmaceuticals or investing in a new clean energy economy had been put into a national permanent trust and distributed to all Americans each year rather than being given to corporations to create profits? The United States would have a guaranteed national income for everyone from our shared commonwealth and would have eliminated poverty. The transformation to a new energy economy, which includes the need to upgrade transit and rebuild infrastructure, creates another opportunity to share wealth by treating taxpayer investment as a commonwealth in which we all should share.

Tension between the market and the commons

There is a conflict between market culture and the commons. Market culture believes in privatizing as much as possible and taking from the commons – whether it is research, access to cheap loans, tax breaks, public land, infrastructure or resources – to make a profit for their owners and investors. The market takes from the commons for free, and whatever liabilities it incurs or whatever it cannot make a profit from, it dumps back into the commons. Some call it privatizing the profits and socializing the risks.

People who believe in the commons recognize the importance of building communities in which we all benefit from protecting, sustaining and expanding the commons. They recognize that the commons should be used in an equitable way so everyone can prosper.

Market culture has colluded with government, sometimes so closely that big business and government seem like a hand in a glove. They work together as partners to expand the market's power over all aspects of our lives. As David Bollier argues: '[t]he state provides a useful fig leaf of legitimacy and due process for the market's agenda, but there is little doubt that private capital has overwhelmed democratic, non-market interests except at the margins' (Bollier and Helfrich 2012).

Often the result seems like legalizing what should be illegal or unethical practices, whether it is massive campaign donations to dominate elections with money, or exempting the oil and gas industry from clean air and water laws so they are not responsible for pollution, or the leasing of public lands at very low rates with no royalty payments for the profits from public lands.

The pressure to privatize the commons is immense. Today, there are efforts to privatize even the most basic of entities: water. Aquifers in drought-stricken areas are being drained by private companies such as Nestlé to sell as bottled water or by farmers to sell to oil and gas companies for fracking. The two trade agreements under negotiation, the TPP and TTIP, are trying to put in place laws that would severely weaken public enterprises and open the floodgates to privatization.

People who believe in the commons seek to get outside of the narrow political discourse authorized by the corporate political duopoly, which does not allow us to examine systematically the abuses of the market and the corruption of the two-party, mirage democracy. Sheldon Wolin, author of *Democracy Incorporated*, describes this 'managed democracy' as 'a political form in which governments are legitimated by elections that they have learned to control' (Wolin 2010). Voters have the illusion of participating but the choices have been vetted by the corporate shadow government and voters are manipulated by the media into voting against their own interests.

Commons advocates seek to open the possibilities of political movements developing around the commons, creating new governance structures and challenging market dominance. A cultural shift and changes in our educational institutions are required to make this a reality.

Economics and political science students are taught from the beginning that treating entities as commons will lead to certain ruin. Advocates of markets have used a 1968 essay by Garret Hardin, 'The Tragedy of the Commons', to make a false case for market ideology. In the essay, Hardin argues that when something is treated as a commons, it will be overused and destroyed by personal interests. He describes a pasture on common land where all those who graze their animals on the land seek individual profit without regard for others. They add more and more animals to make a larger profit and ultimately destroy the land held in common for grazing. The metaphor illustrates his argument that free access and unrestricted demand for a finite resource ultimately reduce the resource to depletion.

In recent years, this argument has been rebutted by Nobel Prize-winning economist Elinor Ostrom, who (with Xavier Basurto 2008) wrote 'Beyond the Tragedy of the Commons'. Ostrom examined how commons were actually used. She found that the so-called tragedy of the commons was not prevalent, nor was it difficult to solve. Indeed, people from local communities routinely develop controls over the commons to protect it from 'the tragedy'. In 1990, she authored *Governing the Commons* (Ostrom 1990), which examined the governance of natural resources. She found that neither state control nor privatization of resources was the appropriate answer and that commons are sometimes governed by voluntary organizations.

She developed eight 'design principles' of stable local management of commons. They are:

1   clearly defined boundaries;
2   rules regarding the appropriation and provision of common resources that are adapted to local conditions;
3   collective-choice arrangements that allow most resource appropriators to participate in the decision-making process;
4   effective monitoring by those who are part of or accountable to the appropriators;
5   a scale of graduated sanctions for those who violate community rules;
6   mechanisms of conflict resolution that are cheap and of easy access;

7 self-determination of the community recognized by higher-level authorities;
8 in the case of larger commons resources, organization in the form of multiple layers situated inside one another, like Russian nesting dolls.

These have been refined to include additional principles, such as effective communication, internal trust and reciprocity, and making connections between the various parts of the resource system as a whole.

Evolving governance of the commons

These principles are applied in the real world to govern the commons. In fact, Bollier argues that using these principles of the commons is the natural default action of people, pointing out that two billion people depend on commons of forest, fisheries, water and wild game. There are an enormous number of functional, successful commons around the world that mainstream economics does not acknowledge. These commons cultures often develop organically and are based in a particular community where they can adapt as conditions change. Compare this set-up to trade agreements such as the TPP and TTIP, which are not connected to local communities but come from hierarchical structures dictating from above.

When we look at the commons, we begin to understand that there is a long history of communal work in the United States and of people building together to benefit everyone, not just a few. John Curl describes this history in his book *For All the People: Uncovering the Hidden History of Cooperation, Cooperative Movements, and Communalism in America* (Curl 2009). In some societies, this was manifested through barn-raisings, and in others it was creating a cooperative market or an educational collective.

Public utilities that provide electricity are a commons of energy. There are 251 municipal utilities, including cooperatives, in the United States and there is a movement to convert private utilities to public ownership in multiple states. FDR created public utilities as part of the New Deal to supply electricity to rural areas that did not have any. A similar battle today is being fought over whether or not cities will be allowed to provide public access to the Internet for everyone.

To develop governance for the commons, people first need to be able to conceptualize it and understand the ways we can legally recognize the commons. One important concept is that responsibility for managing a commons should go to the lowest practical level, so governance is as close to the people using the commons as possible, thereby allowing local cultures and traditions to be incorporated into it. This is a change from traditional hierarchical political institutions to a new bottom-up, networked-based culture of the commons.

Interesting experiments in governance are happening all over the world. There is a huge international interest in developing the commons. One idea from Italy is to take the private-public partnership model that benefits private businesses with tax dollars and apply it to the commons, creating public-commons partnerships so that the commons can be used and developed for the public benefit. People are also chartering a commons just as one would charter a corporation. This provides a legal structure and ensures the commons is used for public benefit.

In many respects, protecting, sustaining and developing the commons brings us full circle, as Jonathan Rowe, author of *Our Common Wealth: The Hidden Economy That Makes Everything Else Work*, wrote:

> Life was once rich in occasions for spontaneous interaction. People shopped on Main Streets, visited on front porches, attended political events in public venues. Abraham Lincoln and Stephen Douglas had their famous debates in county fairgrounds and town squares all over Illinois, and farmers and townspeople sat for hours in the heat and dust to hear.
>
> (Rowe 2013)

But the commons is not looking back to an idealized past; it is looking forward to a vision of an economy of new values, people building community and working together to solve common problems; to a time when all people have access to the information shared on the Internet, and are assured of the most basic of our commons: clean air and clean water. Rowe, who also co-founded the website On The Commons,[2] wrote:

> The commons is real, huge, and invaluable, and it belongs to all of us. It's also being destroyed – not by itself, but by too much privatization. The possibility part is, We have the capacity to save the commons, though time is short. The moral part is, It's our right and duty to save the commons.

We are at an important juncture. The TPP and TTIP are being negotiated in secret to complete the World Trade Organization agenda of nearly complete privatization. If we believe in a more just, sustainable and democratic world, a world based on the common good, then we must mobilize to stop them. In saving the commons, we are actually building the foundation for the new economy. We are building a world in which people work together to solve common problems and create a more equitable economy and better lives for all of us.

Notes

1 www.earthrights.net/docs/alaska.html [accessed September 2013].
2 http://onthecommons.org/ [accessed September 2013].

7 *Autogestión*

Prefiguring a 'new cooperativism' and the 'labour commons'

Marcelo Vieta

Autogestión (self-management) is at the heart of conceptualizing a workers' economy. This chapter reflects on the meaning of *autogestión* for working peoples' struggles against and beyond today's neoliberal economic order. Its roots pre-date the capitalist era in historical practices of self-activity and the commons. Twenty-first-century theories and practices of alternative socioeconomic arrangements advance and prefigure, implicitly and explicitly, an ultimate self-determination and self-management of people's own productive lives. *Autogestión* is the fullest and most promising expression of the 'new cooperativism', infused as it is with practices of the 'labour commons'.

Community- and worker-led struggles for self-determination and experiments with *autogestión* (translated inadequately from the Spanish as 'self-management') are very much present today despite our neoliberal world order. *Autogestión* is inspired by real moments of resistance in the self-activity of labouring people. Its alternative historiography is far older than capitalism. In it working people created and sustained commonly owned and cooperatively based economic models rooted in solidarity and mutual aid. Such inventions always push back against ideologies and practices of hierarchical control and coercion. This 'other' history, in what can be called a 'genealogy of *autogestión*',[1] goes back to pre-capitalist indigenous societies based on community production and led by reciprocity, householding and other forms of non-market redistribution (Heilbroner and Milberg 1998; Kropotkin 1989; Polanyi 1957). It was – and is – present in rural peoples' resistance to the enclosure of common lands and marginalization of traditional ways of life by encroaching capitalism (Bookchin 1990; De Angelis and Harvie 2014; Thompson 1991).

Autogestión was implicit in the Luddites' early struggles against subjecting work to industrialism (Noble 1993; Sale 1996). It existed in the first working-class struggles for better working and living conditions resulting in the emergence of the trade union and cooperative movements (Craig 1993; Hobsbawm 1964; Thompson 1991; Zamagni and Zamagni 2010). Since then, *autogestión*'s evolution has run parallel with that of capitalism.

Autogestión is also a vision of a free society. For the better part of the past two centuries, it has expressed social anarchists' and libertarian Marxists' faith in human beings' capacities for managing their own productive lives together. A stream of radical economic thought runs through theories and practices of *autogestión*, arguing that working people must free themselves from oppressions inherent in hierarchical forms of power. Under capitalism these are largely embodied in the normalized exploitation of wage slavery. Yet pursuit of a free society is inherent in workers' and communities' struggles to determine their own lives by building a people-centred rather than a profit-centred socioeconomic reality.

Defining our terms

The Spanish word '*autogestión*' has Greek and Latin origins (Farmer 1979). *Auto* is from the Greek '*autós* (self, same)' (1979: 59). *Gestión* is from the Latin '*gestio* (managing)', which comes from '*gerere* (to bear, carry, manage)' (1979: 59). *Autogestión* can be conceived as 'self-gestation' – to create, control and provision with others one's own reality, hence to be collectively *self-reliant* and *self-determining*. Its etymology is linked, in practice and theory, with the collective self-determination of working lives favoured in social anarchist and libertarian socialist economics. *Autogestión* alludes, then, to a processual movement of collective and cooperative creation, conception and definition. Since these connotations are largely elided by the English term 'self-management', I choose to use its accepted Spanish translation for its broader and deeper meaning.

Autogestión carries the ethico-political overtones of struggles for freedom from hierarchical systems. It is linked to the ancient philosophical notion of *potentiality* – evolution into something other than what one is now (Feenberg 2002; Marcuse 1964). As practised by groups of people who live in capitalist systems, *autogestión* implies becoming something other than waged-workers bound to produce for others in the capital–labour relation. From this lived perspective, a worker in Argentina's ongoing worker-recuperated enterprise movement offered me a definition of *autogestión* when I interviewed him in 2009:

> *Autogestión* is the possibility that we – all people – have to realize ourselves professionally, economically, and, in our capacities to labor. It emerges from within ourselves together with the people with whom we want to share this realization, but without sacrificing personal freedom, without sacrificing personal dignity, and from our own developmental potential. It is, in other words, about the possibility of the full development of the person.
>
> (De Pasquale 2009 in Vieta 2016)

This articulates some of Peter Kropotkin's vision of an emancipated 'communist' society. Such a society is *prefigured* historically in daily practices of *autogestión*. Prefiguration is the earmark of ethico-political projections of a post-capitalist world. It interlaces alternative futures with the ethics, values, and practices over which workers struggle – to create the new inside of the shell of the old (Boggs 1977; Franks 2006, 2010). Foreshadowing another world within the present one, workers' self-activity and resistances to capital shape those workers as they, in turn, shape a novel socioeconomic reality.

Two common themes course through conceptualizations of *autogestión* and the prefiguration that threads through it and that strives for new people-centred socioeconomic realities:

1   That to struggle for *freedom from* the exploitative society is, most profoundly, to already begin to shape a 'self-governing society' (Horvat 1982: 11; Marshall 1992) in which working people and communities would be co-responsible for the economic realm in their very reproduction of themselves as human beings.
2   That present experiences of workers already sketch, *prefiguratively*, in varied degrees of opacity and clarity, aspects of the future emancipated society.

These two themes have long run through practices and notions of *autogestión*. Indeed, at its core, *autogestión* is the struggle for freedom in a self-governing society, and as such prefigures the desired people-centred economic reality. Struggle for *autogestión* permeates the *lived experiences* of labouring people (Vieta 2016), conditioned as those experiences are by workers' consistent effort to manage their own working lives. Thus, in workers' resistances to capital – implicit in this effort – is a *parallel* striving to *move beyond* the continuation of capitalism and its liberal ideologies of competition in 'free markets'.

Autogestión for the twenty-first century

Today, *autogestión*'s most radical and liberatory conceptualizations and practices focus on problems of transforming the economic realm. More specifically, transforming productive entities into more people-centred and democratic ones tends to be seen as a first step in broader social change away from our worst oppressions and marginalizations.

Basque social economy theorists Antxon Mendizábal and Anjel Errasti (2008), for example, position *autogestión* on two planes. The first is 'cooperative production' at the level of the enterprise, involving 'processes that envision transformation of relations of production'. The other is 'social and participative democracy' at the 'territorial level' involving 'a process that articulates the different workers' collectives to be coordinated and realized within productive structures of cooperation and solidarity'. Thus for Mendizábal and Errasti, *autogestión* entails four key characteristics:

1   organizing productive entities as social(ized) property;
2   directly democratic coordination of productive activities by workers and, ideally, by all people affected by those activities joined in 'common solidarity';

3   respect for the autonomy of each productive entity and the workers therein; and
4   coordination by a type of federated political organ made up of recallable delegates, that democratically configures how production is to unfold socially.

Roots of the Spanish term *autogestión* are partly in the cooperative and collective production practices in parts of revolutionary Spain in 1936 (Broué and Témine 1962; Rama 1962), and partly in older anarcho-syndicalist and council communist proposals. Mendizábal and Errasti begin to allude to how *autogestión* is being taken up today, particularly in Latin America.

Latin American theorists of *autogestión* suggest the term first invokes democratization of the micro-level of productive enterprises: worker cooperatives and collectives, worker-recuperated firms, rural producer collectives, family-based microenterprises, neighbourhood collectives and indigenous community organizing (Cattani 2004). From these often territorially linked experiments, the state, in turn, is often lobbied for support with the goal of making them more responsive to the needs of local community development while at the same time initiatives of *autogestión* struggle for local autonomy and control. For example, in the 1980s and 1990s, Brazil took up this relationship between the state (via the National Secretary of the Solidarity Economy), unions, and rural and urban cooperative movements as landless peasant and worker movements were emerging in anti-neoliberal experiments with *autogestión* (Gaiger and Dos Anjos 2011; Singer and Souza 2000). The aspiration of this bottom-up approach is to foster the spread of a people-centred solidarity or popular economy rooted in economic justice and participative democracy (Coraggio 1999, 2004; Pastore 2010; Sarria Icaza and Tiribia 2004).

Thus Brazilian sociologist Paulo Peixoto de Albuquerque (2004), one of Latin America's most influential theorists of *autogestión*, proposes in a four-pronged definition of that term, a sort of social transformation by 'gradual encroachment'. For him, *autogestión* has:

1   a *social* character in that it engages all social strata in developing a new societal order grounded in self-determination and participation;
2   an *economic* character that weighs production's various social implications, privileging work over capital, as in worker cooperatives;
3   a *political* character as in Porto Alegre's participatory budgeting, by which all affected join in decision-making, collectively constructing a form of parallel popular power; and
4   a *technical* character in (re)designing and (re)deploying new non-exploitative production processes and divisions of labour (2004: 31–38).

Myriad prefigurative seeds of another world have sprouted; many new worker- and community-driven experiments in *autogestión* rooted in these four broad characteristics are blooming throughout the world today. From Italy's *centri sociale* (social centres) and worker- and community-recuperated enterprises,[2] to the de-growth movement, to Latin America's self-managed indigenous villages devoted to *el buen vivir*, to India's Dalit women's agricultural cooperatives organized by village councils called *Sanghams* (Mookerjea 2010), to the Occupy movements – *autogestión* is again attracting the world's formally and informally employed and dispossessed as a means to self-determination. Other promising new forms of *autogestión* are emerging in, for instance: Quebec's *cooperative solidaire* (solidarity cooperatives); guerrilla gardening initiatives in many countries; urban squats; the DIY (do-it-yourself) movement; barter groups; local currency and exchange systems; neighbourhood assemblies; community dining halls; free health clinics; alternative media; radical education experiments; collective farms; intentional communities and housing co-ops, to name only a few.[3]

In Latin America, two renowned experiments with *autogestión* today deserve further mention. With deep roots in its two-pronged genealogical praxis of resistance to capitalism *and* real proposals for alternatives to it, the Zapatistas of Chiapas and Venezuela's movements of socialist production take different approaches. For the Zapatistas, the state has been sidestepped within the movement's radical libertarian socialist tendencies synchronized with indigenous values that have brought local autonomy and control of resources and land to substantial pockets of Chiapas despite the continued presence of a neoliberal Mexican state. At the same time, the Zapatistas are prefiguring the future, liberated society in its horizontal re-organization of territorial control through direct democracy (Khasnabish 2008). On the other hand, in Venezuela, an extensive and new cooperative and social enterprise movement has emerged that has been both facilitated by interventions of the Bolivarian state and by the self-activity of working people in, for instance, the creation of tens of thousands of new worker co-ops and self-managed 'social-ist production' enterprises (Larrabure *et al.* 2011; Malleson 2010). Moreover, in Venezuela, *autogestión* has been re-conceptualized as *'co-gestión'*. *Co-gestión* homes in on collective autonomy from capital in order to 'change the purpose of productive activity' itself into more community-centred and social economic production (Lebowitz 2005: para. 14). In its 'triangle of socialism' – social ownership of production, social production organized by workers and production for social needs – capitalism's triangle of private property, exploi-tation and for-profit production is purposefully contrasted and contested (Lebowitz 2005: para. 3; also see Larrabure *et al.* 2011).

Global community-focused *autogestión* from below, illustrated by these experiments, is creating spaces that at the same time reject neoliberalism's worst *and* prefigure a world without its pursuit of profit and self-interest. Through democratic control of the labour process, sharing of surpluses, inter-cooperative networks of solidarity, and prioritizing needs and desires of individuals and communities, practices of mutual aid rather than competition reach past daily business concerns. From below in our sea of crisis-riddled capitalism, such alternative islands of what have also been called 'solidarity economies' expose and corrode deficiencies in the present socioeconomic order. *Autogestión* answers today's search for socioeconomic self-determination by contesting the logics of neoliberal markets and, at the same time, stimulating its own proliferation locally.

In short, contemporary conceptualizations and practices of *autogestión* have three broad features:

1 *effectiveness* and *viability* of freely associated production in meeting needs and building social wealth;
2 economic justice via *democratic organization* of productive entities by those most affected; and
3 *social ownership* of the means of production.

The 'new cooperativism', the 'labour commons' and twenty-first-century *autogestión*

I have elsewhere called this broad resurgence of myriad projects of *autogestión* 'the new cooperativism' (Vieta 2010). It is opening pathways beyond capitalist exploitation and its circuits of production and exchange.

This new cooperativism is rooted in history's stream of social anarchist- and libertarian socialist-influenced self-determination (Vieta 2015) – with its built-in suggestion that another world is possible. Today's cooperativism is a movement of *autogestión* distinguished by five features:

1 It emerges as direct bottom-up responses by working people and grass-roots groups to the crisis of the neoliberal model.
2 Often without tight links to older cooperative, labour, or social movements, its protagonists' collective projects issue from immediate social, cultural or economic needs rather than from pre-existing ideological commitments.
3 Its politics emerge not from capital-centric frameworks but from every-day experiences, and aim at more equitable distribution of social wealth and more ethical engagements with the other and with the Earth.
4 It fosters more horizontalized labour processes and decision-making, often joined with collective ownership of social, cultural or economic production; gender-sensitive division of labour; and more egalitarian allocation of surpluses – compared both to capitalist production and to more traditional cooperative experiences.
5 It is more connected with its surrounding communities than capital-centric models, usually embracing clear objectives for local community development (Vieta 2010, 2016).

The new cooperativism both responds to neoliberal enclosures and crises, *and* offers a real alternative. It sets in relief the proliferation of desires for economic self-determination and freedom, when people throw off the yoke of capitalist discourses.

Driven by the possibility of another kind of life, *autogestión*, as practised in the new cooperativism, transforms *organizations, communities* and *subjectivities* from within (Vieta 2014). Its radical educative force unleashes in working people the liberatory potential of Paolo Freire's notion of adult education. For its protagonists it prefigures a people-centred world praxically, that is, *from within their moments of struggle*. Instead of preceding those moments, *politicization of these protagonists emerges from them*, often in encounters with crisis.[4]

Their *hope grows from below, in their own responses to their difficulties*, not from above in enlightened vanguards. Cándido González, labour activist and former member of Argentina's worker-recuperated firm Artes Gráficas Chilavert, articulates how a new subjectivity grew from his struggles occupying and taking over the capitalist workplace that had employed him and his *compañeros*, and then proceeding to transform it into a worker cooperative:

> Early in the fight to reclaim our work we fought for our salaries, for getting out of our severe debt-loads left by the boss .... But now I know, looking back on our struggle three years on, now I can see where the change in me started, because it began during our struggles. First, you fight for not being left out on the street with nothing. And then, suddenly, you see that you've formed a cooperative and you start getting involved in the struggle of others. You don't realize at the time but within your own self ... a change is taking place, you don't see it directly at the time. You realize it afterwards, after time has passed ... doing things that you would never imagine yourself doing.
>
> (González 2005 in Vieta 2016)

Yet *autogestión*'s prefigurative potential rests neither on the possibilities of system overthrow nor on reformist hopes for proliferation of cooperatives at capitalism's expense. Its most radical moments arise as pockets of possibility within and against planetary capital, always pointing to a new, more compelling way to satisfy economic and social needs.

Autogestión we now see is part of a clear trajectory of practices fostering solidarity economies, collaborative production, locally based spaces of mutual aid, networks of solidarity and de-marketized socioeconomic relations. Contemporary notions of 'the common', for instance, plot the trajectory that these practices indicate.

For autonomist Marxists Greig de Peuter and Nick Dyer-Witheford, the new cooperativism's prefigurative force lies in its 'circulation of the common' as opposed to 'circulation of capital' (de Peuter and Dyer-Witheford 2010: 45). For this alternative circulation, there are three major areas of the commons whose interplay is crucial: first, the 'eco-social commons' of fisheries and nature reserves, protected watersheds and commonly controlled forestry practices; the 'networked commons' of 'non-rivalrous' digital goods, online resource pooling and copyleft practices; and, most pertinent for us, the 'democratized organization of productive and reproductive work'. De Peuter and Dyer-Witheford call the latter the 'labour commons', most visible in worker cooperatives and labour-managed firms (2010: 45). De Peuter and Dyer-Witheford liken the unfolding of the 'circulation of the commons' to a reconfiguration of Marx's formula for circulation of capital:

> C represents not a Commodity but Commons, and the transformation is not into Money but Association [A]. The basic formula is therefore: A [association] → C [common] → A' [association prime]. This can then be elaborated into A [association] → C [common] → ... P [production] ... C' [common prime] → A' [association prime] ....
>
> (2010: 45)

A worker cooperative's redistribution of economic surpluses and its worker-members' control of their labour processes constitute its 'labour commons'. This commons distinguishes all labour-managed firms as *socialized* productive entities. Thus in a worker co-op the direct producers *hire* capital, not the other way around as in capitalist businesses. This allows worker-members to democratically control both their labour process and the redistribution of surpluses (Craig 1993: 94). So long as this redistribution is equitable and the cooperative does not hire non-member waged-workers, exploited surplus-labour is itself eliminated (Vieta 2015, 2016). In sum, for de Peuter and Dyer-Witheford, a labour commons transforms a workplace into 'an *organizational commons*, the labour performed ... [into] a *commoning practice*, and the surplus generated, [into] a *commonwealth*' (de Peuter and Dyer-Witheford 2010: 45, emphasis in original). These are all central features of the new cooperativism.

The model of the labour commons is not a blueprint to follow; it is rather a framework in which experiments of *autogestión* can proliferate. Thus the new cooperativism opens 'new economic imaginaries'. These already incite invention of alternative spaces using established ones as raw material, in something akin to what J.K. Gibson-Graham calls the 'generative commons' (in de Peuter and Dyer Witheford 2010: 46; also see: Vieta 2010). This potentially fulsome generation of alternative economic possibilities recalls the open-ended and processual 'becoming' of *autogestión* with which we began this discussion. *Autogestión* is not a new 'hegemonic imaginary', as Stevphen Shukaitis reminds us. It is rather a process of 'developing such spaces with the intent of *creating resources and possibilities to expand and deepen other struggles* as well' (Shukaitis 2010: 72, emphasis added). Further, Ethan Miller (Miller and Albert 2009) has called for continual building of a 'wider economic movement' in 'an alternative [solidarity-based] ecosystem' that 'must generate interventions at every point in the economic cycle' (2009: 13).

Instead of accumulating capital, collective self-provisioning of goods and services to meet human needs has begun. Consistent with de Peuter and Dyer-Witheford's, Shukaitis' and Miller's reminders, the new cooperativism and the labour commons help us (re)imagine a self-determining world. These two historical streams converge in today's emergent bottom-up, community-based practices of *autogestión*. And in its convergence, it is starting to map, prefiguratively, the workers' economy as another-world-in-process.

Notes

1 Here *genealogy* means, as it does for Burawoy *et al.* (2000: 5), a 'tracing [of] how we got to where we are'. For the purposes of this article, a 'genealogical approach' looks for historical moments and conjunctures that trace *a possible path* for the emergence of *autogestión* without trying to find the 'authoritative' history of its 'origins' (Day 2004: 720).
2 Community and production spaces that emerge from once-private or abandoned buildings and factories once they are occupied, recuperated and 'commonized'.
3 For a wide range of examples of experiments in self-determination and *autogestión* today, see Buglione and Schlüter (2010), Cattani (2004), Parker *et al.* (2014), Gibson-Graham (2003, 2006), Miller and Albert (2009) and Vieta (2010).
4 For similar arguments emerging out of the struggles of 1968, see Marcuse (1969).

8 Divisions in the commons
Ecuador's FLOK Society and the Zapatistas' *Escuelita*

George Caffentzis[1]

Ecuador needs to become a 'paradise of knowledge'.
(Daniel Vazquez, a Spanish 'hacktivist' and one of FLOK's directors)

In his discussion of 'originary', 'primary' or 'primitive' accumulation (choose your translation from the German and take the consequences) Marx locates, as a crucial presupposition of capitalism, the 'divorce' (using the word with all its legal legacy) of the 'producer from the means of production' (Marx 1976: 874–875). At that time the main means of production was the land (including forests, fisheries, bogs, etc.), and the most important 'marriage' of the producer with the means of production was sited in the lands that peasants held in common. As Marx impressed on us with this memorandum: 'We must never forget that even the serf was not only the owner of the piece of land attached to his house, although admittedly he was merely a tribute paying owner, but also a co-proprietor of the common land' (Marx 1976: 877). Marx's premise of the argument was that in order to initiate and reproduce itself capitalism has needed to break the bond ('marriage') between producers and the means of subsistence and production because no one would become a wage worker if s/he was able to abundantly satisfy his/her subsistence needs without being exploited and commanded; it forced this 'divorce' (separation from the means of production) by means of the 'enclosure' mechanism.

This then suggests that if the 'enclosures' were reversed and commons became a widespread and ever expanding reality, that is, workers would again be able to satisfy their subsistence needs in common without selling themselves to their exploiters, then capitalism would be annihilated.

If one agrees with the Marxian position that the enclosures of the commons (*literally* in Britain, and *practically* in the rest of Europe, Africa and the Americas) was and remains a necessary element in the divorce of the means of production from the producers, then one must also agree that the commons and capitalism are incompatible. That accounts for the capitalist hostility to the commons that has called forth the continued enclosure of existing commons. In other words, a class war was and continues to be required in order to have a capitalist class at all!

In this presentation I will examine not the soundness of the Marxian argument. Is its premise true? Is the recurrent destruction of fully flourishing commons necessary for the continued existence of capitalism? In so doing, I will explore the political implications of an anti-capitalist politics that starts off from positing the commons as the 'primitive' form of the 'dis-accumulation' of capital (i.e. a process that devalues capital and hinders its reproduction) that was always already in action in the sixteenth century as it continues to be in the twenty-first. This examination is useful for deliberating on the following political question:

> Can there be a triune (or triarchic) society comprising a state sector, a market sector and a commons sector? That is, can the commons be compatible with capitalism and its state forms? If so, does this falsify the premise?

In dealing with this complex of questions we confront a serious division in the ranks of the supporters of the commons. For there are many who hold the view that capitalism is perfectly compatible with the commons and, indeed, it requires the commons and the practice of commoning to thrive, especially in this period of 'cognitive capitalism'. These thinkers claim the future of the commons *requires* that commoners collaborate with capital and the state (as 'Partner').

As Massimo De Angelis put it, 'capital needs the commons, or at least specific, domesticated versions of them. It needs a *commons fix*' (De Angelis 2012: 185). Other commoners argue that it is impossible to join together a fully functioning commons with state and market, since positing the former logically repulses the latter two out of existence. I will discuss this division by examining the notion of the anti-state, anti-capitalist commons developed in practice by the Zapatistas and revealed in the *Escuelita* in Mexico versus the notion of the commons that argues for collaboration with certain kinds of capital and 'partner states'. Those who are now working with the Correa government in Ecuador in developing what they call the FLOK Society plan have recently developed the latter view.[2]

The Zapatistas as commoners

The question of the commons' relation to the state and capital is not 'academic'. It has become one of the most discussed issues in the anti-capitalist movement for the last decade in the Americas, especially in Mexico due to the action of the Zapatista movement that 20 years ago, through force of arms and superior strategy, recuperated more than 60,000 hectares of land in Chiapas and affected more than 500 *nucleos agrarios* [*ejidos*] (Stevens 2002: 78). The villagers who began to use the recuperated land revitalized and expanded their commons, extended the practice of commoning in Mexico and inspired many other commoning efforts across the planet (Midnight

Notes Collective 2001). The last 20 years, therefore, has seen one of the most remarkable tests of whether commoning can be 'scaled up', as David Harvey puts it. The answer, up until now, has been 'Yes', even in the face of the enormous pressures the Mexican government and capital have imposed on the Zapatista villages in the form of carrots – offering money for individual Zapatistas or Zapatista villages to defect from the commoning project – as well as a plentiful number of sticks – the deployment of formal army camps cheek by jowl with Zapatista villages and of paramilitary gangs beating and killing individual Zapatistas (the latest being the murder of Galeano, a teacher in the *Escuelita* on 2 May 2014 in the town of La Realidad). The Zapatista project has involved an enormous amount of commonist creativity.[3]

After almost a decade of 'silence' and work on solving the problem of creating a system of governance for dozens of villages and tens of thousands of people (including the young ones, 'Generation 94', who have grown up with Zapatismo as their 'native' political language) the Zapatistas thought they had something to teach the world. I, with thousands of others, went to school with the Zapatistas in the last few months (in their now famous '*Escuelita*') and one of the important lessons I learned is their refusal to take either the state or 'the market'[4] into the *ejidos*[5] on 'recuperated land'. In a textbook the Zapatistas created for the *Escuelita* entitled *Autonomous Resistance* (2013), 'autonomy' is the term the Zapatistas use to summarize their unwillingness to make deals with state agencies and political parties or to register their organizations as capitalist enterprises, which operate with more democratic decision-making procedures concerning the way capital is deployed and work managed. They refuse to do this because it would violate their autonomy through complicity with the '*mal gobierno*' (the state) and with the fraud of equal exchange in capitalism. For at its core capitalism is a systemic violation of equal exchange in favour of the capitalist class, as Subcomandante Marcos points out:

> According to capitalism, everything must be able to be bought and sold. And it hides everything behind the merchandise so we don't see the exploitation that it carries out. And then the merchandise is bought and sold in a market. And the market, in addition to being used for buying and selling, is also used to hide the exploitation of the workers.
>
> (El Kilombo Intergalactica 2007: 71)

Indeed, the term 'autonomy' was not prominent in early Zapatista discourse; terms like 'freedom', 'justice', 'equality', 'democracy' and 'dignity' were much more emphasized.

For example, the 'Demands Submitted during the Dialogue' of 1994 were prefaced by the following: 'We do not ask for charity or gifts. We ask for the right to live in dignity, with equality and justice like our ancient parents and grandparents' (The Editorial Collective 1994: 238). It is only after the Fox government's unspoken, quasi-'settlement' of the Zapatistas in 2001 (when the Zapatista leaders were assured that they could travel out of the recuperated territory in Eastern Chiapas without fear of arrest), that 'autonomy' became a key word in their political vocabulary. As Marcos said, one of the 'great achievements' of Generation 94 was 'to form together this new generation which is the one that created autonomy here' (quoted in El Kilombo Intergalactica 2007: 38).

To sketch out the notion of autonomy in Zapatista thinking, consider this pastiche from the writers of *Autonomous Resistance*:[6]

> When we began to organize ourselves in resistance, we formed our authorities and organized ourselves to work together as villages, regions, municipalities, and even at the zone level. We worked collectively in the *milpa*, cultivating beans, raising livestock, and growing coffee in order to strengthen and exercise our autonomy and to facilitate our authorities' work in each center, region, and municipality. To resist does not mean not to work. To resist is to work, because resistance is made and constructed by the people. That is, resistance is our house, our roof, our shelter where we are together as villages, families, and as *compañeros* and *compañeras*.
>
> (Zapatistas 2013: 38)

> Thus, the bad government could not destroy our autonomy. Why? Because, as we know, it exists in our hearts. When political awareness is mature, when political awareness is not weak, we can keep moving forward collectively, as men, children, women, and elderly all working together.
>
> (Zapatistas 2013: 45)

> Through our resistance as bases of support, we have exercised our autonomy without needing to establish a relationship with the bad government.
>
> (Zapatistas 2013: 50)

These Zapatista voices highlight different aspects of the notion of autonomy. On the one side, autonomy is connected with resistance, i.e. the refusal to accept the command of external authorities (legitimated either by law or money), and on the other side, it means the preservation of the community through common work and common needs, as another Zapatista says:

> In our zone, Selva Fronteriza, there have been many changes. Before 1994, we were organized differently as communities because our grandparents had another way of understanding things. The work that they did in common maintained a community life, but what they didn't practice was women's participation in the assemblies. Women weren't taken into account, as if they didn't have the right to participate. In 1994, with the Women's Revolutionary Law in effect, women's participation became part of daily practice.
>
> (Zapatistas 2013: 21)

There are different kinds of collectives in the villages, with some managed by women and some managed by men. For us, working in collectives is very important because whenever there is a common need in the zone, the municipality, or in our communities, we are able to meet this need with the resources generated through the collectives.

(Zapatistas 2013: 52)

The Zapatistas see *mal gobierno* (bad government) as relentlessly attempting to destroy their autonomous resistance by destroying their common life:

The politics of the bad government is to put an end to life in common, to community life, so that you leave your land, or you sell it, and if you sell it you're screwed.

(Zapatistas 2013: 35)

Now it has a different name [Mesoamerican Integration and Development Project] because the Puebla-Panama Plan was highly criticized, but it is the same thing; they only changed the name so that they could go on individualizing the communities, to put an end to the life in common that still exists.

(Zapatistas 2013: 36)

The Zapatistas' valorization of autonomy is absolute as shown in the refusal to interact with the state (*mal gobierno*) and political parties (including those of the left) from 1994. This refusal led to a major split with the Mexican left in 2006 when the PRD of Obrador and his supporters blamed their electoral loss on the hostility of the Zapatistas.

The Zapatistas also express a deep hostility to capitalism as the subversion of their autonomy. Consider this historical account of the antithesis to capitalism:

[The capitalists] wanted to make us think that in order to live happily and in abundance there had to be inequality, so that some could live in luxury without worrying about those who had nothing. This is the thinking, or the ideology, of the capitalist system today. But our ancestors understood that this was not how life should be, and that they had to struggle against this imposition. Some fled to the mountains to escape slavery on the ranches; in other cases they rebelled against the *patrones* [bosses], killing their oppressors. They risked their lives to maintain their language, their religion, and their knowledges. But resistance is not merely refusing the support of the bad government, or not paying taxes or electric bills. Rather, resistance is constructing everything that we need to maintain the life of our people. That is why resistance is one weapon in our struggle to confront the capitalist system that dominates us.

(Zapatistas 2013: 70)

How does the capitalist system attack our culture? One way is through the media – television, radio, internet, cable TV, magazines – which it uses to confuse and influence the thinking and knowledge of the youth. It also uses modern music trends and instruments, television programs, and youth entertainment centers like discos, the cinema, and bars. Then there are the problems of drug addiction, alcoholism, and drunkenness.

Capitalism also attacks our ways of speaking, of expressing ourselves, what we eat, the way we work, how we are educated, how we impact the environment, and through the institutions of marriage and religion.

(Zapatistas 2013: 83)

This is not to say that the Zapatista communities do not engage in monetary exchanges with the capitalist world around them. Though they have adapted largely an autarkic form of social reproduction, they use Mexican pesos to exchange for commodities they cannot produce, from trucks and computers to certain medical supplies and foods. They mainly earn money through selling coffee beans grown either on individual or collective plots of land. The Zapatistas even have a bank, BANPAZ, with low interest rates and with community involvement in determining why the prospective debtor needs the loan and in enforcing repayment:

the set of regulations we had when we started the BANPAZ [Autonomous Zapatista People's Bank] had to be modified and have gotten better. If a regulation doesn't work for us, we modify and improve it as time and the situation allow. BANPAZ's regulations include several points. For example, if a *compañero* in the zone does not repay his debt, his community must take responsibility in demanding that he repay. In this case we already have the word of the local authority and the local health *promotor* that this *compañero* did in fact need the loan. But if for whatever reason he does not repay, his own community is obligated to demand repayment, because they are the ones who know him best and know why he does not want to comply.

(Zapatistas 2013: 9)

In Marxist terminology, the monetary exchanges the Zapatistas carry on with the non-Zapatista population are not intended for the capitalization of money, i.e. profit-making. They engage in the series of market exchanges C→M→C, Commodity (C)→Money (M)→Commodity (C) and not M→C→M' with M'>M, i.e. their exchanges are finalized as, or are merely, means to the acquisition of use-values and not as a way to create surplus exchange value. Is it possible to have money operate as an intermediary of commodity exchange (C→M→C) and not collapse into functioning as capital (M→C→M')? The Zapatistas are aware of the tendency for C→M→C to be transformed into M→C→M' and they carefully watch the circulation of money in their communities (like the workers in a nuclear power plant who nervously watch the uranium rods, for if they get out of control through their mutual excitation, they can melt down and destroy the whole system, themselves and their regulators).

The Zapatistas are forging a commons-based anti-state and anti-capitalist form of life with international implications. Their political strategy is rooted in a rejection of and hostility toward the state and capitalism. They have had an enormous influence on the politics of the Americas (both North and South). But is such a rigorist path necessary? Could it possibly be politically effective at getting beyond capitalism? I will turn now to those political supporters of the commons who argue against the general position the Zapatistas (among others) support. They – most prominent being Elinor Ostrom, David Bollier and Michel Bauwens – call for various forms of society that would include commons forms of property ownership *with* state and private property as a way to transform the present neoliberal form of capitalism.

The triune system: from Ostrom to Bollier

The Zapatistas have presented the case for rejecting a form of society that would have three kinds of property (state, private and common) and three different 'sectors' on an equal basis at the beginning. However, many theorists and practitioners of the commons do not share this position. Indeed, since 1990 there have been many streams of commons literature that await to be distinguished.

One stream supports the Zapatistas by identifying commoning as antithetical to capitalism and takes the contra-positive reasoning concerning capitalism's origins and reproduction as axiomatic. I will discuss this stream below, in the section 'The anti-capitalist commons', when it comes time to defend the Zapatista position concerning relations of the commons to state and capital. In this section I will present the second stream: the views of those coming out of the research of the International Association for the Study of Commons (formerly International Association for the Study of Common Property) and its founding leader, the late Elinor Ostrom, the political work of David Bollier of the Commons Strategy Group, and the contributors to the FLOK Society Project in Bolivia. I will largely take Ostrom's publication of *Governing the Commons* (Ostrom 1990) as the starting point and Bollier's and FLOK Society Project's work as the present point of the trajectory of the irenic commons politics. I am not suggesting, however, that Ostrom, Bollier and the FLOK Society were self-consciously allied in an organization.

Ostrom begins her project of making a conceptual place for the commons by responding to the 'tragedy of the commons' paradox that Garrett Hardin posed in his infamous 1968 article of that name in *Science* (Hardin 1968). In that article Hardin aimed to show that commonist modes of production lead to a practical dead-end – a position Ostrom wanted to counter. Hardin, an ecologist, imagined the following scenario: there is a meadow that is accessed by two or more cow herders who are intending to sell their animals in the near future.

It appears reasonable to each individual herder to add another cow and still another to graze on the meadow since each additional cow grazing costs him/her little while the fattened cow would be worth much more at the meat market. Inevitably, however, if each herder follows the same logic the field becomes overgrazed and useless to all the herders.

What looks like rational action individually turns out to be collective folly. Hardin called this situation 'the tragedy of the commons', because he referred to the meadow in question as 'a common' and the 'tragedy' as the destruction of the meadow ecosystem due to the actions of the 'rational decisions' of the herders. How is this tragedy to be averted in the interest of both the herders and of the ecological system?

Hardin, and those who turned his performance into a founding myth of neoliberalism, saw only two ways out: (1) divide up the meadow and privatize it (so that individual proprietors who would be concerned to preserve 'their own plot' would be careful not to overgraze) or (2) have the state police the herders and punish any herder who broke the state-imposed rules intended to stop overgrazing.

The problem with (2), the state solution, from a neoliberal perspective, is that it would soon degenerate into a set of corrupt deals between some unscrupulous herders and the cow-police. So, given the well-known problems of state regulation, this tale implies that the best way to use land and other 'natural resources' is by privatizing access to them. Of course, a presupposition of this tale is that the herders were clearly directing their thought to trading beef in a market for money and not to their subsistence needs even before the privatization; because if they were concerned with subsistence, then once the need for meat as a use value was satisfied, the herder would turn his/her attention to other non-cow-feeding activities and help reduce the pressure on the meadow.

The burden of Ostrom's paradigm-defining 1990 book, *Governing the Commons*, was to prove that alongside the state solution and a privatization solution offered by Hardin there is room for a 'commons' solution. That is, the herders could come together in a democratic assembly, pose the problem of overgrazing collectively, and agree to a set of self-imposed rules for accessing the meadow and a set of penalties for those who violate the rules. Is this just wishful thinking? Doesn't Mammon with his loyal subject Leviathan rule? Ostrom's book is filled with historical studies of actually existing and long-lasting commons fisheries from Turkey to Nova Scotia and Sri Lanka, of Philippines farmers' commons irrigation schemes, of the groundwater commons in parts of California as well as theoretical efforts to counter the framework imposed by Hardin and his neoliberal descendants (Ostrom 1990). *Most of these commons are used for commodity production*, as was Hardin's meadow.

Ostrom's commons solution to the 'tragedy problem' is thus not just a theoretical possibility, but a practical one, often superior to both the state solution (which is heavy on sanctions and prone to corruption) and the privatizing one (that often leads to uneven income results and class conflict). At the least, the commons can be considered alongside the state and private solutions. But 'alongside' implies a lack of antagonism that is present in Ostrom's writing concerning these different 'solutions'.

A similar sense of nonconfrontation can be seen in her analysis of the Eight Principles for Managing a Commons (Ostrom 1990):

1   Define clear group boundaries.
2   Match rules governing use of common goods to local needs and conditions.
3   Ensure that those affected by the rules can participate in modifying the rules.
4   Make sure the rule-making rights of community members are respected by outside authorities.
5   Develop a system, carried out by community members, for monitoring members' behaviour.
6   Use graduated sanctions for rule violators.
7   Provide accessible, low-cost means for dispute resolution.
8   Build responsibility for governing the common resource in nested tiers from the lowest level up to the entire interconnected system.

These seem reasonable enough as 'design principles'. However, they ignore the conflictual element involved in creating and preserving commons in or around a capitalist society, especially commons that give power to workers to refuse the wages offered and the dangerous working conditions in the capitalist sector. Or, at best, we hear some muffled noise of class conflict in Principle 4, For how does one 'make sure' that the 'outside authorities' will respect the rule-making rights of the commoners? Through reasoned discourse? Tell that to the Native Americans past and present and to the English commoners of yore.

In fact, though the state (or government) is referred to often in *Governing the Commons*, there is almost no mention of the corporation – local, national, multinational and global – which has a major stake in the privatization of access to what had been common property resources. There is little mention either of war, or slavery, or racial, class and gender divisions among the commoners even though these gigantic forces were quite central to the life and death of commons past and present. The grand enclosures of recent history, organized by governments in the interests of their capitalist clients, are not given a mention either. On the contrary, Ostrom concentrated on the commodity-producing commons as the empirical basis of her response to Hardin.

This is understandable, for after all, Hardin's rational herders were fattening their cattle for the beef market, so Ostrom in *Governing the Commons* barely touches the non-market, subsistence commons that have been the main form of commons throughout history. As a consequence, Ostrom founds commons studies on the commodity-producing commons and, as a corollary, she shows that in many cases these kinds of commons are often more efficient, sustainable and profitable than comparable corporate efforts. So for her there is no need to protect commons from capitalism, on the contrary, Ostrom argues that they need to be given a legal structure in order for them to compete fairly with corporations.

The commons research programme that Ostrom launched in the 1990s has produced evidence showing that the 'commons can in certain circumstances do it better than corporations and the state'.

The commons discourse has developed a political character, because many supporters of Ostrom's design principles realized that the neoliberal turn of capitalism was increasingly pulling off a 'silent theft' (as David Bollier entitled his 2003 book) of the commons resources of the planet, from land, forest, fisheries, deep seas, to the electro-magnetic spectrum, the genetic code and so on.

It has become increasingly more difficult to have 'outside authorities' respect the rule-making rights of commoners (Principle 4). The commons everywhere have been under threat and the 'you don't know what you've got 'til its gone' adage has seemed to apply to this period with a vengeance.

David Bollier, by identifying himself so consistently and publically as a spokesman for the commons, marks for me the present moment of the conceptual trajectory beginning in 1990. I will use his work (including his joint work with others like Silke Helfrich) to trace the path of the political development of the notion of the commons, for there have been some major changes occurring in this period.

In 2003, Bollier was anxious to defend the commons against the neoliberal assault. He wrote:

> So the issue is not market versus common. The issue is how to set equitable and appropriate boundaries between the two realms – semi-permeable membranes – so that the market and the commons can each retain integrity while invigorating the other. That equilibrium is now out of balance as businesses try to exploit all available resources, including those that everyone owns and uses in common.
>
> (Bollier 2003: 4)

Although the levelheaded Bollier was far from taking a harsh apocalyptic tone, there was a sense of 'clear and present danger' in the face of rapacious market institutions. His structural conception at that time was that the market 'realm' depended on the commons 'realm' and was not in competition with it. Indeed, in the neoliberal corporate order's totalitarian drive to privatize the commons in all its appearances lies the seeds of its own destruction, Bollier warned (as Polanyi did in the midst of the Second World War) that the free marketeers are on the verge of killing the goose that laid the golden egg (to put another goose besides the goose on the commons into play!) (Polanyi 1944). His major political effort was to appeal to the state to protect the commons against the rapacious corporations and their neoliberal advisors.

By 2012, four years after the latest financial crisis, Bollier speaks in a different key in a volume he edited (with Silke Helfrich) *The Wealth of the Commons: A World beyond Market and State* through its title, ending and introduction. It is a rich book that includes articles from many different tendencies in the increasingly self-confident movement that is calling for commons 'solutions' for contemporary socioeconomic problems. The subtitle of the 2012 volume speaks of going 'Beyond Market and State' while the subtitle of the 2003 book is 'The Private Plunder of Our Common Wealth'.

Instead of ending, as did *Silent Theft* with a chapter entitled 'Strategies for Protecting the Commons', *The Wealth of the Commons* ends with an 'Epilogue' written by Bollier and Helfrich (dated May Day 2012) that lists a series of commons-based conferences, demonstrations and organizations. These events were taking place from Bangkok to Paris to Cape Town to New York and so on, giving a graphic testimony of 'the beginnings of an international commons movement'. What a difference a world financial crisis and a movement makes! (Bollier and Helfrich 2012: 438).

The 'introduction' of the 2012 volume also speaks volumes about the increase of self-confidence among the supporters of the commons in less than a decade. For example, the title of the introduction in the 2012 book is 'The Commons as a Transformative Vision'. And in that introduction there is a remarkable boldness of expression compared to the modest language of the 2003 introduction (which had no title):

> This book, then, is a first rough draft of that much larger project, the reclamation of the common wealth – and the reinvigoration of the commonwealth.
>
> (Bollier 2003: 11)

> Now that the severe limitations of the market system under capitalism have been made abundantly clear, the question we must confront is whether the commons can become the dominant social form.
>
> (Bollier and Helfrich 2012: xix)

In 2003, Bollier was speaking of returning to the past by '*re*-claiming' and '*re*-invigorating' whereas in 2012 Bollier is looking to the future where the commons literally conquers the world, that is, it goes beyond equality of sectors to dominate the triune society.

But as with any movement there are usually profound strategic conflicts and the one Bollier comments on is exactly the division that the Zapatistas present. Bollier cautions:

> There is an inherent tension in seeding new sorts of commons initiatives, however, because they must often work within the existing system of law and policy, which risks co-optation of the commons and the domestication of its innovations ... some commoners prefer to have little or no

intercourse with markets while others believe that their communities can better thrive if they interact with markets.

(Bollier and Helfrich 2012: xviii)

Bollier makes clear which side of this 'creative tension' he is on: '[Bollier and Hilfrich] believe it is entirely possible to create commons-based innovations that work within existing governance systems while helping bring about a new order' (Bollier and Helfrich 2012: xix). In the next section we investigate this claim, by examining the other side of the commons. Thus the tremendous work done by social scientists and social activists in the Ostrom research programme leads to the willingness 'to work within existing governance systems'. But is this possible 'while helping bring about a new order'? Can the capitalists and the state bureaucrats be tricked into working for the commons revolution?

The anti-capitalist commons: the Ecuadorian FLOK Society or the Zapatistas' *Escuelita*?

In order to answer these questions I now turn to another train of thought concerning the commons. For there is no unequivocal definition of the commons. Indeed, the word 'commons' in the early twenty-first century has become something like 'socialist' was in the nineteenth century, a term that could include followers of Robert Owen, Marx and Engels, and Georgi Plekhanov among dozens of others.

There is an anti-capitalist, Marxist perspective on the commons that includes Peter Linebaugh, Silvia Federici, Massimo De Angelis, Steven Colatrella and Monty Neill, who contributed books and articles to this anti-state, anti-capitalist train of thought as did online journals such as *The Commoner* (De Angelis 2006; Federici 2004; Linebaugh 2008; Neill 2001). This tendency was inaugurated with the Midnight Notes Collective's publication of the *New Enclosures* in 1990 (the same publication year as Ostrom's *Governing the Commons*).[7] It argued that in order to understand the class struggle of the post-1970 period we had to see past the terminology of 'structural adjustment', 'new international division of labor', 'post-Fordism' and even 'neo-colonialism' to recognize that we were living *once more* through a new era of primitive accumulation on a large scale and a keystone of this process is the enclosure of common resources. Although the wage struggle is central to the class struggle, its presupposition – the creation of the waged worker – is also an essential aspect of the class struggle. For no people are 'naturally' waged workers. They must be made into workers in the face of much resistance and the closing of the doors of escape, the most prominent exit being access to a functioning and abundant commons.

In this view the commons is brought to the centre of the class struggle, not only in the sixteenth century, but throughout the history of capitalism.

Whenever the working class struggles for and creates a commons that can provide reliable and abundant subsistence, capitalism is threatened, especially if this struggle is generalized. So in the 1960s and 1970s, after the combined struggles associated with the anti-colonial movement, the factory workers' refusal of work, the welfare mothers' and student movements that led to wage hikes and increases in the 'social wage' (think Medicare in the US), capital launched a counter-revolution that continues down to this day. As the Midnight Notes Collective summarized in the 1980s by the Reagan and Thatcher regimes: 'the last decade has seen the largest Enclosure of the worldly Common in history' (Midnight Notes Collective 1992: 319).

This insight has led to a whole literature on the commons that is radically different in tone and purpose from the work done in the name of the research programme initiated by Elinor Ostrom and developed by Bollier and many others.

1   Instead of asking whether the commons is more productive, more sustainable and more equitable than ordinary capitalist firms, as Ostrom's followers do, this approach asks whether the commons gives the commoners more power to refuse poor wages and working conditions and, in the extreme, to refuse to be workers for capital at all. In a word, does the commons support the dis-accumulation of capital? If not, then it is not an anti-capitalist common (Caffentzis and Federici 2013).
2   Instead of proclaiming the ability of commons to stimulate the capitalist sphere (something that both Ostrom and Bollier often do), the anti-capitalist commons is judged on the basis of the maxim: 'more power to the commons and the commoners, less power to capital and the capitalists'.
3   Instead of taking the commons as the end of politics and economics as the supporters of the Ostrom paradigm seem to, the supporters of the non-capitalist commons see them not as ends, but as means to the ending of capitalism.

This study of the conditions required for an anti-capitalist commons has led to re-examining the role of the state. For clearly there has been a profound transformation from the Keynesian state that injected the class struggle into itself in order to stimulate production and periodically 'shake up' the capitalist class.

This form of the state ended decades ago, however, beginning with its self-proclaimed termination in the 1980s with the Reagan and Thatcher regimes. This change in the nature of the state has been expressed by Bollier and Helfrich in their phrase 'market/state duopoly', that is, the state becomes marketable while the market becomes the form of the state, and even more openly in the rhetoric of the Occupy Wall Street movement, with its claim that the 1 per cent have now purchased the state apparatus so thoroughly that their relation to it is no longer one of representation, but of direct presence (exemplified by the thousands of corporate lobbyists descending daily on the Congress and White House in Washington DC and the large number of very wealthy elected politicians). And indeed, recent Supreme Court decisions, especially *Citizens United v. Federal Election Commission*, 558 U.S. (2010), have granted full personhood (hence having First Amendment protection, thus equating money with speech) to corporations, a process that has been in the making since the early nineteenth century.

It is clear that the so-called 'market sector' would not be interested in cooperating with an anti-capitalist commons network unless capitalism would transit from its present 'cancer stage' to becoming both senile and suicidal.

With the above evidence, it would be folly to try to 'partner' with the other side of the duopoly, the state. But there apparently is still hope among many supporters of the commons that at least some states can be somehow persuaded to untie themselves from capital enough to become a 'partner' to the commons, which would open and protect a space for a triune society that includes a commons sector alongside the state and the private capital sectors. Because this strategy is difficult to apply with respect to Western Europe and the US, regions where neoliberalism is dominant, the hope for some commoners like Michel Bauwens has shifted to the leftist governments of Latin America, especially Rafael Correa's government in Ecuador. Correa is interested in making Ecuador the centre of research projects using commons notions of property in the sphere of what is often called 'immaterial' production (biotech, computer design, etc.).

Correa is inviting prominent supporters of the commons from around the world to the City of Knowledge on the outskirts of Quito to propose plans for research and communications that would transform Ecuador's economy into a 'knowledge-intense' one. Indeed, the Ecuador government's offer of safe haven to Julian Assange is one part of this effort to make the country into a centre of 'free thought' attuned to the latest technological transformations. One major project is the work of the FLOK Society that is researching the legal and economic consequences of changing 'intellectual property' laws into new forms of copyright that would in effect be making knowledge a common.

FLOK gets funding from the Ecuadorian government and grew out of speeches Correa had made calling for a 'social knowledge economy', according to Michel Bauwens, a founder of the Peer2Peer Foundation hired to work on the FLOK project for Ecuador. According to an interview given by Daniel Vazquez, a Spanish 'hacktivist' and one of FLOK's directors, 'Ecuador needs to become a "paradise of knowledge"'. The idea also springs from Ecuador's five-year *Vivir Bien* (living well) Plan introduced in 2009 (Gray 2013).

These developments pose the question: should commoners take passage to Quito or to Chiapas or to both?

However, given such different theoretical perspectives that I sketched above it is inevitable that political, even philosophical differences would arise within the heart of the supporters of the commons at this moment. In fact, when we contrast the Zapatista *Escuelita* with the government-sponsored FLOK Society supported by Correa we see tensions everywhere, and it remains to be seen whether they will be 'creative'. For example, the model of epistemology used by these two projects and the role the commons should play in learning and knowing are quite different. The Zapatistas' *Escuelita* looks to the everyday life of Zapatistas as the source of knowledge that gets communicated only through the direct experience of living with Zapatista families in Zapatista *ejidos*. There is no substitute, neither via books nor DVDs, nor the Internet. Of course, this does not imply some sort of anti-intellectualism on the side of the Zapatistas, who are indeed credited with some of the most sophisticated political use of communications technology (Cleaver 1994), but it does imply the recognition of the limits of the so-called electronic social networks.

The FLOK programme, on the other side, is inspired by the work of Michel Bauwens of the Peer2Peer network who, in turn, has as his model for the contemporary knower a worker involved in computer-intense forms of production and world-wide internet-mediated cooperation. For example, he argues that because of the technological possibility afforded by these machines and networks a commons-oriented society 'is possible because producers are much more in control of their own means of production, i.e. personal creativity, computers, and access to networks. We propose to extend this vision and reality to the totality of the means of production' (Bauwens and Iacomella 2012: 327).

Thus the creative, computer savvy Internet voyager is now to be the model of production (goodbye to the factory worker, the miner and the farmer). This is an unprecedented development according to Bauwens:

> What is important, and to some extent historically novel, is the rise of equipotential cooperation mechanisms that function beyond the local level; the generalized possibility for stigmergic [social insect like, CGC], horizontal communication among large numbers of people; the legal protections for maintaining commons that open licenses provide; and the choice that commoners always have to fork a collaborative project.
>
> (Bauwens 2012: 377)

One way of describing the situation is that this mode of commons production will bring about something of a socioeconomic version of Kurzweil's notion of 'the Singularity' (Kurzweil 1999).

Whether this is an accurate picture of the job conditions of the average worker in a computer-intensive production or not, this generalization repeats the mistake that is made again and again by many productivists who take the most productive capitalist forms of work to be uniformly hegemonic. For Bauwens' view is that commons forms of production will out-compete standard industrial capitalist forms of production by 'out-cooperating' them (Bauwens and Iacomella 2012: 326). Consequently, the most productive workers would have the power to negotiate with and move the capitalist class.

But this is not always so, for being 'productive' for capitalism hides other notions of 'productivity' and other notions of power. As feminists like Silvia

Federici have soundly argued, capital often imposes on workers in the reproductive branch radically different roles and values and forms of work that are
not even counted as work, like child rearing, hence are not even considered to
be on the scale of productivity (Federici 2012). So who are more productive
here, mothers or programmers?

In fact, the Zapatistas have inverted Bauwens' logic of power for their ideal
teachers of freedom and autonomy are the *ejidatarios* and their communities
in the mountains of the Mexican Southeast who often neither have a computer nor are computer savvy, but do have a long history of anti-capitalist
cooperation (Cleaver 1994).

There are other differences as well, of course. For example, bodily presence
is important for the Zapatistas' conception of democracy. That is why there is
so much expense paid (in the form of gasoline and transport vehicles) by the
communities to have 'their' members in the various committees. Of course,
for the workers in 'immaterial production' their presence is not necessary, on
the contrary, it is somewhat reactionary. If you can 'Skype' a meeting, why
go through all the trouble and expense of bringing material bodies together?

The key difference, however, concerns the relation of the Zapatistas and the
FLOK proponents to the state and capital. The Zapatistas have refused to formally recognize the authority of the Mexican state in their *ejidos*. They refuse
to accept its legitimacy. If the government in Mexico City votes down a law
the Zapatistas support, they put it into action in their territories anyway. They
reject the blandishments as well as the assaults of capital and the state. Why?
Because their aim is to be a part of the long struggle for the end of the era of
capitalism and the state. They are 'planting the seeds of the trees of the future'.

This is in stark contrast with Correa's project of turning the productivity of
the commons into an engine of economic growth in Ecuador by leaping over
the industrial stage of capitalist development and arriving directly in an era of
'cognitive capitalism' (with the help of an indeterminate period of extractivism).
Is the commons to be the vehicle of anti-capitalism or of a hyper-capitalism?
These two experiences then are embodiments of the present division in the common and it is clear to me that the Zapatistas are the realistic ones here, for the
following reason: the ability to use the power of cooperation to out-compete
'traditional industrial capitalist' enterprises, as Bauwens and his co-workers
propose, forgets that there is capitalist cooperation aiming to produce surplus
value and there is anti-capitalist cooperation that, like Bartleby the Scrivener,
'prefers not to' contribute to capitalist accumulation (Melville 1961). They are
by no means identical; in fact, in most cases they are antithetical.

In conclusion is a triune society possible? Not, if the commons in question is
anti-capitalist and negates a necessary condition for the existence of capitalism.

Postscript

We are at a 'fork' in the life of the commons as a concept and a reality. After
centuries of neglect, it is now becoming an essential concept for discussing

contemporary society. But at the moment of its re-emergence, deep and growing divisions are appearing among the commoners concerning their very self-definition. These divisions can be expressed in pairwise alternatives. They include:

- commodity-producing commons versus anti-capitalist commons;
- state as partner to the commons versus state as nemesis to the commons;
- the hammer (or silicon chip) versus the sickle.

It is time we acknowledged these divisions and act on their consequences: 'Which sides are you on?'

Notes

1 I would like to thank Steven Colatrella, Ryan Conway, Silvia Federici, Max Haiven, Hans Widmer, Peter Linebaugh and Harry Cleaver for their comments and criticisms.
2 'Free, libre, open knowledge' society.
3 Given all this, one would think the Zapatistas are at the centre of commons studies. However, the huge academic literature on the commons has not included much on the Zapatistas. In fact, in the Digital Library of The Commons none of the thousands of titles of books, articles and conference papers dealing with the commons have the feared word 'Zapatista' in their confines. I suppose that when the commons comes armed, anxiety and timidity scales up as well.
4 I write the phrase 'the market' with scare quotes in order to alert the reader that I am a critic of the use of this phrase as a synonym for capitalism. 'The market' gives a sense of equal exchange relations, whereas capitalism requires workers to receive less value for their labour power than the value they create. Otherwise, the system does not work. In the text below I will use the terms 'capital' and 'capitalism' in most places where 'the market' is normally used. However, there are occasions when I am referring to the realm of equal exchange, and there I use the phrase 'the market'.
5 *Ejido* – a classification of the post-revolutionary Mexican Constitution of 1917 which recognized and protected collectively held lands so that they could not be bought from or sold by their communal owners nor titled by an individual owner. This prevented their expropriation as collateral or debt payment. An *ejidatario* is a member of an *ejido*.
6 This textbook is one of four produced in a commonist manner for the *Escuelita*. I mean by this that first, there is no 'authorial voice' proclaiming the 'official' Zapatista view on this or that subject. On the contrary, the voice is constituted by Zapatistas (with the emphasis on the plural) presenting their views on freedom and autonomy. It remains nominalist throughout. Second, contributors come from all five *caricoles* and give their views from their perspective and experience, there is no editorial committee that claims to summarize and iron out differences in individuals' approaches to defining 'autonomous resistance' (Zapatistas 2013). So in adding my effort of learning in the *Escuelita* to the discussion in the US, I too do so in a commonist spirit I learned from my *votan* and the village, the 8th of March, assigned to me.
7 In the interest of full disclosure, I should mention that I was a founding member of the Midnight Notes Collective.

Part III

Alternatives to a system in crisis

Cliff DuRand

In the post-Second World War period, Western nation-states, international institutions and major foundations promoted what were called developmental policies throughout the global South. In the context of the Cold War, this was a strategy to prevent them from following a socialist path and to bring former colonies into the capitalist orbit. Massive assistance was given to build the physical, cultural and institutional infrastructure to link their economies to capitalist markets. Developmentalism promised modernization, economic growth and rising living standards. However, their incorporation into a neoliberal globalization has not been so beneficial. In recent years these goals have come under challenge in parts of the global South. The quality of life, solidarity, reciprocity and sustainability are seen as higher values for a human-centred society. Human developmentalism is replacing economic developmentalism as they move beyond capitalism.

9 Economic crises, environmental crises

Moving beyond capitalism

David Schweickart

> The big challenges that capitalism now faces in the contemporary world include issues of inequality (especially that of grinding poverty in a world of unprecedented prosperity) and of 'public goods' (that is, goods people share together, like the environment). The solution to these problems will almost certainly call for institutions that take us beyond the capitalist market economy.
>
> (Sen 1999: 167)

This is Amartya Sen, Nobel laureate economist in his well-known treatise, *Development as Freedom*, published in 1999, at a time when no 'reputable' scholar dared question the supremacy of capitalism. Interestingly – tellingly – Sen does not emphasize this striking remark, nor elaborate on it. Not so hesitant was Brian Barry, Lieber Professor of Political Philosophy, Columbia University, Professor of Political Science, London School of Economics, and former editor, while at the University of Chicago, of *Ethics*, the most influential journal of moral philosophy in the English-speaking world: 'The need for another revolution should be obvious to all those who are not willfully blind. It is not, I fear, probable. But without doubt it is possible' (Barry 2005: 272).

These are the closing words of his beautiful, angry book, *Why Social Justice Matters*, published in 2005 – his last book. Barry died in 2009. These words were foreshadowed by his remarks in the book's preface:

> One thing can be stated with certainty: the continuation of the status quo is an ecological impossibility. The uncertainty lies with the consequences of this fact. It is quite in the cards that the response will be the further retrenchment of plutocracy within countries and an ever more naked attempt by the United States, aided and abetted by a 'coalition of the willing', to displace the costs onto poorer countries. Whether it succeeds or fails, the results will be catastrophic. But I shall argue that there are some grounds for hope, which include growing discontent within rich countries with politics as usual.

Barry notes that this book may not be as well received among professional philosophers as his earlier work, but he will say bluntly what needs to be said. One guesses that he knew that his time on Earth was running out.

Economic crisis/ecological crisis

Barry's book was written *before* the global economic meltdown, which would suggest that things are even worse now, since addressing climate change and other ecological disasters requires money, and *everyone* – governments as well as private citizens – are strapped right now.

Not quite 'everyone'. Charles and David Koch, for example, clocked in this past year at $40 billion each. If they make a modest return of 5 per cent on their combined wealth, that'll give them $4 billion to play with this year, which means – do the maths – they can donate a million dollars to each of 4,000 political candidates this year – and next year and the next …, so as to make our country – or at least they themselves – prosper. They are but two of the 545 billionaires in this country today. But that's a discussion for another time.

Unfortunately, the current economic malaise is not going to end, not unless there is a *fundamental* restructuring of our economic system.

Let's remember the deep cause of the present crisis – about which left economists have been far more perspicacious than their mainstream counterparts. Consider Figure 9.1 – a plot of productivity and wages (adjusted for inflation) in the United States since 1945. If you want to understand the Great

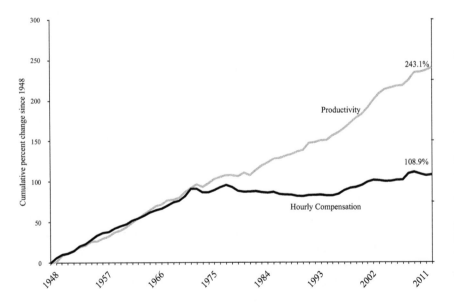

Figure 9.1 Rise in productivity vs rise in pay, United States, 1948–2013

Recession that began in 2008, and, for most people continues to this day, stare at this graph. Forget about fraudulent mortgage brokers, paid-for rating agencies, mortgage-backed securities, credit default swaps and other financial chicanery that were so much talked about back then, and stare at this graph.

Now ask yourself, 'If incomes have been flat since 1975, and yet we've been producing more and more stuff ... who's been buying it?'

Let's back up a bit and put this into historical perspective. Remember, long ago, Marx talked about those strange new economic crises that began appearing in the nineteenth century, crises caused not by some sort of material cause, like drought or disease or war, but because people didn't have enough money to buy all the stuff that was being produced. But when people don't buy enough, existing businesses lay off workers, who now can't buy anything at all, and so more workers are laid off, which makes the situation even worse, then worse, then worse. We get an economic crisis of a most peculiar sort. We still have all the natural resources, all the factories and machinery, all the workers and with all their skills that we had before, and yet prosperity has turned into misery.

Marx called these economic crises 'crises of overproduction'. Moreover, said Marx, although there are temporary recoveries, these crises will tend to get worse and worse, since ever advancing technology allows us to produce more and more with less and less labour.

And you know, Marx seemed spot on when, in 1929, the bottom fell out of the world economy. In the US we went from prosperity to massive unemployment almost overnight, over a quarter of the workforce losing their jobs. And the Depression wouldn't go away. Ten years passed. Still in crisis.

But then, lucky for us, the Second World War. Millions of men were drafted. Women surged into the factories. Unemployment disappeared. And when the men came home, jobs remained plentiful – for we kept up military production and the draft (the Cold War was now under way); women were pressured to leave the factories and return to their homes, and the government launched the largest public works project in human history – the interstate highway system – to encourage (and accommodate) affordable automobile production, which in turn required gas stations and their attendants, auto repair shops, car dealerships, etc. And the automobile made possible – and desirable – the suburbs, and so a huge construction boom was soon under way.

Not only were jobs plentiful in those days, but wages kept going up. Millions of workers joined labour unions. Before long a third of the workforce was unionized. Unions bargained for higher wages, longer vacations, more benefit. We had entered what is sometimes called capitalism's 'Golden Age', or, in France, *'le trente glorieux'* – the 30 glorious years.

That's the first part of our graph: productivity rising, wages rising. As someone who grew up during that period, I can attest, it was a 'Golden Age' of sorts – provided, I should add, you were white and male. In those days no one worried about getting a decent job, whether you went to college or not. White- and blue-collar jobs were plentiful. And we were all confident that our children would have even better lives than we were living, just as we were so much better off than our parents had been, who themselves were so much better off than their parents. Back to the graph. If the party ended in the mid-1970s, at least with respect to wages, *why didn't we have a crisis of overproduction decades ago*? To repeat the earlier question: If wages have been flat, but production has kept rising, who has been buying all the stuff?

You know the answer. We were! *On credit!* That is to say, to keep up effective demand, the wealthy (the capitalist class) have been *lending* money to the rest of us – to us individually, and to us collectively, to our local, state and national governments. Essentially they said,

> No need to raise your wages *or* our taxes – indeed, we can slash the graduation in the graduated income tax and cut those corporate taxes as well. But don't worry. We'll make credit readily available to you so you can keep spending, and we'll buy up all the bonds that governments want to issue.

Such was the claim, but do the maths. Ever mounting, interest-compounding debt is unsustainable, and so the bubble popped. And there would seem to be no way out of the mess we are now in. *Globalization* now keeps downward pressure on wages, and also renders the Keynesian multiplier less effective. Moreover, there are no new technologies on hand or on the horizon that will create lots of new enterprises that will create lots of new jobs. The Internet and i-gadgets are no match for the automobile. As MIT economists Erik Brynjolfsson and Andrew MacCaffey (2011: 34) note, the last decade was the first since the Great Depression for which there was no net job creation.

Let me throw another grim consideration into the mix. Suppose I'm wrong. Suppose we do get the global economy growing again, and are able to keep it growing. I don't think this will happen, but suppose I'm wrong. That will bring us face to face with a crisis of a different sort, a crisis based on the very fact of relentless, limitless growth: the environmental crisis. This one is real in a more profound sense than our current economic crisis, in that it has a *material* basis, as opposed to a 'merely' structural one. We *are* pouring too much methane and carbon dioxide into the atmosphere, using too much fresh water, etc., depleting our fisheries and forests.

Of course some will say we can 'grow' our way out of this crisis by investing in green technologies, but that's a fairy tale. To be sure, green technologies are important. They help. But it is obvious to all who think seriously about this issue that a long-term solution requires shifting our economy to one that does not depend for its health on ever-increasing rich-nation consumption – a consumption that doesn't make those living in rich nations happier anyway.

So we are in a tight corner. Those concerned about large-scale unemployment tell us we need to spend, spend, spend, while the environmentalists scream back that our consumption-addiction is killing the planet. And both sides are right. Moreover, both sides really want the same thing: a healthy, stable full-employment economy that treads lightly enough on our fragile planet to be sustainable. This is what we all want, isn't it?

(A side note: Even the rich are at least subliminally aware of the economic/ecological contradiction, though, of course, they don't want to dwell on it. Consider these two sentences from a long article in the May 2014 issue of *Forbes*, celebrating oil tycoon Harold Hamm – the only mention of the problem: 'Sure', the author writes, 'there remain legitimate concerns about the environmental impact of fracking. But you wouldn't want to see what the American economy would look like without it' (Helman 2014: 79).)

It is no accident that governments in the US and Europe, the heartlands of capitalism, are deadlocked to the point of dysfunctionality over what to do about the state of the economy *and* what to do about climate change. The capitalist class no longer has a coherent plan. The days when certain rational capitalists had influence – those who worried about the long-term viability of the system – are gone. Marx's observation in *Capital*, seemingly refuted by history, has gained new currency: '*Apres moi, le deluge*, is the watchword of every capitalist and every capitalist nation' (Marx 2003: 257).

So, as Brian Barry said, we need a revolution.

Is another world possible?

How do things stand now? What alternatives are we facing? At least four come to mind:

1   A return to Golden Age social democracy? I've argued that this is out of reach.
2   Fascism – friendly or otherwise? This option would not seem likely either – although the rise of the Tea Party Movement in the United States and anti-immigrant parties in Europe is somewhat unsettling. But fascism as an economic model (authoritarian capitalism) has been tried, not only by Mussolini and Hitler, but also by scores of anti-communist military and civilian dictatorships since the Second World War. None of these economies has flourished. None of the instigating regimes has survived. I don't see fascism as a threat, at least not at this point in time – although one should not disregard the ugly, race-tinged virulence being stirred up now in the United States and Europe.
3   Managed stagnation? This is Nobel laureate Paul Krugman's current prediction: 'disastrously high unemployment persisting years into the future'. All the wise heads will tell us that 8 or 9 per cent unemployment – maybe even 10 per cent – is the 'new normal', and that only irresponsible people will want to do anything about the situation (Krugman 2009). In my view, this is our most likely short-term future. But what about in the longer term?
4   A new form of democratic *socialism*? An economic system beyond capitalism? Hmmmm. Let's think about that.

If we look at world history over the course of the past several centuries, it is hard to miss the fact that democracy has been advancing. The notion that people have the right to rule themselves is an idea of near-universal currency at present, and it shows no signs of weakening.

Democracy has not only extended itself geographically, but in most countries it has deepened internally. Property qualifications have been dropped. Women have been granted the vote. Racial minorities are no longer excluded.

This deepening of democracy has changed the nature of the state. We no longer tolerate a minimalist government that does nothing but maintain our national defences and enforce law and order. The state is also supposed to provide certain economic services: ensure that our children are educated, our elderly receive pensions, our workplaces are safe, our wages are at least above a bare 'minimum', our air and water are clean and more.

This extension of democracy into the economic realm is far from complete. Of course further expansion will be resisted. Democratic rights have rarely been granted without a fight. It will always be said that further democratization is unworkable, and, if attempted, will have dire consequences. Such arguments are always made, and yet, to date at least, they (and the powers they represent) have not been able to hold back the democratic tide.

I want to argue that a much fuller *economic* democracy is on the horizon. It will probably be a while before we get there – although it should be noted that the rhythms of history are not constant. Long periods of relative structural stability are punctuated by periods of rapid transformation (consider the sudden, wholly unexpected, collapse of the Soviet empire). In any event, if we know where to look, we can discern, even in the present, economic experiments, political reforms and intellectual shifts that point to an economic formation vastly more democratic than the one in which we live today, an economic formation that goes beyond capitalism, an economic formation that is, in fact, a form of *socialism*.

Is this plausible? Here is Krugman again in a book published in 2008:

> Who now can use the words of socialism with a straight face? As a member of the baby boomer generation, I can remember when the idea of revolution, of brave men pushing history forward, had a certain glamor. Now it is a sick joke ... The truth is that the heart has gone out of the opposition to capitalism.
>
> (Krugman 2009: 14)

Yet surprisingly Krugman strikes a different note, just a paragraph later:

> Capitalism is secure, not only because of its successes – which have been very real – but because no one has a plausible alternative. *This situation will not last forever.* Surely there will be other ideologies, *other dreams*, and they will emerge sooner rather than later if the current economic crisis persists and deepens.

There *are* other dreams, and they are emerging sooner rather than later. Let me spell out one of them in some detail. It's an economic model that should be called *socialist*. But before laying out the specifics of an alternative economic model, let me say a few words about that term so demonized in mainstream culture, at least in my country (the US): 'socialism'. Let's be clear as to what socialism is *not*.

What socialism is not

Socialism is not *anti-religious*

The fundamental values of socialism are in no way incompatible with the basic moral principles of Christianity or any of the other major religions. That the most influential of the early socialists, Karl Marx, was an atheist is an historical accident. Marx, while a student, came under the influence of a group of German atheists (the Young Hegelians), but he eventually broke with them, because he didn't buy their line that religious superstition was the root cause of Germany's problems. For Marx the root cause was the *economic structure*, not religion. (You may have heard Marx's famous phrase, 'religion is the opiate of the people' – but you probably weren't told that in Marx's day, opium was not regarded as a delusional drug, but as a painkiller. And I'm sure you weren't given the sentences that preceded his famous phrase: 'Religion is the sigh of the oppressed creature. It is the heart of a heartless world. It is the spirit of spiritless conditions' (Marx, 'Toward a Critique of Hegel's *Philosophy of Right*' in Simon 1994: 28).

Socialism is not *opposed to freedom or individuality*

To the contrary, classical socialism regarded capitalism as a hindrance to real freedom and genuine individuality. As the two young authors of *The Communist Manifesto* announced, we want a society in which 'the free development of each is a condition for the free development of all' (Marx and Engels 1988: 74).

Socialism is not *anti-democratic*

Prior to the advent of the Soviet Union, socialism was explicitly democratic. In the *Communist Manifesto*, Marx and Engels (1988: 74) urge workers to 'win the battle of democracy'.

Socialism should not *be identified with what developed in Russia and Eastern Europe in the twentieth century*

Marx expected socialism to triumph first in the advanced capitalist countries that had already industrialized and developed sophisticated technologies.

Instead, the first 'socialist' revolution occurred in a backward country surrounded by hostile powers that had intervened against the revolutionaries during the Civil War. Feeling the need to industrialize rapidly, the leadership (primarily Stalin) put the country on authoritarian, military footing, and proceeded – at horrific human cost – to do just that: industrialize at breakneck speed. And when, following the Second World War, the Russians insisted on keeping the Eastern European countries in their 'orbit' – for self-protection – they were equally ruthless. The democratic component of socialism was, for an historical epoch, quashed.

Socialism is not *opposed to inequalities based on genuine differences of productive contribution to society*

Marx called the levelling down of everyone to a common level, 'crude communism', a form *inferior to capitalism* (Marx, 'Private Property and Communism' in Simon 1994: 69). Democratic socialists recognize the need for economic incentives, to encourage people to develop their talents and to employ them productively – as did Marx himself (Marx, 'Critique of the Gotha Programme' in Simon 1994: 321). What we *don't* want, however, are the massive inequalities that keep compounding, so that the more you have, the more your fortune grows.

Socialism is not *about the wholesale replacement of competition with cooperation*

Socialism wants a balanced mix of the two. Certain forms of competition are healthy: we want enterprises to compete to see who can use their materials most efficiently, who can innovate most productively, who best responds to what consumers need and want. Other forms of competition are not healthy: status competition based on consumption levels, and above all competition among workers to see who will work for the lowest wage.

A viable alternative

But does there exist a viable alternative to capitalism, a new system that would preserve the strengths of competitive capitalism while at the same time eliminating or at least mitigating its worst features?

It is important to be clear and unequivocal: that answer is 'Yes'. What we need to do is extend democracy to the economy itself. Consider the structure of free-market capitalism. It consists, essentially, of three kinds of institutions:

1   Markets for goods and services: enterprises compete with one another to provide consumers what they need or want.
2   Wage labour: in order to work, one must have access to the 'means of production'. One's 'capacity to work', one's 'labour-power' – to use Marx's

term – is a commodity like any other, to be bought and sold; people must compete for jobs, and, once hired, do what they are told.

3   Private allocation of investment funds: private financial institutions raise money from those who have excess, and allocate it to businesses promising the greatest profitability.

Let us imagine a form of socialism, which we will call economic democracy, that keeps the first set of institutions in place, i.e. competitive markets for goods and services, but (i) replaces (most) wage labour, by cooperative labour, and (ii) replaces those out-of-control financial markets with a more democratic mechanism for handling investment. Let us add (iii) the government as employer-of-last-resort, and (iv) public provision of basic education, health care and pensions. Thus our new economy would be:

- a competitive market economy; with
- democratic workplaces;
- transparent public banks, answerable to their communities, which allocate investment funds in accordance with long-term development needs;
- full-employment; and
- basic human needs guaranteed.

Such a socialism would be economically viable, and would not suffer the massive evils of capitalism.

Economic democracy: more details

Let me say a bit more about the institutions defining economic democracy. Let's begin with the 'basic model'. Let me be clear. I will set out a simplified model of an alternative, socialist economy. Real-world economies will always be more complicated than the models that describe them. But, if we are going to comprehend the essential dynamic of an economy, modelling is necessary. Marx gave us a 'model' of capitalism that remains, to this day, at least in my view, indispensable for grasping the workings of our current system. I propose a model for a different system – one that goes 'beyond capitalism'.

By way of comparison, consider the standard model of free-market capitalism. Such an economy consists of three types of markets:

- markets for goods and services;
- labour markets;
- capital markets.

Economic democracy will retain the first set of markets, but replace the latter two with more democratic institutions. Thus our basic model of economic democracy also has three components:

1   markets for goods and services, which are essentially the same as under capitalism;
2   workplace democracy, which replaces the capitalist institution of wage labour;
3   democratic control of investment, which replaces capitalist financial markets.

Let me elaborate briefly on each of these key institutions.

1   Historical experience makes it clear that markets are a necessary component of a viable socialism. Central planning does not work for a sophisticated economy. The knowledge and incentive problems are too great. But these markets should be largely confined to goods and services. They should *not* embrace labour or capital. And, of course, they should be regulated so as to protect the health and safety of both consumers and producers.
2   Enterprises in economic democracy are regarded, not as *properties* to be bought or sold, but as *communities*. When you join a firm, you have the right to vote for members of a worker council – just as you have the right to vote for the city or town council governing your place of residence. This council appoints upper management and oversees major enterprise decisions. Although managers are granted a degree of autonomy, they are ultimately answerable to the workforce, one-person, one-vote.

As for income: all workers share in the profits of the enterprise. These shares need not be equal, but everyone's income is tied directly to the performance of the firm – hence the incentive to work diligently and efficiently – and to see to it that your co-workers do the same.

3   Some sort of *democratic control of investment* is essential if an economy is to develop rationally. This has always been the case, but, given the ecological problems we face, never before has rational development been more urgently needed. But control of investment is exceedingly difficult if we must rely on *private investors* for these funds. The solution to this problem is simple. Don't rely on private investors. Generate your investment funds publicly – via taxation. I would argue that a *capital-assets tax* is the best tax for this purpose – a flat-rate property tax on all businesses. In effect, this tax replaces the 'returns to capital' represented by interest and dividend payments in a capitalist economy, this money going, not to private 'suppliers of capital', but to the central government.

These revenues constitute the *national investment fund. All* of these revenues are reinvested in the economy. They are not used for other governmental services (a separate income or consumption tax will fund on-going governmental expenses).

Each region of the country gets, as a matter of right, its *fair share* of the national investment fund – *prima facie* its *per-capita* share – although democratically-determined exceptions can be made. The important point: regions do not compete for capital. Each and every year they get their rightful share of the capital-assets-tax revenue.

These funds go to *public banks*, which channel them back into the economy, utilizing both economic and social criteria – including, importantly, employment creation and environmental sensitivity. Coherent long-term investment planning, at the national, regional and community levels, becomes possible.

The three basic institutions – markets for goods and services, workplace democracy and social control of investment – constitute the defining features of economic democracy, but there are other structures that should be part of our 'new socialism'. Let me comment briefly on two of them:

- *The government as employer-of-last-resort*

It has long been a tenet of socialism that everyone who wants to work should have access to a job. Everyone should have a genuine *right-to-work*. The government will ensure this right. If a person cannot find work elsewhere, the government will provide that person with a job, low-wage, but decent, doing something useful.

- *An entrepreneurial-capitalist sector*

In my view, Marx's critique of capitalism remains unsurpassed, but there is an important economic issue that Marx neglected, namely the function of the *entrepreneur* in society. Marx's analysis of capitalism focuses on the capitalist *qua* capitalist, as the provider of capital. This is a *passive* function, one that can readily be taken over by the state – as is the case in our basic model.

But there is another role played by *some* capitalists – a creative, *entrepreneurial* role. This role is assumed by a large number of individuals in a capitalist society, mostly by 'petty capitalists', who set up their own small businesses, but by some 'grand capitalists' as well, individuals who turn innovative ideas into major industries. Although workplace democracy should be the norm throughout society, we needn't demand that *all* businesses conform to this norm. The petty capitalist, after all, works hard. He (or she) is anything but a parasite. It takes energy, initiative and intelligence to run a small business. These small businesses provide jobs for large numbers of people, and goods and services to even more (it is important, politically, for socialists to realize that small business owners – however deeply ingrained most are with 'free-market' ideology – are not, structurally, the enemy, and would continue to play a vital role in 'the next system').

Petty capitalists may provide important services to society, but they do not provide much in the way of technological or organizational innovation. There is also an honourable role to play in a socialist society for *entrepreneurial capitalists who operate on a grander scale*. Such an entrepreneurial capitalist class need not pose a serious threat to a society in which democratic workplaces are predominant. Democratic firms, when they have equal access to investment capital, need not fear competition from capitalist firms. On the contrary, since capitalist firms must compete with democratic firms for workers, they will be under pressure to at least partially democratize their own operations, by instituting profit-sharing and more participatory work relations.

Moreover, there is a rather simple legal mechanism that can be put in place to keep this capitalist class in check. The basic problem with capitalists under capitalism is not their active, entrepreneurial role (which relatively few capitalists actually play), but their passive role as suppliers of capital. Economic democracy offers a transparent, rational substitute for this latter role – the capital-assets tax. So the trick is to develop a mechanism that would prevent the active, entrepreneurial capitalist from become a passive, parasitic one.

Such a mechanism is easy enough to envisage: a simple, two-part law stipulating that (a) an enterprise developed by an entrepreneurial capitalist can be sold at any time, but, if it exceeds a certain size, *only to the state*, and (b) the enterprise *must* be sold when the owner retires or dies. When the state purchases an enterprise, it turns it over to the enterprise's workers, to be run democratically.

Thus the entrepreneurial capitalists serve two socially useful functions. They are a source of innovation *and* an incubator for new democratic enterprises. Entrepreneurial capitalists have a significant, honourable role to play in our democratic *socialist* economy.

Economic democracy and economic/ecological crises

I have argued at length elsewhere that economic democracy would not only be efficient and innovative; it would be much more democratic than capitalism, vastly more egalitarian and far better able to provide everyone a reasonable balance of work and leisure (Schweickart 2011).

It is also the case that economic democracy would not be vulnerable to the kind of *economic* crisis we are now experiencing. The basic reason is simple. There are no private financial markets in economic democracy. Wall Street is gone. Markets for goods and services remain, but there are no stock markets, bond markets, hedge funds or private 'investment banks' concocting collateralized debt obligations, currency swaps and the myriad other sorts of derivatives that preoccupy investment bankers today. Thus, *there is no opportunity for financial speculation*.

Our financial system is quite transparent. A capital-assets tax is collected from businesses, then loaned out to enterprises wanting to expand or to individuals wanting to start new businesses. Loan officers are public officials, whose salaries are tied to loan performances. The loans they make are a matter of public record. There is nothing *mysterious* about finance in an economic democracy.

Immunity to speculation is not the only strength of economic democracy. Even more important, it is not vulnerable to a *deep problem* we have noted: insufficient effective demand, due ultimately to the fact that wages tend not to keep pace with increases in productivity. Since wages are a cost of production in a capitalism firm, capitalists strive to keep wages down.

But wages are *not* a cost of production in a democratic firm. Workers receive a specified share of the firm's profit, not a wage – so all productivity gains are captured by the firm's workforce. Worker income always keeps pace with productivity gains.

Capitalism, as we have seen, faces an even deeper problem than the one responsible for the economic crisis now holding us in its grip. Should we succeed in getting our economies growing again (indeed, even if we don't), we will soon find ourselves in an ecological crisis (more precisely, ecological crises – large global ones, many smaller, more regional ones).

Economic democracy is far better positioned than capitalism to avoid ecological crises. First of all, democratic firms lack the expansionary dynamic of capitalist firms. They tend to increase in size so long as there are increasing returns to scale, but stop when returns-to-scale are constant, whereas a capitalist firm will keep expanding until decreasing returns to scale sets in – which in the real world rarely happens. A simple example: You're a successful entrepreneur. You set up a hamburger stand and call it 'McDonalds'. It's a hit. So you set up another. It too is a hit. Your profits double. So you set up another and another and another … McDonalds grows and grows. But consider now a successful democratic 'McDonalds' cooperative. Would the workers vote to set up another one? Why would they? True, total profits would double – but so would the number of workers with whom to divide the profits. In essence, capitalist firms strive to maximize total profits, whereas democratic firms aim to maximize profits-per-worker. Hence democratic firms tend to grow to a certain point, and then stabilize. Capitalist firms are more like cancer: cells multiplying exponentially; democratic firms are healthy, stable cells.

A second feature of economic democracy that enhances ecological sustainability is democratic control over investment, which means control over development. We can aim for healthy, equitable, sustainable development, not the mindless consumption endemic to contemporary capitalism. (Needless to say, democratic control does not *guarantee* that people will make the right choices, but the system is not biased against collective rationality – as is a system in which the relevant actors, the private corporations, must 'grow or die'.)

A third feature contributing to the possibility of ecological sanity: since funds for investment in an economic democracy do not come from private investors, the economy is not hostage to 'investor confidence'. We need not worry that an economic slowdown will panic investors, provoking them to pull their money out of the financial markets, triggering a recession – for there aren't any private investors. Economic democracy can be a healthy, sustainable, 'no-growth economy', whereas capitalism cannot.

Actually, 'no-growth' is a misnomer. Productivity increases under economic democracy can be translated into increased *leisure* instead of ever-increasing *consumption*. When introducing a more productive technology into their enterprise, workers in a democratic firm have a choice not available to workers in a capitalist firm: they can choose to take those productivity gains in the form of shorter workweeks or longer vacations, rather than higher incomes. Given the importance of scaling back excessive consumption, the government can encourage such leisure over consumption choices. The economy will continue to experience 'growth', but the growth will be mostly in free time, not consumption.

Conclusion

Such a world is possible. Will it become a reality? That is impossible to say with any certainty, of course. But let me mention three things that I would worry about if I were a member of the capitalist class.

The first is the mushrooming sense that the current system is no longer working, and the increasing sense that the upper 1 per cent is implicated in this dysfunction. That a 685-page treatise by a young French economist on this topic should become a national bestseller – #1 on Amazon for a while, fiction and non-fiction – might well disturb my sleep.

The second is all those students out there, saddled with debt – which now totals $1 trillion, more than all the outstanding credit card debt in the country. Students were told to borrow to finance their education. By increasing the value of their 'human capital', they would earn a healthy return on their 'investment', since there would be all those nice, high-paying jobs waiting for them. But those jobs aren't there. They feel betrayed. At least three polls in recent years have shown increasing sympathy to socialism among young people. A 2011 Pew Research poll, for example, found 49 per cent of Americans under 30 having a favourable reaction to 'socialism', as opposed to only 46 per cent having a favourable reaction to 'capitalism' (cited by Gar Alperovitz 2013: 195).

The third thing I'd worry about concerns nationalism. It has been argued, correctly, in my view, that Marx vastly underestimated the appeal of nationalism as a counter to socialist internationalism. The workers of the world did not unite to overthrow the capitalist classes of their countries in 1914, but instead enthusiastically (in Europe at least) rushed into battle, to slaughter one another. And of course during the Cold War American workers (unionized or not, it made no difference) rallied to defend 'the American Way' against the menace of International Communism.

But it is now crystal clear that capitalist corporations have no loyalty to their communities, or even to the nation as a whole. They play one city or state against another – legalized bribery and blackmail. They out-source and off-shore American jobs; they play accounting games to avoid paying taxes.

It is also becoming clear that the capitalist class as a whole has no 'grand plan' for resolving any of the deep problems now surfacing – not only in the poorer regions of the world – but in capitalism's heartland: the United States and Western Europe.

I would argue that, as mentioned earlier, there once existed a 'rational' segment of the capitalist class, a segment with major political influence that concerned itself with the overall well-being of the country – so as to inoculate American workers against that Communist 'virus' that might take hold among them, if sufficient care were not taken. That rational segment no longer exists, or at any rate, has dwindled to the point of insignificance. In the words of Marx and Engels in the *Manifesto*, the ruling class is showing itself to be 'unfit to rule'. They no longer have a 'grand plan'.

So, what will be our future? Let me close with a couple of poems and a thesis. The first is by a writer not usually thought of as a poet. It's from a book published in 2005, the same year as Brian Barry's *Why Social Justice Matters*. He titled it, *A Man without a Country*. Like Barry's book, it was his last. The book is not a happy book. The poem is not a happy poem – but it does highlight what is at stake. Kurt Vonnegut entitled his poem 'Requiem' (Vonnegut 2005).

> The crucified planet Earth,
> Should it find a voice
> And a sense of irony,
> Might now well say
> Of our abuse of it,
> 'Forgive them Father,
> They know not what they do.'
>
> The irony would be
> That we know what
> We are doing.
>
> When the last living thing
> Has died on account of us,
> How poetical it would be
> If Earth would say,
> In a voice floating up
> Perhaps
> From the floor
> Of the Grand Canyon.
> 'It is done.'
> People did not like it here.

The second is a short, more optimistic poem by the Irish poet, Seamus Heaney (also recently deceased), quoted, interestingly enough, by Amartya Sen in his latest book, *The Idea of Justice* (Sen 2009: 27).

> History says, Don't hope
> On this side of the grave,
> But then, once in a lifetime
> The longed-for tidal wave
> Of justice can rise up,
> And hope and history rhyme.

Lastly, a quote – one that electrified me when I first read it 44 years ago, as a first-year graduate student in philosophy: 'The philosophers have interpreted the world in various ways. The point, however, is to *change* it' (Marx, 'Eleventh Thesis on Feuerbach').

Postscript

At the last meeting of my undergraduate social-political philosophy class two years ago, we had a wrap-up discussion. Toward the end, I told them that I'd had a hard time sleeping the night before. I'd just read the *Forbes* article I mentioned earlier, I told them, with its ecstatic account of Harold Hamm – 'the most disruptive oilman since Rockefeller, [who] has made $17 billion from the domestic energy boom – and he's just getting started' (the *Forbes* cover tells us) and the author's rapturous description of the 100,000 barrels of oil *a day* Hamm's company is pumping out of North Dakota's Bakken oilfield, and the one *billion* barrels of proven reserves it now holds.

I told them how that article had lodged in my brain next to the editorial, authored by the full editorial board of *The New York Times* just a few days earlier, entitled 'Running Out of Time'. The editorial was based on three recent reports. One points out that 'annual emissions of greenhouse gases have risen *almost twice as fast in the first decade of this century as they did in the last decades*', another that global warming is caused largely by the burning of fossil fuels by humans, and a third – the key finding of which they underscore: '*The world has only about 15 years left* in which to bend the emissions curve downward' (*New York Times*, Editorial Board 2014: A20).

I told them that seeing Hamm's smiling face on the cover of the favourite magazine of billionaires made me feel what a German Jew must have felt on seeing Hitler on the cover of a prominent German magazine celebrating his having been named Chancellor of the Reich – the holocaust still some years away.

I ended with an excerpt from a recent article by Chris Hedges, entitled, 'The Myth of Human Progress and the Collapse of Complex Societies'. Let me end this discussion with it as well:

I do not know if we can build a better society. I do not even know if we will survive as a species. But I know these corporations have us by the throat. And that they have my children by the throat. I do not fight fascists because I will win. I fight fascists because they are fascists. And this is a fight, which, in the face of overwhelming forces against us, requires us to embrace this sublime madness, to find in acts of rebellion the embers of life, an intrinsic meaning that lies outside of certain success. It is to at once grasp reality and to refuse to allow this reality to paralyze us. It is, and I say this to people of all creeds or no creeds, to make an absurd leap of faith, to believe, despite all empirical evidence around us, that good always draws to it the good, that the fight for life always goes somewhere – we do not know where – and in these acts we sustain our belief in a better world, even if we cannot see one emerging around us.

(Hedges 2014)

10 The left and a Green New Deal

Jerry Harris

Can capitalism find a way out of its current economic problems, or is stagnation and high unemployment the new normal? One possible solution is a Green New Deal. But does capitalism have the capacity to turn away from the fossil fuel era in time to prevent major environmental catastrophes from occurring?

Most left critics answer no, and point to the inherent need of capitalism to consume ever-greater inputs of energy, land, resources and labour (Foster and Clark 2012; Magdoff 2013; Rogers 2010). As Murray Bookchin argues, 'Attempts to "green" capitalism, to make it "ecological," are doomed by the very nature of the system *as* a system of endless growth' (1990: 94).

Other environmentalists argue that the growth cycle of capitalism provides room for investments in green technologies. Capitalism can grow in ways that reduce the use of energy and resources by expanding solar and wind power, as well as an array of new technologies that can convert the current systems of transportation, architecture and agriculture (Hawken 1993; Lovins and Lovins 1997). Such theoretical arguments are finding their way into policy studies and advocacy by established voices within the inner circles of capitalism. Al Gore long stood out as a lone voice in the wilderness. But an op-ed piece in the *New York Times* by a trio of billionaires urging a tax on carbon is a clear indication that some capitalists are ready to make the shift to green capitalism (Jasper 2014). The trio consisted of Hank Paulson, ex-CEO of Goldman Sachs and Secretary of the Treasury under George W. Bush, former mayor of New York and political independent Michael Bloomberg and San Francisco liberal Democrat Tom Steyer. Both Bloomberg and Steyer are already big-time funders of environmental groups and political candidates.

Other voices within the capitalist class have joined the choir. Robert Rubin, President Clinton's Treasury Secretary and Citicorp executive wrote in the *Washington Post*, 'We do not face a choice between protecting our environment or protecting our economy. We face a choice between protecting our economy by protecting our environment – or allowing environmental havoc to create economic havoc' (Rubin 2014). And the Rockefeller Brothers Fund, a family fortune founded on Standard Oil, committed to divesting all of its investments in fossil fuels (Schwartz 2014).

The green wing of the capitalist class developing a strategic vision may solve three major problems facing the system: stagnation, legitimacy and defence. In terms of economic stagnation new investments in green technologies can set off a renewed cycle of accumulation, creating an expansion of new industries, jobs and profits. The next problem, rapidly disappearing political legitimacy and trust in government, is in Gramscian terms a crisis in the ideological hegemony of the ruling class. But green capitalism can reestablish the system's identification with democracy, and extend its political legitimacy to the grand issue of saving the planet and building a better future. Lastly is the question of defensive stability. For the past decade the Pentagon and CIA have been warning of possible social and political chaos as the result of global warming. They have predicated economic collapse in ecologically vulnerable countries, and the movement of vast amounts of environmental refugees creating instability across wide areas of the planet. Addressing the most pressing environmental issues can help reduce this threat and create a more stable and manageable global situation.

The question for the left is how to relate to this wing of the capitalist class. Tom Hayden poses this problem in sharp terms. As he writes:

> As more finance capitalists go green, the trend will be problematic for those with an anticapitalist or socialist agenda. They blame capitalism for the unfettered exploitation of the Earth's resources and life-supporting ecosystem. History shows that fundamental critique to be on the mark, though it can be dogmatic in its assumptions. To demand that the environmental movement turn socialist – or anarchist – as a precondition of progress, however, is a hopeless venture. Socialists and progressives of all stripes need to recall the lessons from history where capitalists surprised their detractors by incorporating substantial reforms, partly in order to save capitalism itself. The New Deal was such a model. We are entering another historic moment of potential market adjustment born out of necessity. Progressives can play a vital role in the unpredictable transition ahead. They can help broker a Green New Deal.
>
> (Hayden 2014)

There is no question that the Green New Deal faces significant obstacles. For all the international conferences, treaties and rhetoric generated over the past 20 years, little has been accomplished. In the last ten years fossil fuel emissions have risen at almost double the rate of the preceding decade. Leading United Nations scientist Dr Ottmar Edenhofer stated the world is 'in the middle of a fossil fuel renaissance' (Gillis 2014). And the UN warned renewable energy is being overwhelmed by fossil fuel emissions and the rapid growth of fracking. If there is any hope of keeping to internationally agreed limits of a two degree Celsius rise, 75 per cent of all fossil fuel reserves need to stay in the ground. But much of these huge reserves are already on the books of oil and energy transnationals, and account for billions in the valuations of these corporations. Replying to the UN, Exxon issued a report in which it stated, 'The scenario where governments restrict hydrocarbon production in a way to reduce GHG (greenhouse gas) emissions 80 per cent during the outlook period is high unlikely .... We are confident that none of our hydrocarbon reserves are now or will become "stranded"' (Crooks 2014). In other words, in the immortal chant led by Sarah Palin at the 2008 Republican National Convention, 'Drill, Baby, Drill!'

Another obstacle facing the Green New Deal is the cumulative effect of economic recessions. While left critics have looked at the problems inherent in capitalist-driven growth, little attention has been paid to the crisis side of the economic cycle. Recessions produce three major problems for green capitalism: cuts in subsidies; protectionism; and overproduction and a crisis in profitability. Solar and wind are still dependent on state subsidies for the development of their technologies and gaining market shares. Funders also keep close watch on government support to judge the viability of their speculative investments into the industry. When economic recessions hit, subsidies tend to disappear or suffer cuts, often resulting in lay-offs, and a general slow-down of overall development.

Protectionism was the next problem to rear its head during the recession, as Chinese solar panels became a hot issue in both Europe and the US. In the space of five years China became the world's biggest producer of solar panels, lowering costs and making them competitive with fossil fuels. In the US Solar World, a German company, initiated a lawsuit against China and was joined by other manufacturers. But the suit was opposed by companies that install panels because prices had come down and the market expanded. The case went to the World Trade Organization (WTO) with a lot of rhetoric about saving American jobs and companies. But the largest US-owned solar panel manufacturer, First Solar, has production units in Malaysia where they employ ten times the number of workers they do in the US. The biggest stockholder of First Solar is the Walton family of WalMart fame. Although the WTO case was nationalist in form it was transnational in content. Fundamentally it was all about transnational corporations fighting for market share and profits, not employment.

The rapid rise in solar panel production also caused overproduction and a profit crisis in the industry. Global production of panels could power 70 gigawatts of energy, but worldwide demand was only at 30 gigawatts. With supplies running ahead of the market by over 100 per cent prices crashed and so did companies. Bankruptcy spread throughout the US, Europe and China. But such a crisis could only happen under capitalism. In reality, to combat global warming the world needs to produce much more than 70 gigawatts of solar power per year. In the US, solar power only accounts for about one-fifth of 1 per cent of energy use. Cheaper prices should encourage widespread adaptation, not bankrupt companies and lead to the shutdown of capacity. These problems of subsidies, protectionism and overproduction reveal some of the inherent economic problems blocking a Green New Deal. Market forces have to be controlled and capitalist rationality replaced by the rationality of environmental sustainability.

Such changes would necessitate a virtual political revolution. A green political movement would have to capture hegemony and become the dominant wing of the Democratic Party. And the majority of the Republican Party would have to accept the scientific basis of environmental science. This would be possible only with a powerful environmental social movement, and large-scale changes in mass consciousness. Currently about one-third the US population rejects the science of global warming, and provides the social base for political deadlocks and backward economic and social policies. All of the above would entail the defeat of fossil fuel industry influence over political policies, and its ideological hegemony over society. Lastly, within finance capital the willingness to invest in large-scale environmental projects and technology would need to occur.

Sectors of the capitalist class will attempt a move to green capitalism with or without the left. But a *progressive* Green New Deal depends on the participation of the left and a number of important contributions it can make. This means a tactical alliance with the green capitalist sector and a strategic alliance with its most progressive wing. To paraphrase Mao when he advanced the united front, the left needs to unite the many to defeat the few and aim the main blow at the most reactionary sector of capital. Such a policy was already called for in the WTO solar panel case of the US against China. Which side should the left have supported? The WTO ruled against the US, a ruling I think was correct and that the left should have thought about and taken a stand. Objectively, that would have meant supporting Chinese private producers of solar panels and the installation companies against the production companies inside the US. Unfortunately, the Obama administration has moved ahead and set tariff charges ranging from 27 to 78 per cent on the importation of Chinese-made panels. But there are other fundamental issues for us to consider, such as:

- labour rights and the struggle against neoliberalism;
- building a broad environmental movement;
- supporting a decentralized energy system and creating green cooperatives.

James O'Connor wrote about the first and second contradictions of capitalism (O'Connor 2014). The first was the exploitation of labour, the second the exploitation of the environment. Green capitalism will attempt to solve the second contradiction, but makes no commitment to stop the exploitation of the working class. This is already evident in First Solar's use of low-cost Asian labour to produce its solar panels. Only a red/green strategic orientation will address the problems labour faces with capital. Some of the most well-known capitalist supporters of a green conversion, Rubin, Paulson and Bloomberg, are also among the biggest advocates of working-class austerity and neoliberalism. They see no particular contradiction between such economic attacks on workers, and investing in green corporations and supporting government policies to address global warming. The left must fight green neoliberalism in the same manner that it has carried out the struggle against austerity for the past two decades. That means supporting progressive policies, while organizing alternatives and solutions to the anti-working class line of attack.

In order to do so means building a more powerful and deeply rooted environmental movement – but an environmental movement that understands its links to other social movements and issues. Only by creating a synergy of movements can the left hope to be successful. This was achieved in the 1960s when the civil rights movement, the anti-war movement, Native American struggles, Asian activists, feminists, the farm workers' struggle and gay pride movement collectively posed a challenge to capitalism. The green movement needs to be dynamic and independent, work with all progressive forces, and be taken into the labour movement as well.

The left also needs to be actively building and supporting cooperatives as alternatives to capitalist corporations. This is particularly important in the area of green industries. The Evergreen Corporation in Cleveland is a good example, bringing together the issues of minority urban employment with sustainability (Evergreen Cooperative 2014). Other important actions are supporting innovative and independent entrepreneurs, and fighting for a decentralized system of energy production. An interesting example is the German government's requirement that corporate utilities buy excess solar energy produced by homeowners, at a price set above market value. The policy was so popular in encouraging homeowners and farmers to install solar panels that Germany now leads the world in solar energy use, although its latitude is similar to Canada's Hudson Bay.

Among the various possible actions and policies that the left can promote, a decentralized energy system is an important way to mark a progressive approach. This is important for two different reasons. The first is that it undermines monopoly control, centralized into the hands of a few big providers and producers. The main focus of both solar and wind corporations is to build large-scale energy farms, which after construction employ very few people in operations and maintenance. But if solar panels existed on the roofs of millions of homes, schools and businesses, people would have a largely independent supply of energy. This would push utility delivery networks into a backup system and make fossil fuel corporations secondary providers. A decentralized system would also prevent the rise of new green energy monopolies. While supplying sustainable energy, these corporations could still follow neoliberal approaches to labour costs and market prices. Already, Malaysia is the world's second largest producer of solar panels, attracting

US, European and Japanese transnationals by offering a dollar an hour wage structure for factory workers (Bradsher 2014).

Another key reason to fight for a decentralized system of energy is that it links to a strategy of creating synergy between movements. There could be thousands of small installation cooperatives in communities across the country, particularly in low-income neighbourhoods. Such cooperatives could be built around hiring and training members from the local community. The creation of jobs and the circulation of money into the area would help to undermine economic incentives to join gangs, undercut the rationale for increased police presence and disrupt the school-to-jail assembly line. It's certainly not the whole answer to these problems. But it ties job creation to worker empowerment, combats racism rooted in economic discrimination, begins to address youth unemployment and challenges the use of police violence through community development and empowerment. It offers a strategy that can tie the economic exploitation of capitalism to racism, while presenting a concrete strategy for oppositional institutional development. Van Jones and Green for All have been promoting a strategy along these lines for a number of years (Jones 2008).

Such an approach also fits into a Gramscian vision of creating popular institutions within capitalism that can provide a base to further the fight against the system (Gramsci 1971). The left is good at producing newspapers, web sites, holding discussions and conferences, and marching in the streets. But it is weak in creating an organizational structure, whether political or economic. The above strategy links back to the Black Panther Party and their 'serve the people' projects that provided health care, free legal advice and free breakfast programmes. The left must have a day-to-day practice that helps people survive in solidarity with each other, moving from protest to power. To do so, the left needs a network of institutional base building in various areas that can link together. Green cooperatives can certainly play an important role. With a broad strategic outlook, a united front policy and base-building efforts, the left's influence in a Green New Deal can be a transmission belt to a system beyond capitalism.

Without a strong left presence, green capitalism will offer too little too late, and the world will certainly suffer massive disruptions. Immigration is already a hotly debated issue, supplying the right wing with energy and activists. But the flood of people crossing borders due to environmental disasters will likely provide rocket fuel to the reactionary movement. A dystopian future may also include large-scale migration within the US. Texas, Arizona and California are huge population centres already suffering serious environment problems that are bound to get worse. People may move in large numbers to areas like the Great Lakes, further north and near huge bodies of fresh water. This massive move will surely cause an urban crisis in cities like Chicago and Milwaukee in housing, jobs and infrastructure. Will states demand ten-year residency records or state birth certificates to qualify for jobs or home ownership? Will Illinois or Wisconsin tell people from Texas and Arizona that they are crossing the state border illegally and deport them back to Houston and Phoenix? There may be some ironic justice in contemplating such a future. But in reality the tense social conflicts created by environmental catastrophes may push the US to the hard right or progressive left. Under such circumstances the road to a society beyond capitalism lies through a Green New Deal and a red/green movement willing to make allies of those who move in the same direction.

11 Alternatives to development in Latin America

Rebecca Hollender[1]

The concept of sustainable development[2] has been weakened and even rejected after decades of failed attempts to meet environmental and social objectives. This rejection comes from diverse actors ranging from civil society movements to academic sub-disciplines including post-development, political ecology and de-growth. While the international sustainable development agenda has made progress in some areas, in most regions of the world social inequality and poverty have worsened, and a global environmental crisis is imminent. Despite myriad attempts to make the development system more inclusive, representative and sustainable, the root causes of social and environmental problems have not been addressed.

As a result, a gradual exhaustion and shifting away from official development processes is taking place among civil society groups around the world. Instead of continuing efforts to improve and change the development system from within, alternatives are being deliberately elaborated outside of the system. Alternatives to Development (A2D) proposals were born from the post-development (PD) school of thought, which cites the current development model as a root cause of social inequality and environmental problems, reflecting four decades of failed prescriptions designed to promote economic growth (Escobar 2010; Esteva 2013; Gudynas 2012; Lang 2013). Post-development questions much of development's underlying logic about participation, decision-making, hierarchy, human–nature relationships, governance structures, the [economic] value of nature, etc. Post-development sees the development system as a tool employed by capitalism in order to fulfil its constant need for expansion and domination over other forms of economic and social organization.

Alternatives to Development are concrete proposals for transitioning toward an environmentally sustainable, post-capitalist society. They address the urgent need to limit economic activity to within the biophysical limits of the planet. Broadly labelled 'post-growth', they posit (1) that current growth patterns cannot be sustained and (2) that the primacy of economic growth in public policy must be undone. Post-growth recognizes that growth patterns will inevitably change and proposes transition measures that could mitigate a complete economic crisis and/or ecological collapse.

Alternatives to Development originates in the global South and thus holds a unique place within post-growth thinking, because its analyses take into account the poverty, inequality and environmental problems of Southern societies, thereby involving different audiences and policy frameworks than proposals constructed in the global North. The development lens allows for an analysis of the expansion of the growth-based economy (including current extractive models) from the standpoint of the global South, whose encounter with modern economic globalization has been most often mediated through development policy. It is striking that in their efforts to address unique, local circumstances, A2D are tracing the root of their problems to a global system; they recognize that the capitalist system is the root cause of ecological and social crises, and view the development system as part and parcel of the problem.

However, these shared historical factors do not overlook the diversity of experiences that Southern countries and communities have had with development, and therefore their current priorities and needs. This is best illustrated by the multiplicity of Alternatives to Development initiatives that are emerging out of dramatically different contexts across the global South.

Introducing Alternatives to Development: concepts, processes and actors

This section will introduce the types of Alternatives to Development approaches that are present in Latin America and outline three examples of A2D proposals that are rising in popularity at local levels and gaining recognition from international academic and policy audiences.

Theorizing alternatives to development in Latin America

Although A2D groups differ in their claims, processes and goals, they agree that:

1   development is grounded in a universal conceptualization of modernity and progress that mimics Northern models of industrialization, consumption and economic growth; which
2   necessitates the use of top-down, coercive, forceful or hegemonic implementation mechanisms and the elimination or cooptation of alternatives;
3   development policy furthers the global embedding of capitalist systems, norms and institutions that serve and protect the interests of powerful elites;
4   development directly clashes with its own stated environmental and social goals (Escobar 2010; Esteva 2013; Gudynas 2012; Lang 2013; Pieterse 1996).

A2D theories question development's underlying logic about participation, decision-making, hierarchy, human–nature relationships, governance structures, the economic valuation of nature, etc. New frameworks for imagining alternatives include conviviality, super-strong sustainability, biocentrism, deep ecology, feminist critique, the care economy, dematerialization of the economy, de-growth, interculturalism, pluralism, relational ontologies, expanded forms of citizenship, etc. (Gudynas 2012: 33). A wide range of themes are being explored by A2D groups that involve restoring and incorporating diverse epistemologies, including indigenous and gender-based knowledge, into longstanding discussions of transformation:

- reframing historic debates about the roles of states and markets using marginalized lenses and practices, such as barter, reciprocity, self-sufficiency, gift and others;
- building practical ways to delink development, economic growth, consumption and well-being, for example via new indicators that go beyond material and individualistic measurements of well-being to include collective, spiritual and ecological dimensions;
- exposing and overcoming the false dichotomy between environment and 'development' by recognizing intrinsic values of nature and questioning the role of technology in environmental problem-solving;
- reexamining definitions, relationships and processes of politics, citizenship and justice (Gudynas 2012: 36–37).

In practice, the construction of A2D initiatives involves diverse actors, including communities, NGOs, academics and policymakers. They form a vast web of activity that extends beyond the global South to interact with wider transformational processes, such as the global climate justice movement. The three most visible expressions of A2D in Latin America are post-extractivism, *Buen Vivir* and Solidarity Economies.

Post-extractivism

Post-extractivism proponents link the dependence of resource-rich countries on natural resource extraction to a conventional development agenda that has failed to address the structural causes of poverty and environmental crisis. They propose a series of transitions, including economic policies, education programmes and public participation, aimed at moving from the current, *'predatory'* extractivist model to an initial *'sensible'* extractivism and a final *'indispensable'* extractivism phase. The characteristics of sensible extractivism include the deliberate selecting of extractive projects that meet strong environmental and social criteria, such as those outlined in national and international legislation. Extractive projects that risk irreversible environmental damage or species loss should be immediately halted. During this phase, a country would implement additional macroeconomic reforms such as price correction for primary materials, tax and royalty reforms, subsidy reductions, etc. The transition to an indispensable phase of extractivism involves eliminating all extractive activities that cannot be directly linked to human needs and quality of life improvements. Each policy phase would require complementary socio-cultural measures to facilitate the gradual transformation of consumption patterns and materialistic values (Gudynas 2012).

Reducing the dependence of countries on the export of extractive goods involves reforms and transformations across society and economy, which must be applied in coordination across national borders. The joint implementation of post-extractivism policies is necessary due to the highly competitive nature of globalized capitalism and the financialization of capital, which allow for the easy relocation of investment to the most auspicious economic climates. The post-extractive proposal includes strong national-level regulations for environmental and social control, price correction to include externalities, the elimination of subsidies and redistribution of royalties from extractivism, the diversification and expansion of other economic sectors (agriculture, tourism, services, manufacturing), regulations on markets and capital, strengthening of Solidarity Economies, recognition of non-monetary values of nature, resources, quality of life, selective decoupling from globalization, dematerialization of production and changes in consumption patterns. Post-extractivism authors highlight the need for parallel cultural changes, social participation, regional coordination and democratization in order for transitions to be effective. They also acknowledge that the process of change will be lengthy and diverse.

In summary, post-extractive policy proposals aim at gradual transitions away from the current development model and eventually from the capitalist system, in which the structural drivers of extractivism are rooted. While they do not deny the positive contributions of reformist policies to improving transparency, income distribution, consumer awareness and production practices, post-extractivist proponents seek above all to transform the growth-based development model. Until this is done, social and environmental problems will only deepen.

Buen Vivir

The literal translation of *Buen Vivir* is 'Living Well'. It was originally made popular by Kichwa, Quechua and Aymara populations in the Andes, but similar concepts can be found in diverse indigenous cosmovisions around the world. Unlike post-extractivism, which offers concrete policy proposals, *Buen Vivir* has become a political ideology, used as the basis for progressive agendas in South American countries including Bolivia, Ecuador and Venezuela.

There is no single definition of *Buen Vivir*. As Gudynas and Acosta (2012) show, *Buen Vivir* incorporates a plurality of concepts, allowing for an intersection of indigenous and occidental knowledge. *Buen Vivir* focuses on human well-being, the 'fullness of life', the need to coexist with nature, recognize its intrinsic value and respect its physical limitations. *Buen Vivir* also focuses on the need to change the market's role, position and mechanisms, and the way in which humans relate to each other economically.

The electoral platforms of presidents Correa and Morales brought *Buen Vivir* into regional and international spotlights. Correa and Morales promised to construct a new socio-political-economic system based on *Buen Vivir* and to reject the destructive model that enabled the opulence of industrialized countries. The incorporation of *Buen Vivir* into legislation implies an emphasis on food security and sovereignty; autonomy in education, governance and justice; making Mother Earth a subject with rights, etc. *Buen Vivir* has also found its way into the discourses of other Latin American governments (Cuba, Venezuela, Argentina, Paraguay, Uruguay and Peru) and regional integration organizations such as ALBA, UNASUR and CELAC (Rodríguez 2013), and has become a unifying concept for different groups working on Alternatives to Development.[3]

Solidarity Economies

The term Social Solidarity Economy was coined in Lima, Peru at the First International Meeting for the Globalization of Solidarity in 1997. It was originally defined as 'all economic activities and practices with a social finality, which contribute to building a new economic paradigm' (RIPESS 2013). Currently, the umbrella of Solidarity Economies encompasses the myriad alternative approaches towards sustainability, self-sufficiency and economic independence that are being practised at local scales around the world. Examples include communal resource ownership and management, local/ regional production and consumption of organic foods, fair trade, harnessing renewable energies, the revaluation and use of traditional and ancestral knowledge, non-monetary barter, community networks of mutual support based on local needs and the provision of basic services (education, health, childcare, domestic work, etc.), the formation of community cooperatives for industry and financial services, and, more generally, recognizing the value of traditionally unpaid services, such as care-based activities, natural resources and ecosystem services (Perkins 2007).

The importance of Solidarity Economies to A2D lies in their potential to transition society beyond capitalism 'to a fairer and more sustainable society based on popular mobilization to meet local needs' (Amin 2009: 16). Mance (2007) and Gibson-Graham (2006) characterize Solidarity Economies as post-capitalist because they are based on the redistribution of wealth, not the accumulation of capital. The compatibility with post-extractivism and *Buen Vivir* is striking.

Certain examples of Solidarity Economies are well known because of their role in responding to dramatic economic crises, such as the 170 'recovered' firms which employed more than 9,000 workers in Argentina in 2003, and the explosion of barter groups with 2–5 million participants in response to the Argentine currency crisis. In Brazil, it is estimated that 1.2 million workers are involved in the Solidarity Economy and over 1,250 worker-owned enterprises exist. In Venezuela, Brazil and Mexico, there are vast networks of community banks that issue local currencies (Mance 2007). In many Latin American countries, Solidarity Economies have grown so much that they have become a sector in themselves, influential enough to warrant the creation of government departments and legislation, such as a Special Administrative Unit for Solidarity Organizations in the Colombian Ministry of Labor.

International organizations like the Intercontinental Network for the Promotion of Social Solidarity Economy (RIPESS), Grassroots Economic Organizing (GEO) and International Cooperative Alliance (ICA) track the spread of the Solidarity Economy movement and mention thousands of initiatives on their web sites. In 2013 the UN founded the Inter-agency Task Force on Social and Solidarity Economy with the aim of promoting international and national political frameworks hospitable to Solidarity Economies. The mainstreaming of Solidarity Economies into national and international governance structures may eventually undermine A2D principles, insofar as they are co-opted or reoriented to fulfilling capitalist objectives of accumulation, profit and growth. This progression will be important to monitor and evaluate.

Conceptual and practical impediments to post-growth and A2D

The main conceptual dilemma facing post-growth frameworks is whether the failure to reach sustainability objectives lies in fatal flaws of the capitalist system or in poor policy implementation. Authors who trace the root causes of global environmental problems to the capitalist system view at least five characteristics of capitalism as being incompatible with sustainability:

1   the tendency toward commodification ('marketization of social life');
2   dependence on continued growth;
3   the tendency towards inequality;
4   the elimination of other options ('universalization of economic contexts'); and
5   the amoral nature of capitalism and the pervasion of this into social norms (Arrighi 1994; Beckert 2012; Gibson-Graham 2006; Hodgson *et al.* 2001; Lang 2013; McMurtry 1999; Posner 2010; Reich 2007; Streeck 2011).

Capitalism's dependence on perpetual growth and expansion of the market creates the basis for continued instability and crisis (Arrighi 1994; McMurtry 1999; Streeck 2011). There is an interesting convergence between economic stagnation theorists (Foster and Magdoff 2009; Gordon 2012) and post-growth theorists (Heinberg 2011; Miller and Hopkins 2013) who predict the end of capitalist growth. Both call for deliberate steps to transition away from capitalism as the dominant paradigm.

A contrasting group of reform-oriented post-growth proposals do not see sustainability as being incompatible with the capitalist model. Post-growth proposals, such as Herman Daly's (1997) Steady State Economy and Jackson's (2009) Prosperity without Growth, do not challenge the fundamental organization and characteristics of capitalism, but call for reforms to decouple throughput from growth. These authors argue that ecological concepts such as the source and sink functions of ecosystems, carrying capacity, adaptation and resilience should be used to calculate appropriate limits for human activity and economic growth (Daly 2005). This viewpoint clashes with the post-development view, which argues that while reforming the system from within may bring initial benefits (such as incorporating principles like participation, gender and sustainability into development), they are ultimately limited by the overarching logic of capitalist accumulation (Blauwhof 2012).

Post-growth approaches face considerable challenges due to the pervasiveness of growth across social, political and economic structures and processes. Post-growth claims note the limitations of using GDP as the universal measurement for success and giving economic growth primacy over social and environmental priorities. The negative effects of the economic influence over politics are widely recognized. However, financial resources cannot be replaced with idealistic post-growth principles. The daily lives of nearly every person on Earth are structured around meeting their financial needs for survival. In addition, public institutions, especially in the global South, are seriously lacking the financial resources they need in order to provide basic services, infrastructure and social programmes. Blanket de-growth prescriptions will not be acceptable. The point is to place strict criteria on where growth is allowed to happen.

Perhaps the biggest challenge facing post-growth frameworks is the way that growth has become embedded in cultural norms, values and behaviours.[4] A2D authors including Escobar (2010), Gibson-Graham (2006), Gudynas (2012) and Sousa Santos (2007) emphasize the importance of making visible the myriad alternative approaches towards sustainability, self-sufficiency and independence that are already being implemented at local scales around the world. Feminist authors promote the use of feminist economics as a bridge to sustainability, and cite numerous examples of communities recognizing the value of unpaid inputs into local economies, such as care-based activities, natural resources and ecosystem services (Perkins 2007). However, it is not clear how locally generated solutions will achieve the scale necessary for global sustainability (Harvey 2008). Moreover, it is uncertain whether local initiatives can spread fast enough to match the urgency of the problem.

Another key issue is redistribution policy, which is an important component of any post-growth strategy. Originally championed by Chenery *et al.* (1974) for use within conventional growth-centred development, redistribution has taken on many forms in different political economic contexts and has resulted in criticism on economic and ethical grounds, in both the North and South (Pieterse 1996: 19). Its importance in the post-growth debate stems from the question of whether redistribution policy (either within or between countries) is an effective and appropriate substitute for economic growth, whether it is politically feasible and whether it is even possible without continued growth. The current model of the 'compensatory state', exemplified by redistribution programmes in Bolivia, Brazil, Ecuador and Venezuela, is critiqued as a way for Southern states to gain legitimacy through cash-transfer and social bonds without having to address underlying class structures. The social gains from these programmes are used to justify increasingly predatory forms of extractivism, further embedding the very models that A2D initiatives seek to dismantle (Gudynas 2012; Harvey 2003; Webber 2012b).

In addition, Barnet (2004: 530–531) argues that post-growth proposals are not fully developed and may have unacceptable economic side effects. Additionally, he is pessimistic about solutions that involve putting too much faith in the UN or multilateralism, such as those found in alternatives to globalization proposals (Cavanagh and Mander 2004). This concern is also relevant for A2D proposals, due to the heavy reliance they place on regional integration. Given the radical nature of post-growth alternatives, Barnet doubts that many of these changes are likely to happen, but believes they are worth considering.

Echoing this concern, Svampa (2012) states that a major challenge facing post-growth proposals, and post-extractivism specifically, is the 'horizon of desirability' of such proposals in terms of lifestyles and quality of life. She calls for redefining human and social needs in a way that supports sustainability as well as cultural diversity. She suggests three possibilities for re-framing human requirements including:

1   the human needs approach (Max-Neef 1993), which includes the process by which human needs are fulfilled;
2   the economy for life approach (Hinkelammert and Mora Jiménez 2005), which requires that the organization and social division of work allow for the reproduction of life over time; and
3   the ethics of care approach of eco-feminists (Aguinaga *et al.* 2012; Perkins 2007, etc.), which places the culture of care at the centre of a sustainable society.

Svampa's proposal for redefining human needs, while necessary for the sweeping cultural transformation called for by post-growth, will not be easily accepted. This will pose a significant impediment to the possibility of post-growth.

A final concern with the feasibility of post-growth strategies refers to their reliance on intensive political intervention and public regulation, which clash with the increasing corporate drive toward deregulation (Reich 2007; Shutt 1998). Blauwhof (2012) points out two obstacles to state-interventionist approaches:

1   The state is directly dependent on financial capital, which makes acting against economic growth directly counter to its interests.
2   Reforms that limit the growth prospects of businesses will eventually be evaded, overturned or co-opted in order to return to growth.

Like Blauwhof, Streeck (2011) identifies the state's response to capitalist crisis is increased regulation, capitalism cannot function under any restrictions on growth and expansion. This dynamic is exemplified in the expansion of extractivism by the progressive governments of Ecuador, Bolivia and Venezuela, despite their stated intentions to do otherwise.

Up to now, post-growth policies (including A2D) either have not yet been implemented, or face significant obstacles to implementation, or have not been in place long enough. Also, little has been done to evaluate the specific proposals put forth by groups who argue that growth must be limited or halted. The discussion about the technical, political and popular feasibility of post-growth proposals is more developed for the global North than for the global South. Additional work is needed to explore Southern-oriented policy proposals and, when possible, analyse their outcomes. Such work must take up the question of political will.

Conclusion

Regardless of whether Alternatives to Development are born out of the necessity to survive or from ideological convictions, they have important potential in contributing to wide-scale socioeconomic transformation, far beyond Latin America. A2D are just one example of a series of post-growth frameworks that are burgeoning on every continent in response to increasing recognition of the inevitability of change and/or collapse of the current growth-based global economy. The quantity of post-growth initiatives around the world is striking. It is also significant that diverse local initiatives recognize the systemic roots of local problems. The growing global concern is reflected by the steady increase in protests every year, especially since the onset of the 2008 financial crisis. A 2013 study (Ortiz *et al.* 2013) of 843 protests in 84 countries from 2006 to 2013 identified four main causes of outrage:

1   economic injustice and austerity;
2   failure of political representation;
3   global (including environmental) injustice;
4   human rights violations.

The acceptance of plurality or 'otherness' is a central component in the building of A2D, and a marked contrast to the top-down, one-size-fits-all tools of the growth-based development paradigm.

Among the obstacles to A2D, perhaps the least thoroughly discussed are those involving the issue of consumption. The growing middle class in countries of the global South will soon surpass middle-class populations in the global North. A2D thinkers believe that a mix of strict policies and popular education has the potential to catalyse change, but this debate requires a much deeper practical and logistical examination.

Continued political analysis and development of advocacy strategies by A2D groups will be just as important as fine-tuning technical proposals and garnering public support. While many A2D initiatives, such as Solidarity Economies and the Zapatista movement (cf. Chapter 16), have enjoyed successes while skirting the traditional policy process, this will not be possible for all A2D approaches. Even if A2D are taken up at national levels, few Latin American countries have sufficient geopolitical clout to have an impact in international arenas. This is yet another reason why A2D thinkers emphasize the importance of strengthening regional integration initiatives (Cerezal 2013; Gudynas 2013).

Despite the failure of Latin American governments to reverse the subordinate position of their countries in the global economy, the political climate of the region continues to offer interesting possibilities for change. The progressive environmental legislation in Bolivia and Ecuador, such as recognizing Mother Earth as a subject of rights that can be fought for legally, is an important step towards eventually adopting sustainable policies, even if it has not yet resulted in changing priorities on the ground. In addition, the mission, discourse and political experiments taking place among different integration bodies such as CELAC and UNASUR offer potential spaces to advance innovative regional policy frameworks, such as those developed by postextractivism. Although the transformations envisioned by A2D thinkers will not take place in the short term, the political environment in Latin America is certainly more conducive to alternatives than that of other regions. Despite the barriers, work on A2D continues to expand in Latin America and beyond. The magnitude of the change needed to reach sustainability and equality warrants the total commitment of civil society.

Notes

1 Abridged from Hollender, Rebecca, 'Post-Growth in the Global South: The Emergence of Alternatives to Development in Latin America', *Socialism and Democracy* 29(1), pp 73–101. http://www.tandfonline.com/doi/full/10.1080/088543 00.2014.998472.

2 Sustainable development, as defined by the UN, is development that meets the needs of the present without compromising the ability of future generations to meet their own needs.

3 Influential authors include Gudynas (2012, 2013), Dávalos (2008), Acosta (2012), Sousa Santos (2007), Ibáñez (2012) and Boff (2009).

4 Some authors note that the pervasiveness of growth has even influenced childrearing methods (Streeck 2011).

Part IV
Bringing politics back in

12 The limits of localism

Gregory Diamant

[T]here exists an indissoluble tie between social reforms and revolution.
The struggle for reforms is its *means*; the social revolution, its *goals*.
(Rosa Luxemburg 1899 [2004: 129])

[T]he present tactic of Social Democracy does not consist in *waiting* for
the antagonisms of capitalism to develop to their most extreme point and
only then transform them. On the contrary, the essence of revolutionary
tactics is to recognize the *direction* of this development and then, in the
political struggle, to push its consequences to the extreme.
(Rosa Luxemburg 1899 [2004: 143])

The wish to move beyond capitalism arises in the tension between the possible
and the actual. This tension is between two major contradictions: that between
capital and labour, and that between capital and nature. Capital exploits
both labour and nature in its relentless drive to accumulate profits. Labour
creates value and thus the surplus, the ultimate area of contestation. Our
goal of moving beyond capitalism (or transcending capitalism as I prefer)
can only be achieved by keeping these contradictions in the forefront of our
(labour's) struggles to democratically take control of the surplus and in so
doing transform the relations between people and nature in a thoroughgoing
and self-conscious way. My argument is that local initiatives alone, without
an educational and political movement rooted in solidarity and with the goal
of socialism in the forefront, are doomed to failure. Horizontality alone is not
the answer and the question of taking state power cannot be pushed to the
recesses of our mind.

The foregoing being said, local initiatives and struggles can be great and
necessary tools, acting as educational and physical incubators of new and
progressive ways of being within capitalist society, 'the seeds of the new' as
they have been characterized. They have the potential to help build a better
world. They will have to be cultivated with great care: much can and will be
learned by their successes and their failures. But how to evaluate what is a
success and what is a failure? That is a task we must set ourselves. It will be
well nigh impossible to evaluate these initiatives unless they are judged as

part of an overall movement toward socialism steeped in progressive class politics.

Evolutionism, whether overtly advocated or immanent in many local projects, for many years has been a dominant outlook on the left in the advanced capitalist societies. Whether the projects are community gardens, projects to improve human health, co-ops, a myriad of environmental improvement projects and so on, most seem to assume that capitalism will die out due to major crises and that the new potentialities expressed will lead to 'the *progressive emptying out* of the power of capital and the state' (Porcaro 2013a). Many on the left feel that we can create a life that is independent of capital and the state; the need to conquer political power is not only *not* on the immediate agenda, but is rarely discussed. Questions such as who owns the means of production (and how to change that on a macro level) and who will lead the state are not often addressed. Somehow, by an evolutionary process, the new associative forms that have been created are supposed to overcome capitalism as it is in its death throes. The constructive/destructive energy of capitalism in crisis will be expressed in many forms that will require fluidity in our tactics and strategy. The general crisis of political legitimacy has to be addressed and not just through electoralism.

One of the main tensions on the left is the search for a balance between pragmatism and utopianism. We are engaging in everyday struggles around concrete issues and simultaneously need to project a transformative vision. This vision needs to be allied with a structural analysis that illustrates how capitalism regenerates the problems that have to be faced again and again on a local level. Not the least of the problems we face may be the failure of our local initiatives or the unintended consequences of a local success. As an example of the latter, the repurposing of abandoned or neglected facilities and land by community-based organizations or co-ops can and have led to an increase in rents and a subsequent move to gentrification. Such 'successes' can lead both to the failure of our project (inability to cover the rent) and/or financial pain and evictions in the local community. This does not mean that we have to abandon these projects. However, if we are not constantly aware of the power of capital and do not have an understanding of rent and its role in capital formation, how can we project a transformative vision that illuminates both their power (capital and rent) and the need to overcome them? How do we collectively provide a vision of a society of associated producers in control of the surplus it creates and the formation of new relations between people and their creations (that is, a lessening of alienation)? Further, small is not always better. As an example, the drive for local health centres and the dismantling of public health infrastructure, which have the benefits of scale, are not always a positive. Such actions too can play into the hands of local real estate interests in league with local municipalities and toadying politicians.

Local initiatives have particular difficulty in resisting the market discipline that mediates capital's ruthless and incessant drive to accumulate. The need for credit, not only in the production of commodities but also in their circulation, becomes another disciplining force. Even the largest and most long-lasting positive local initiatives, such as Mondragon in Spain, can become seriously weakened as they are exposed to the vagaries of the financial circuits. Our local initiatives are not immune to the crazy self-enhancing circuit of capital that is often expressed in wild speculation and the creation of waste (not just pollution, but advertising and marketing costs). The internal drives of capitalism limit the potential for small-scale alternatives. Small projects can become self-justifying and are not in and of themselves the means to build broad movements for social change. Many of these projects, especially those with a great component of 'do-it-yourself-ism', can conceal a deep pessimism about the possibility of collective agency and come out of a profound internalization of individualism. There is a great (and understandable) wish to delink from the global economy with all of its confusions and injustice. This desire can lead to what Marx characterized a 'Robinson Crusoe economy', an ahistorical concept that leads us nowhere. We need to look at the relational aspects of the local: how do the projects collectively prosper and simultaneously advance a class-based political transformative project?

In the North American left there is an especially strong moralizing streak that all too often substitutes individual choice for class politics (compare McCabe, Chapter 14). We concentrate on such topics as 'ethical shopping' but does this really change the circuits of production and distribution of capital (Sharzer 2012)? We rightly critique consumerism and ecological waste, but have we developed a way to tie that critique to our transformative project? Do we know how to convince the mass of people that we do not just criticize but have a vision of the future that will seem attainable? After all, it is they who will actually have to struggle and keep creating and renewing that vision. All too often, we project guilt and pessimism; these are not strong political bases for organizing. Related to the foregoing is a sense of catastrophism that often engenders a sense of guilt. How should we approach this? By recognizing that, yes, the catastrophes will come, whether ecological or economic (truthfully one cannot disentangle them), and thus we need to show that there is *no* future within the system. This creates an opening for radical change.

People with precarious work lives often have to hold down multiple jobs just to reproduce themselves, and they probably need to consume *more*, not less. Worldwide, their level of consumption needs to increase. Recently, proposals have been made (and in Brazil instituted) to give to the poor a basket of money or goods, in short a dole. When even the likes of Milton Friedman push this project we need to understand it for what it is: the welfare state reconfigured for the financial market capitalist state. Give the citizens a minimal dole; increase automization in manufacturing and in service areas and thus lessen the need for variable capital. This fits well with more precarious work and we end up with no or few workers, a partial realization of the dream expressed by Margaret Thatcher that there is no society, just individual citizens. This is a profoundly reactionary plan. In fact, we need more work for ecological conversion and infrastructure building and improvements. It should be those who create value, and not the 1 per cent, who should determine the distribution of the surplus (Wolff 2012a).

Women have it doubly hard: they often have poorly paid and unstable work and then have to work in the home maintaining their families. They and all those who live in the new, precarious economy are often exhausted and turn to drugs and other entertainments to deaden the pain of alienation. An irony is that we on the left understandably and rightly use the word 'participatory' as a positive modifier in our projects, but how much time do workers have to participate? For the most part, working people suffering under the blows of increased austerity and loss of dignity have little time to devote to growing their own food. That doesn't mean that community garden projects are a bad idea, they have a lot of positive attributes. But the potential for limited, healthy food consumption is not a substitute for income security and the large-scale social planning of agricultural production and distribution. Urban agriculture cannot guarantee that.

Since I have mentioned precarious labour, let's speak a little about technology, labour and capitalism. 'Restructuring' has become a bourgeois buzzword repeated ad-nauseam in both the business and mainstream press. It means what it says and changing the structure of work is one of its goals. Let's not forget that the main purpose of technology is to increase the value given to capital. Smaller high-tech workplaces have the effect of breaking up the concentration of labour and thus hindering the drive to solidarity and reducing workers' bargaining power. Now the workplace is shrinking even further by going back to the home: Internet sites such as TaskRabbit in the US are matching workers with employers. The new/old wrinkle is that the work is done at home and it has led to the revival of piecework. It is creating a high-tech home of work that is socially redolent of pre-Industrial Revolution days and is putting a downward pressure on wages. Further, this project strengthens individualism while reducing the space for collective action. Time is compressed and the search for work becomes all-consuming. Even sleep now is being perceived as an affront to capitalism: it is 'unproductive', 'a waste of time', much as Locke viewed the lack of intensive cultivation by native societies as unproductive, thus providing an ideological and moral justification for colonial expropriation. Time is becoming an area of contestation unseen since the clock was mated to the factory 200 years ago.

As Samir Amin has written in *Monthly Review*, 'There is no possible revolutionary advance of the movement toward socialism without construction of strategic unity of action linking together the needed critical mass of diverse social forces in conflict with the dominant capitalist system' (Amin 2014). The task before us is to go beyond localism; to transcend capitalism we will have to engage in a self-consciously political project to contest for power; not only or even principally in the electoral arena whose own logic can distract us, even in subtle ways, from the logic of the larger struggle. As inspiring as many of the worldwide protests have been, such as Occupy, 'they are revolts without the spirit of revolution' (Žižek 2012). As we view the Arab Spring revolts they bring to mind the insight commonly ascribed to Walter Benjamin that 'every rise of fascism bears witness to a failed revolution'. The counter-revolution is proof of the left's failure but it is also proof that there was revolutionary potential that we were unable to mobilize. Bertolt Brecht gave a poetic and dialectical illustration of failure in one of his Anecdotes of Mr. Keuner entitled 'The Exertions of the Best People'.

'What are you working on?' Mr K was asked.

'I'm having a lot of trouble: I'm preparing my next mistake', answered Mr K.

As mentioned earlier, we will have to move beyond horizontality to have a chance of success. We will have to move beyond rejection and protest (a necessary first step) to positing a vision of a future society. Many of our local projects do that in various ways but a form of evolutionism seems to be at the root of them. David Harvey, among others, has put his finger on some of the problems of the strictly local and horizontal approach:

> in some sense 'hierarchical' forms of organization are needed to address large-scale problems such as global warming. Unfortunately the term 'hierarchy' is anathema in conventional thinking, and virtually unpopular with much of the left these days. The only politically correct form of organization in many radical circles is non-state, non-hierarchical, and horizontal.

And further,

> What looks like a good way to resolve problems at one scale does not hold on another scale. Even worse, patently good solutions at one scale (the local, say) do not necessarily aggregate up (or cascade down) to make for good solutions at another scale (the global, for example).

In an even more explicit way Harvey goes on to write:

> This is also, incidentally, why the valuable lessons gained from the collective organization of small-scale solidarity economies along common-property lines cannot translate into global solutions without resort to 'nested' and therefore hierarchical organizational forms. Unfortunately, as already noted, the idea of hierarchy is anathema to many segments of the oppositional left these days. A fetishism of organizational preference (pure horizontality, for example) all too often stands in the way of exploring appropriate and effective solutions. Just to be clear, I am not saying horizontality is bad – indeed, I think it an excellent objective – but that we should acknowledge its limits as a hegemonic organizational principle, and be prepared to go far beyond it when necessary.
>
> (Harvey 2012)

The important point Harvey makes here needs to be applied to our political work as well. In our collective transformative project, one cannot ignore the power of military force. Both the police and military personnel are simultaneously enforcers of the current order and members of communities where they and their families are subject to the same ecological, political and economic degradations as everyone else. In one fashion or another, some of them will need to become supporters of our progressive goals.

In 1968 there was a slogan, 'demand the impossible', that can inspire us today to demand things that are perfectly reasonable and materially possible, but well nigh impossible to deliver under capitalism (such as universal health care, affordable housing for all, free and excellent education for all). This again exposes the inability of capitalism to truly satisfy the needs of the majority of people. We will have to create a political formation that will express our *collective* solidarity and become a vehicle for political education and national and transnational struggle. As Žižek (2014) has argued, '[w]e will have to posit a positive universal struggle that can be shared by all participants'. Just as transnational capital recognizes no boundaries or time zones neither can we on the left. In our struggles, we need diversity and respect for differences to become not the supreme goal and principle; rather the achieving of unity, the theorizing of what is common, among the broadly defined working class has to become the central self-conception. We will begin at the local but create political formations that can contest the power of capital in multiple arenas. We will have to make the long march through the institutions, as Gramsci has noted, for where else will we help gain the knowledge and experience to change society?

13 Getting past capitalism
History, vision, hope

Cynthia Kaufman

I first became political around the struggle against US support for dictatorships in Central America. At that time, many of us on the left in the Americas saw armed struggles to overthrow pro-capitalist dictatorial governments as important pieces in the process of overthrowing the capitalist system. We believed that nations would be liberated one at a time. As those movements largely failed, and as neoliberalism gave pro-capitalist forces new energy to crush the imaginations of the populations living under it, many of us on the left were without a clear sense of a path forward.

Like many others, I soldiered on doing good work engaging in struggles such as the fight against the North American Free Trade Agreement, against police abuse and against displacement and gentrification. For those years, I, like many on the left, did that work without any hope that my work would add up to much of significance.

Then, following 1 January 1994, when the Zapatistas made their bold debut onto the world stage, many of us were woken up to a new and deeply inspiring way of understanding our roles in the world. The Zapatistas boldly claimed that 'another world is possible'; that we need to build a 'movement of movements'; and that we needed to 'build a new world'. From that moment, it has seemed that we were in a new and very promising period, one where we could see our work as building a new world one step at a time, one where we didn't need to wait for the revolution that wasn't coming. In the period that has followed, many people have begun to theorize ways that we can see our progressive work as building a new post-capitalist world.

Non-capitalism and anti-capitalism

There is a lot of important work being done these days related to building non-capitalist alternatives to our present economy. In the global South, people talk about an emerging 'solidarity economy'. In the north, the same concepts are often referred to as 'new economy'. Both stress the importance of cooperatives, of economic forms that build community and what the Ecuadorian constitution terms *Buen Vivir*, a way of living in harmony with nature, in ways that produce more happiness with less economic throughput.

In what follows I will refer to these moves collectively as the solidarity economy.

One important author in this area is J.K. Gibson-Graham (2003, 2006), who wrote a few books that started from the premise that when we see the world as 'capitalist' we miss the many forms of non-capitalism all around us, and this makes the problem we are up against seem much more overwhelming than it needs to be. She claims that more than 50 per cent of the US economy is non-capitalist, meaning: gift-based and household economies, socialist (meaning done by a state) and communal, such as worker-owned cooperatives. Gibson-Graham talks about capitalism as a set of practices that can be interrupted, rather than as a system that can be overthrown. This work is what got me started on this project. She does an amazing job laying down a theoretical paradigm that opens up new and productive ways of understanding the nature of non-capitalism all around us. Many people working toward a solidarity economy argue that if we want to move beyond capitalism, we need to build non-capitalism.

Developments in the solidarity economy often offer means of subsistence to people who otherwise do not have them, they allow people a sense of agency and power in their lives, and they can spill over into taking more power in other aspects of their lives. But there is a piece that is missing from much of the analysis of the power of non-capitalism, and that is the relationship between non-capitalism and anti-capitalism. We can create economic forms so that people who work too many hours can work less, and people who consume in unsustainable ways can waste less, and we can build economic forms that employ people who are under-employed, and build meaning and community in our economic processes. All of that will lead to better lives for those of us living that way. But how are we going to stop ExxonMobil and the US Chamber of Commerce from destroying the atmosphere? What do we do about the fact that these same forces dominate the political landscape in many countries, and thus have to a large extent captured and control the US government, the Mexican government and many transnational organizations? How do we make our vision spread when the World Bank spreads transnational capitalism throughout the world and the IMF enforces capitalist practices on states that try to break away from that?

We need to think about ways to take down the old, even as we build the new. In my experience those who are working to build the new tend to not talk very much about how to take down the old, and the discussions we have on how to take down the old are quite under-theorized and based on understandings of how capitalism works that were formed about 100 years ago, and have since become ossified. That older paradigm assumed a social totality that would eventually be moved to an inevitable social rupture that would move us to the next social totality, socialism.

Most anti-capitalists have given up on the theory of an inevitable move from one mode of production to the next. And yet that paradigm haunts us and makes most conversations among anti-capitalists about what to do to challenge capitalism feel stilted and unproductive, as we feel uncomfortable with 'reformism', and yet don't know what to do to make a positive revolution happen. It is time that we did for anti-capitalism what the solidarity economy theorists have done for non-capitalism. Once we give up on theorizing capitalism as a social totality, we can begin to theorize anti-capitalism as a practical, realistic set of practices that we can engage in right now.

Four forms of agency that constitute capitalism

Helpful in this process is the concept of social formation, borrowed from the framework that Omi and Winant (2014) develop for analysing racism in their book *Racial Formation in the United States*. What Omi and Winant argue in their analysis of racism is that it is constituted by a variety of intersecting forms of agency. The analysis of racism proceeds then by the study of the historically contingent outcomes of these forms of agency. Expanding this idea beyond the analysis of racism, social formations are the results of the historical trajectories of a variety of forms of agency operating over time. Capitalism can be seen as a social formation, that is, as a set of historically contingent interrelated practices that have no necessary common core to them.

If capitalism is something like a social formation constituted by a multiplicity of forms of agency then there is no one core place to go to destroy capitalism. This is why it cannot be overthrown – why a coup against it won't work – and why even having a group of anti-capitalists take state power will not mean that it has been destroyed. Even countries like Bolivia, which has elected an anti-capitalist government, have to deal with local wealthy landowners, pro-capitalist media, the transnational capitalist ruling class and transnational corporations, all working to undermine their progress to a solidarity economy. Capitalist logics have woven themselves deeply into the social fabric. Much like the work done by public health officials in virus eradication, anti-capitalists must use a multiplicity of means and they must be ever vigilant against the continual reemergence of new ways in which capitalist forms of destruction emerge.

I would like to begin a conversation about the forms of agency that constitute capitalism, and the practical political implications of that analysis, by focusing on four of what surely are a myriad of forms of agency that constitute capitalism: systems of desire, the intentional actions of the owning class, the state and the economic dependency trap of capitalism.[1]

Living in a society dominated by capitalism, we inhabit a world where pleasure is increasingly structured as something to be bought. Fulfilment is conceived as something to be attained through the consumption of commodities. Our time is so colonized by our work, that many of us don't have time for the slow pleasures in life, and so must buy fast pleasures like premade food and expensive vacations. Our sense of self comes to be thoroughly mediated by the kinds of products we buy, the ways we decorate our living spaces, the cars we drive or bikes we ride, how we dress and do our hair, the things we do for fun – the texture of our day-to-day lives becomes caught up in the process of buying products.

Because of the ways that capitalism provides us with what we need and what we believe we need, those opposed to it cannot count on others to join their side out of any simple, objectively determined set of interests. People at all levels of society work to reproduce capitalist forms of agency through many activities, including their consumption, their beliefs, the ways they vote and the ways they engage in leisure. Members of the owning class are not the only ones acting to reproduce capitalism. We all reproduce it through our everyday activities.

Thus capitalism is partially reproduced by the ways most people in a society dominated by capitalism live their everyday lives as consumers. This form of pro-capitalist agency is challenged by moves to live outside the system, both culturally and economically. This form of anti-capitalist agency is the one most likely to be addressed by those who focus on building a solidarity economy.

The second form of pro-capitalist agency is the intentional actions of the owning class. There are a variety of ways that the owning class comes to work as a coherent actor. At the most macro-scale, large actors realize that they need coordinated action to further their collective interests and many agents of large-scale capitalism work hard to make sure there are transnational structures that promote their common interests. That the 1 per cent comes to act in coherent and cohesive ways is powerfully seen in transnational apparatuses such as the WTO, Davos and major trade agreements. Powerful work has been done in the past 20 years in the global justice movement exposing what happens at the summits where the transnational owning class works out common agendas. Exposing their work to the light of day and challenging the owning class' ability to coordinate, as well as the long slow work of challenging the trade agreements the transnational owning class push through our nominally democratic governments, are powerful ways to challenge capitalism. And we constrain the actions of the 1 per cent to the extent that we control the state.

That gets us to the third form of pro-capitalist agency: the state. Applying pressure through nation-states is a powerful way to constrain the transnational ruling class. To the extent that states come to be captured by local or transnational owning classes, they are powerful vectors of pro-capitalist action. While in some of his work, Lenin saw the state under capitalism as a 'capitalist state' that needed to be overthrown, Marx and Engels actually had a more nuanced view. They saw the state as a site of struggle. In the *Manifesto* they wrote:

> The first step in the revolution by the working class is to raise the proletariat to the position of ruling class, to win the battle of democracy. The proletariat will use its political supremacy to wrest, by degrees, all capital from the bourgeoisie, to centralize all instruments of production in the

hands of the State, i.e., of the proletariat organized as the ruling class; and to increase the total of productive forces as rapidly as possible.

(Marx and Engels [1848] 1972: 490)

Marx and Engels saw the modern nation-state as rising in tandem with capitalism, and as largely offering the framework in which capitalism could function. But they also believed that the state could be captured by the working class and made to serve the needs of a society undivided by class. They saw governments in capitalist societies as being dominated by capitalist forces, but not as mere puppets of the capitalist class. This view of Marx and Engels is often forgotten, or is minimized, and the dominant view among Marxist-influenced revolutionaries has been closer to Lenin's.

The Leninist view that the state functions to serve the needs of the bourgeoisie has led to a polarization in anti-capitalist circles around the concepts of reform versus revolution. There is a tradition on the left of dismissing as reformist any action not specifically designed to instigate a revolution to smash the state and overthrow capitalism. Early theorists of capitalism believed that the only two options were violent revolution to overthrow capitalism or a reformism that accepted capitalism as a given. Current critiques of reformism often rely for their rhetorical force on some very stale understandings of what happened in the German Social Democratic party more than a hundred years ago. The binary of reform versus revolution, and the unthinking ways anti-capitalists repeat those terms is a huge part of why it is hard for anti-capitalists to have productive discussions on how to get past capitalism.

The state is an important site for anti-capitalist work. So the question becomes how anti-capitalist forces can do better in our challenges around the state. Very helpful for answering that question is *Capitalism and Social Democracy* (1993) by the Polish-born political theorist Adam Przeworski. Przeworski criticizes the ways that Marxists have tended to see the state as nothing but an agent of the ruling class. He argues that many are attracted to this sort of analysis because they have not been able to explain why it is that socialist parties in Europe throughout the twentieth century accommodated themselves to capitalism rather than overthrowing it.

Przeworski shows that in Europe there is a basic paradox for socialist parties: to win elections they must stand for improving the lives of the majority. The best way to improve the lives of the majority quickly enough to win reelection is to gain concessions from the owning class, such as higher wages, a social safety net and better working conditions. The European social democracies have accomplished this to a high level without challenging the private ownership of the means of production (Przeworski 1993).

Przeworski argues that many attempts to nationalize the means of production led to capitalists withdrawing from their side of the bargain and not investing in the national economy. Anti-capitalist organizing faces the challenge of what I call the economic dependency trap of capitalism, wherein it becomes difficult to move stepwise away from capitalism since getting a job from a capitalist is the most likely way one can get what is needed to survive in a society dominated by capitalist processes. People in a largely capitalist society will generally see that their interests are served by the election of candidates who are able to provide a context in which business can be successful.

Przeworski shows that we don't need a functionalist theory of the state that posits an all-powerful bourgeoisie invariably getting its needs met by the state to understand why European voters have not chosen to abolish capitalism. Instead, the explanation for why people choose capitalism is quite simple: it is often in their short-term self-interest (Przeworski 1993: 202).

This leads us to the fourth form of pro-capitalist agency: an economic dependency trap that emerges in capitalism, whereby people's ability to meet their needs comes to be dependent on the success of capitalists in needing to hire people in wage labour.

Once a society comes to have a large enough capitalist sector, the economic dependency trap thus functions passively as one of the most powerful tools favouring the interests of capitalism. The economic dependency trap of capitalism needs to be taken into account when constructing anti-capitalist strategies. Anti-capitalist organizers will be severely limited and not likely to find much support if they advocate for policies that will run directly against the ability of people to maintain their standard of living.

Proponents of solidarity economies argue that it is better that most people with a full-time job work less and, for most of us in the global North, consume fewer low-quality disposable goods, while also arguing that people in the global South can be brought out of poverty without moving to high GDP, high employment or high carbon-producing economies. And yet how do we explain this to people who believe that more employment and more GDP are the ways to a better life?

One aspect of escaping from the economic dependency trap is to develop coherent narratives that help people understand the path out of dependency on capitalism. The more coherent and plausible we can make that alternative economic narrative, the more likely it is that our views will find traction in the political sphere. We need to do more to have powerful answers to the questions of how our policies will not lead to the devastations of unemployment in the short term. In order to make that case we need to spend more time talking about alternative ways of understanding large-scale economic practices and policies. We need to promote the use of alternative economic indicators.

We also need to develop practical projects that shrink the economic dependency trap of capitalism, such that moving in the direction of solidarity economics will not make people's lives worse. Some of those practices are the promotion of work-time reduction, so more people can work in an economy with less economic throughput; national health care, so people are not dependent upon a full-time job to have their medical needs met; strengthening systems of social security, so that people do not need a job to have a secure old age; etc. Also important are projects that develop non-capitalist ways of meeting our needs, such as worker-owned cooperatives that allow for work outside of capitalist relations, and public banks, that allow resources to flow to non-capitalist projects.

Actions to get past capitalism

From within this framework of understanding pro-capitalist forms of agency, we can begin to see how a variety of forms of action are important for challenging them. The work promoted by theorists of solidarity economics toward building alternatives in the here and now is powerful for a number of reasons:

1   It helps break the hold of consumerist desire on people.
2   It refutes the argument that 'There is no alternative'.
3   It is valuable for lessening people's vulnerability to the economic dependency trap of capitalism.

But equally important to building those alternatives, and working on non-capitalism, are strategies that are more directly anti-capitalist:

1   We need to make states as democratic as possible so that we can promote laws that constrain the ability of capital to control us.
2   We need to work to develop alternative ways of understanding the economy so that people are less willing to vote for pro-capitalist candidates in the belief that they will provide needed jobs.
3   We need to begin to name capitalism. If, like the anti-racist and feminist movements, we are able to get to the point where it is common knowledge that capitalism is a destructive social form, and where many people understand the ways it works, more people will be able to decode pro-capitalist manipulations.
4   We need to challenge the major processes of capitalist reproduction in respectful coalition with others, working for shorter work hours, working against free trade deals, etc.
5   Finally, we need to think strategically. Fighting against an enemy that is dispersed through the whole fabric of society, that is implicated in our own desires, and that has no central core holding it together and making it function, requires subtle forms of analysis. We need to give up on the binary of reform versus revolution and look to build revolutionary reforms: actions that step by step begin to liberate us from capitalism. We need to avoid looking for simple solutions, fulcrum points, or a black-and-white understanding of what we are doing. In all of our work, we need to think about what we are doing and how it will add up to meaningful change. If we want to get past capitalism we need to be clever, flexible, perceptive and brave.

A postscript on engaging the state

I see in many people who have been politicized by the Zapatista and Occupy movements a deep distrust of forms of struggle that engage the state or that involve taking on macro level institutions such as transnational capital. Some of this seems related to an attraction to the sense of healing that comes from building something positive in a world awash in processes that lead to cynicism and apathy. Some of it is probably also a result of decades of neoliberal ideology according to which the state is seen as the enemy of all things good. And most of our states have mostly been largely captured by pro-capitalist forces and are largely unaccountable to democratic forces. And yet we need to build another world by pushing back on the old as much as by building the new.

To take climate change as an example: we need to delegitimize the fossil fuel industry, make its destruction of the atmosphere illegal and minimize the political power of the small number of companies that are ultimately responsible for the destruction of our atmosphere. We need to embrace this less aesthetically pleasing part of our struggle even as we embrace the more attractive ones. We need to contest the state and transnational apparatuses of capitalist power, even as we embrace the more personally transforming actions that build horizontal power among our communities.

Our politics needs to be guided by a deeply strategic approach that looks carefully at the situations before us and asks hard questions about the best ways to move forward. At this propitious time we need to be much more creative in our thinking than we have been as a community for a long time. We need to develop our understandings of how the different parts of our movement of movements can create synergies. After years of coasting on old analyses because we knew the stakes were not very high since no one was listening to us, we need to ask deeper questions and ask them more seriously.

An anti-essentialist approach to anti-capitalism can help us get past the binary of reform versus revolution and help us focus on revolutionary reforms. We don't need to wait for 'the Revolution' to begin to get past capitalism. Getting past capitalism happens as we build economic forms based on community forms of capital, gift-based economies, worker-owned cooperatives and government actions that serve human needs. We get past capitalism when we work in coalition with others to constrain the ways that capitalism is reproduced at all levels of society, from cultural memes that promote consumerism, to economic structures of dependency, to transnational legal apparatuses. We build a movement to get past capitalism as we spread realistic analysis of how capitalism functions, what is wrong with it and how we can push it back.

Rather than undermining practical political activity by pointing out that it is not revolutionary, as traditional Marxists have tended to do, or undermining challenges to the structures that reproduce capitalism by pretending we can ignore them, as many building a new world seem to think we can, anti-capitalist analysis can help inspire the work people are already doing on many fronts. We can show how other forms of struggle can be part of a movement for a truly better world: one without alienation, without exploitation and one based on sustainable economics.

As we build that movement, at every step along the way life can be made better for those who are now unable to gain minimal means for a healthy existence as well as for those who are privileged. Life can be more secure, more interesting, more environmentally sustainable and more equitable. It can be less alienating, less exploitative and less dominated by the race for profits at all cost. And perhaps one day it can be completely free from capitalism.

Note

1 A more developed version of this analysis can be found in Kaufman (2012).

14 Toward a stronger, more influential political left

An appeal for critical self-reflection

Michael P. McCabe

This chapter begins with the understanding that we face no greater threat or challenge than anthropogenic climate change. Each year, increasing sophistication of climate models forces past global warming-related projections once considered 'dire' to be reclassified as 'conservative', or worse, antiquated. Indeed, the latest AR5 report from the Intergovernmental Panel on Climate Change (IPCC) provides the clearest example of such revisions. Much of this sophistication is based on the inclusion of a growing number of 'positive feedbacks' found in the natural environment, but revisions in climate change projections are also attributed to other factors including a growth in observable data that shows an increasingly unstable climate at temperatures below the popular 'rise of two degrees Celsius' threshold previously considered 'safe,' and endorsed by major international bodies including the United Nations (Hansen *et al.* 2013). Perhaps most striking, however, is the understanding that we are triggering an unprecedented mass-extinction event that includes the near-term death of our oceans. Unlike other social crises, anthropogenic climate change offers a limited time for intervention before we reach a 'tipping point' when positive feedbacks caused by greenhouse gas (GHG) emissions trigger a process of 'runaway' climate change – a situation whereby *mitigation* and *adaptation* will be effective only at retarding inevitable social and ecological catastrophe.[1] Failure to avert such an event or to highlight the specific need for immediate intervention is unacceptable.

Concurrent with the environmental crisis of climate change is a global crisis of capitalism. The lack of an effective political response by the left to the 'Great Recession' has provided neoliberal planners with a monopoly over policy intervention, globally. As such, bailout packages and quantitative easing focus on resuscitating capital while leaving untouched the neoliberal features of financialization, privatization, monopolization and acutely exploitative global production practices that have, in their totality, made the global political economy increasingly inequitable and prone to systemic failure. Additionally, unprecedented rates of unemployment in conjunction with neoliberal austerity measures have served to further exacerbate structural inequalities by shifting the burden of crisis onto the working class and the public sector more generally. By packaging austerity as a technical necessity born out of budgetary restraints, neoliberal strategists and governing elites have concealed neoliberalism as a political project designed to restore class power (Harvey 2005), successfully restructuring the state into an aggressive facilitator of market imperatives with wide public support. Consequently, the state is no longer *perceived* to have the necessary institutional capacity or a legitimate claim over the mechanisms required to mitigate social inequities, such as wealth redistribution, market regulation and more direct interventions in the market economy. Neoliberal state restructuring also presents profound challenges beyond the pursuit of equity, as the advancement of adaptation and mitigation strategies for climate change also requires a strong interventionist state and a retreat from the primacy of markets that have hitherto failed to avert or remedy social problems. The development of this alternative paradigm is predicated upon the left's ability to develop a counter-hegemonic movement capable of redirecting the state to simultaneously confront the failed paradigm of neoliberal political economy and the imminence of abrupt climate change by legislating a more socially equitable and ecologically sustainable model of political economy. The goal of this chapter, then, is to present my view of how we may come to build a stronger, more influential political left.

A great amount of energy has been spent by the left analysing and confronting the pathologies and social crises that are born out of capitalist social relations. While such efforts are indeed useful and pertinent, I argue that we, the left, must also direct our focus of analysis inward. For although it is accurate that the market has failed to correct climate change and the most recent global crisis of capitalism, so too has the left. And yet, if the rapid growth of Occupy Wall Street (OWS) as a national and international social movement is any indication, there is a strong desire among large segments of the population for progressive change. Given this reality we must acknowledge that OWS was a squandered moment for which the left should be held accountable. This, however, is not intended to understate the importance of the Occupy movement. Any critical assessment of OWS must also acknowledge that following the Great Recession, the rhetorical slogan 'we are the 99 per cent' served the important role of moving the public debate away from technical questions about austerity, and toward political questions centred on political and economic inequality. Additionally, Occupy gave rise to a new generation of political activists who, prior to OWS, were largely marginalized or otherwise removed from the political process, and who did not have a conception of the legitimacy and importance of disruptive protest as a means by which to advance a political agenda. Though despite these important accomplishments, like the majority of social movements following the 1960s birth of the New Left, Occupy Wall Street ultimately fell short of transcending or even modifying structural social relations. Therefore, I argue that the left must engage in a process of critical self-reflection, to which I hope to make an initial contribution.

Methodologically, my argument is largely built according to observations made at the height of the Occupy Wall Street movement. My reason for focusing on OWS is twofold:

1   OWS is the most recent, significant manifestation of the anti-capitalist left in the United States – and in many instances, globally – and as such, should be critically evaluated as a means of furthering the socialist project.
2   OWS is an embodiment of the left – both in the United States and abroad – whereas its tactics, strategies and general ideological makeup are largely (but not entirely) characteristic of today's broader anti-capitalist left.

Therefore, Occupy Wall Street is both a subject of critique as well as a window into a broader discussion about the state of prevailing left tactics and strategies.

The critique

We have witnessed a resurgence of the 'post-political' social movement form that defined much of the 1960s and 1970s New Left. Rhetorically, Occupy Wall Street was often discussed by its core cadre as being a 'post-political', *cultural* movement intended to transcend the limits of ideology; and its tactics and strategies support these claims. This raises a question of fundamental importance: if a social movement is 'post-political' but we define politics as being a process of power relations, then is not the logical conclusion that any ideology structured upon a position of post-politics is incapable of conceiving of and contesting power relations? Thus, if a movement is post-political, can we expect from it a concrete programme for change and demands? This is hardly semantic, as the ideology of post-politics in OWS and the broader left is not confined to rhetoric, but instead informs the theory–praxis dialectic.

Anti-organization

Social groups lacking organization are forced into a subordinate position, devoid of the capacity to challenge power relations by the nature of their atomized social position. Gaetano Mosca demonstrates in his masterpiece, *Elementi di Scienza Politica* (Mosca 1960), that the ability of a ruling class to hold power over the majority depends upon its active dis-organization of society at large. Troubling, then, is the ethos of anti-organization that is dominant in contemporary left theory and praxis.

A major factor that drives the rejection of political organization is the concern that political organizations threaten to ideologically contaminate or co-opt collective action. This fear is channelled through a politics of neo-anarchism that celebrates the dynamism of the 'organic' social movement, free of organizational burden. Such sentiments are popularly theorized by social movement scholar Francis Fox Piven (Piven 2006), and they are embraced by much of the contemporary left. However, emphasis on the *organic* reduces the birth of social movements to a personal and interpersonal cognitive awakening to relations of domination, grossly underestimating the contributory factor that political organization lends to the development of a social movement and the social consciousness (or false consciousness) of its participants. For example, are we to believe that the 2006 immigrant rights protest movement, which *appeared* to be a spontaneous phenomenon, was in fact organic? Or, might we acknowledge that this protest movement was the result of decades of on-the-ground organizing by a multitude of community-based organizations including workers' centres and immigrant rights organizations whose successful collaboration resulted in what is now a historic moment of protest? Certainly the latter is the case, and it is by no means a deviation, but is instead the formula for successful political action (De Leon *et al.* 2009).

Furthermore, organizations such as labour unions, progressive community organizations and left political parties have the necessary ability to lend specifically left ideological focus to social movements that may otherwise be guided by populist or even reactionary discourses. If we redirect our attention to the wider body politic, we again see clear evidence of the great necessity for this interpellative function of an organized left to train political discourse according to emancipatory principles of social justice. Many leftists incorrectly theorize the 'grassroots' as an organic locus of a politics rooted in equity, but prefigurative analysis ignores social reality. The history of local politics exposes 'community' as being fertile ground for political projects that are equally likely (or perhaps more likely) to be hostile to social justice rather than a producer of it. Indeed, the prevalence of conservatism in the United States owes much of its success to localism (DeFilippis *et al.* 2010). The conclusion to be drawn from this observation is not the abandonment of the local; after all, the local is where people live, work and socially reproduce, and as such, is also the place where the arduous process of political organizing must take place. Instead, this social reality begs that the left rediscover political organization, as the ability of left organizations to interpellate a politics of social justice onto otherwise ideologically diffuse populations is to confront the limits of populism and the threat of reactionary political forms, by establishing an explicitly *left* social bloc, armed with the cognitive and political ability to identify, critique and confront relations of domination. Here I borrow from De Leon, Desai and Tuğal (De Leon *et al.* 2009) to additionally argue that it is not unreasonable, but rather necessary to pursue a paradigm wherein a party strategy is developed that serves to institutionalize these *left* social blocs; at which point a genuinely counter-hegemonic challenge can be levied against established institutions of domination, perhaps leading to their eventual expropriation and democratization.

It is important to note that beyond active attempts to resist political organization, other ideological trends within the contemporary left have undermined the need for organization in less intentional ways. Specifically,

I want to make brief mention of the effect that post-modernism has had on the ways in which the contemporary left addresses questions of identity. The emphasis that post-modernism places on multiculturalism has exacerbated the prevalence of identity politics that challenge the development of political organization that is ideologically guided by a class-based analysis of social relations. Politically, this elevated importance of individual identity makes the forging of solidarity along class lines exceedingly difficult (if not entirely impossible), as a politics centred on class is perceived to be suppressive of, rather than incorporative of, multiple identities and cultures. As such, class politics becomes subordinate to the politics of multiculturalism that in recent decades has proven to disorganize rather than unite the left; the consequence of which is the preservation of elite rule.

Anti-statism

The dominance of anti-statism in the contemporary left theory–praxis dialectic is the starkest manifestation of both a reluctance to embrace formal organization, as well as a failure to adequately theorize power relations. Indeed, the left has largely abandoned the state as a necessary institution and a legitimate target of our political practice. Citing the historical record of state repression, singularly theorizing the state as an appendage of capital, or viewing the state as being incompatible with participatory forms of democracy, what unites each of these positions is the naïve assumption that it is possible, let alone desirable, to 'smash the state'; establishing what can reasonably be assumed only to be the left's endorsement of the Hobbesian, *bellum omnium contra omnes*.

Let us imagine more concretely a scenario where the state withers away tomorrow. What are we left with? Will we establish a governing structure that utilizes the romanticism of the general assembly? In this scenario, do Goldman Sachs and Citigroup wither away as well? What about the fossil fuel industry? What institutions will meet the need for climate adaptation, or respond to social crisis following *natural* disasters? Do states around the world wither away simultaneously? If not, what prevents a still-existing state, reactionary political groups or counter-revolutionary bourgeois interests from taking advantage of such a gaping power vacuum? Will it not still be required of us to address the reign of terror imposed by the market, but now without the regulatory capacity of the state? Doesn't this position of a withered state paradoxically support more the *rhetorical* aspirations of the neo-liberal project than any political project seeking emancipation from capitalist social relations? My point here is not to simplify state theory, but instead to expose the lack of responsible, intellectual thought governing the position of anti-statism.

Only the state can rival the all-encompassing Leviathan of capital and address the pathologies born out of it; climate change being the clearest modern example of such externalities. The state is also the institution best suited to guard against any reversion back to inequitable class relations once a socialist political economy takes root; for despite recently fashionable post-modern incantations that frame culture as the ultimate determiner of equitable social relations, history demonstrates that class interests transcend culture and must be democratically regulated accordingly. Classical liberalism birthed an acute awareness of the most necessary concern over arbitrary, repressive state power and it will forever be the duty of a democratic society to regulate the state. But, not all state coercion is to be feared or abandoned. The nation-state is the only modern institution with the coercive ability to expropriate capital and to ensure a balance between productive forces and environmental sustainability, be it within a capitalist or socialist framework. Therefore, we should not be 'smashing' the state but instead commanding it to redirect political economic forces toward sustainable and democratic ends rather than oligarchic ends (Thompson 2011). And, this should be done in coordination with the simultaneous expansion of people's access to policy-making processes. In doing so we utilize the necessary organs of state power for waging a counter-hegemonic insurgency against capital while creating a more inclusive and accountable state and policy-making process, albeit in a context that transcends the preservation of private interests championed by classical liberalism (Barber 2003).

Finally, a disclaimer regarding the state: it must be noted that the left cannot not be drawn into deterministic interpretations of historical materialism which posit that once production is democratized the state will no longer be required to carry out its regulatory duties. Indeed, we must ask the question: is a political economy assumed to be socially just simply because it is collectively owned or managed? What prevents a cooperative enterprise owned by workers in location 'A' from dumping toxic production-byproduct in location 'B'? What prevents a cooperative enterprise from hiring a set of exploited, second-class wage earners as we saw happen in the Israeli Kibbutzim (Dahl 1985), especially in the context of the capitalist superstructure? What about the regulation of food products? Do we assume that food produced in a socialist or otherwise communitarian economy is free of pathogens simply because it was produced under more democratic conditions? Certainly, the answer to each of these questions is no, we should not assume that socialist or otherwise communitarian social forms transcend the requirement of government oversight and regulation simply because of their model of ownership. Given these conclusions, a defence of the state also requires a critique of 'direct action'.

Direct action

The term direct action is often attributed to confrontational, disruptive protest that includes civil disobedience and even violence. But within the anarchist tradition direct action is expanded to include efforts to develop 'direct' alternatives to state-based action in areas such as social service provision and institution building (Graeber 2009). Thus, in this latter instance, direct action, is the philosophy of 'be the change you want to see in the world' in practice. It is this specific expression of direct action that I will focus my critique on. Accordingly, in the following pages the term 'direct action' refers specifically to direct alternatives to state action in the areas of social service provision and institution building.

A most extreme example of the relationship between anti-statism and direct action was presented to me several years ago by a leading anarchist theorist at a discussion on anarchism. Taking place in the immediate aftermath of the devastating 2010 earthquake in Haiti, the presentation began with a discussion of the goals of a small group of cooperative bookstores in New England that had been attempting to develop a cooperative-based inter-library network, capable of sharing resources. The conversation was celebratory and hopeful despite years of sustained failure by these cooperatives to achieve their goal. Later in the talk, the response to the earthquake was discussed with strong (and justifiable) condemnation of the international community's failure to respond adequately to the humanitarian crisis. The proposed solution by this leading anarchist theorist, and supported by most of the audience: the development of horizontally organized citizen response teams that can be dispatched to humanitarian crises around the globe without the colonial prejudices and aspirations of international aid organizations. Now perhaps such aspirations for direct action can be accomplished once the plans for bookstore coordination are ironed out. Or, maybe there are alternative means by which we can achieve the goals set forth by an agenda of social justice that are not blatantly thoughtless and irresponsible.

Rather than seeking to replace institutions such as the United Nations or FEMA, we should be demanding that they improve their efficiency and engage in an equitable distribution of humanitarian resources. Though I am not willing to go so far as to equate the efforts of Occupy Sandy with those aspirations discussed in the aftermath of Haiti's earthquake, we must acknowledge a fundamental point: the role of an oppositional social movement is not service provision, but instead to make demands on the state and to push for new institutional forms that can enhance democracy. Particularly today as neoliberal state restructuring has shifted the burden of social service provision to non-state actors, oppositional social movements must defend the state-based model of social goods provision rather than attempt to replace it. Indeed, it was the embrace of such 'shadow state' politics that crippled much of the urban social movement organizations in the United States that were vibrant and often militaristic up until the 1980s and 1990s (DeFilippis *et al.* 2010).

If we expand our scope of analysis to incorporate efforts such as the establishment of credit unions or cooperative enterprises, we come to find deep flaws in direct action. Chartering a credit union does not cause Goldman Sachs or Bank of America to dissolve, nor does it challenge the hyper-financialized and increasingly privatized world that neoliberal political economy has thrust upon us. Equally so, building a worker-owned cooperative does not lead to the collapse of the capitalist mode of production. Treating these projects as an end rather than a means establishes a system of what I refer to as *membership justice* whereby particular rather than universal emancipation is achieved, thus speaking directly to the critique presented by Marx in his seminal essay 'On the Jewish Question'. In other words, those who are lucky enough to, for example, gain access to employment in a producer-cooperative might escape some of the trauma inflicted upon them by capitalist employment, but this does not change the suffering of everyone else.

My point here is not to undermine the benefits of the sorts of institutions that practitioners of direct action seek to construct. Worker-owned cooperatives have both economic and social benefits, and credit unions have enabled marginalized populations to access credit when it was otherwise unavailable. Additionally, many of these projects serve as models for organizers to point to when presenting the argument that 'Another World is Possible'. However, unless the development of institutions like cooperatives is coupled with a state-based public policy approach that supports their growth, while also seeking to fundamentally alter the broader political economy to support public rather than private interests, these efforts pose no challenge to hegemonic social relations. To put it bluntly – direct action is not a threat to capitalism, and may in some instances even serve to reify market relations by seeking to compete with capitalist institutions rather than transform and appropriate them.

Consensus-based deliberation and direct democracy

There is a popular belief on the left that democracy benefits from increased localization (Purcell 2006) and elevated deliberative participation based on consensus. OWS came to be known for its 'general assemblies', often proclaiming that in an ideal world there would be a general assembly in every neighbourhood. For most people outside of this insular thinking, the romanticism of the general assembly quickly fades after the third, fourth or tenth hour of consensus-based deliberation. Though I raise this point in a comical vein, it does present a question regarding efficiency that is worthy of consideration. Attempting to achieve consensus on minor issues is difficult enough, as was demonstrated by a group from OWS who required two months to 'consense' on the abstract for their upcoming presentation at a conference of left politics.[2] But how is it possible, nay, how is it democratic, to expect all participants to reach consensus on contentious and complicated issues that very much require democratic debate? Is it not more reasonable to conclude that consensus-based deliberation is structurally hostile to pluralism by forcing the minority to submit to the majority will without any recourse such as partial representation or the mere right to hold a minority view, thus producing a system of conformity superficially presented as pluralistic? Despite neo-anarchists' expressed concern over sectarian politics and the splintering of the left that has historically contributed to its weakness, the deliberative process largely inspired by anarchist and neo-anarchist thought, and practised by OWS, ironically resulted in the astonishing fracturing of the movement. Indeed, the need to establish consensus forced the creation of increasing numbers of homogenous 'working groups', often working toward similar or even identical goals but from a slightly different ideological or tactical perspective, in order to avoid the paralysing chaos wrought by pluralism within a consensus-based deliberative format.

Like pluralism, representative democracy does not suffer from any fundamental deficit in its ability to foster an inclusive, participatory process. A social movement such as Occupy Wall Street would benefit from a representative framework because it would increase efficiency with respect to basic decisions that do not require intense deliberation. Perhaps more importantly, a representative model would institutionalize and make transparent and accountable the de facto leadership by which rhetorically 'leaderless' movements are commonly shaped by; and OWS is no exception in this respect. Indeed, representation should be supplemented by a participatory framework that is inclusive and provides participants agency to shape the direction of the movement and provide regular input on decisions made by leaders. However, this arrangement should part from any emphasis on consensus, to instead provide a deliberative platform where ideas can be debated rather than repressed or pushed into alternative venues. It is also important to note that although this model of participatory representation is being discussed in the context of democracy within social movements, such a socially responsive model of representative democracy must also be pursued in the larger body politic. A democratic framework that builds upon the benefits of representation *and* participation such as the one I have presented here would be difficult to label undemocratic. Indeed, it would be more democratic, transparent and efficient than the form of democracy practised in the crowded general assemblies that served as the cornerstone of OWS. It would also be a more desirable model of democracy to export to every neighbourhood.

Going forward

Most succinctly expressed by Marx in one of his earlier essays 'For a Ruthless Criticism of Everything Existing', the purpose of critique is to reveal the obstacles to achieving universal emancipation from social relations of domination. In this sense, critique must be directed at the external world, exposing the mechanisms and logics of inequitable or otherwise unjust social arrangements, in order to dialectically inform their replacement. But critique must also be levied internally, and here I am referring not to Marxian psychoanalytic theory spearheaded by the Frankfurt School – the importance of which cannot be overstated – but instead, to the overarching theme of this chapter. In other words, critique must be equally applied to the socialist project itself, so as to produce a more theoretically and empirically grounded left theory and praxis, not burdened by prefigurative dogmatism or an incomplete analysis of power relations.

I believe this chapter presents useful critical observations of dominant trends in contemporary left theory and praxis. However, it would also remain incomplete were it not also to include suggestions for how the left might proceed in its attempt to confront the dual crises of global capitalism and the spectre of abrupt climate change. Therefore, I have developed a set of suggestions in the form of policy proposals that are informed by the critique laid out in the previous pages. While they serve as illustrative examples that help to contextualize the importance of the state as an organ of counter-hegemony, my ultimate hope is that they serve as a legislative platform for future left praxis. Of course, the following list should be seen as incomplete. To develop a complete vision for a new society is both dialectically impossible and socially undesirable, as was demonstrated by twentieth-century communism. But although we cannot develop a full blueprint for what a more equitable and environmentally sustainable world might look like, we should continue to build dialectically upon the ruins and contradictions of existing society. The following pages do just that by presenting both reformative and transformative policy recommendations that address climate change as well as the failures of neoliberalism. A weakness in my proposal has to do with the broad goal of economic democracy. Although I address the question of economic democracy and propose ways in which the state can facilitate the growth of democratically governed workplaces, this chapter, like much of the work governing this particular area of political economy, falls short of explaining how we might fully democratize now-existing traditionally organized workplaces. To this point, I am not only referring to what can be considered *large* capitalist firms: multinational corporations, publicly traded firms and the like, but also those businesses owned by the petit bourgeoisie: small businesses. Indeed, although this latter category of producer firm is celebrated by the mass of society including many on the left, it must be acknowledged that these firms are dictated by the same market imperative as large firms, and as such, tend to be equally exploitative and undemocratic, but are shielded from scrutiny due to the romanticized modifier, 'mom and pop'. Finally, although I make specific reference to my incomplete theorization of a complete transition to democratic economic production, there are many other undeveloped areas within my proposal that I trust will be expanded upon by the broad community of leftists with whom this chapter is written in solidarity.

Several of these policy proposals are particular to the American political system, but many of them are not. This focus on the US political system rests heavily upon the understanding that if international progress is going to be made with respect to political, economic and social equality, and environmental sustainability, then the US hegemon must be confronted directly. In other words, the power of the American state to shape global hegemony is not confined solely to oligarchical interests, but can instead be redirected toward more socially just ends if it is appropriated by the left. It must be emphasized, however, that although the American state is an instrumental apparatus for shaping global hegemonic relations, the national government remains the optimal vehicle for advancing the socialist project. Toward this end, the left might demand or legislate:

1 A steep progressive tax on income and wealth, and a flat tax on financial transactions – the latter contributing to an initial restriction on speculative financial practices; the former two serving to reduce income inequality and fund redistributive efforts including the expansion of the welfare state and the development of a democratically governed *social*, rather than *private*, sector of economic production.

2 Publicly-funded elections and a national model of fusion voting to reduce the marginalization of political parties outside the bourgeois electoral arrangement, and to prevent the need for casting 'safe votes' for bourgeois political parties despite the existence of radical alternatives.

3 A *new* New Deal that creates tens of millions of 'green' jobs, but that transcends Keynesian economics by (directly or indirectly) developing permanent, democratically governed workplaces. In conjunction with this project, the state will simultaneously implement a Second World War-style mobilization of the industrial sector, not for the production of wartime goods, but instead for the development and production of the infrastructure required for a sustainable energy economy. A staple of this effort will be the development of a comprehensive, modern public transportation system that benefits from steep subsidies making ridership affordable (Van Arsdale and McCabe 2012).

4 The establishment of a federally based community development model based on the Community Action Program (CAP) established during the US War on Poverty. This initiative will build upon the strengths of the CAP and correct its limitations including the lack of a focus on job creation, instances of limited community participation (Arnstein 1969) and local political tensions born out of a *bypass* approach to local political machines. By drawing upon the resources and redistributive capacity of the federal government, community development efforts can be relieved of the economic burden caused by 'new federalism' whereby subordinate scales of government, lacking resources and redistributive capacity, are unable to fund social programmes and socially-oriented development initiatives effectively. It will also foster a more inclusive paradigm of governance through direct public participation within a larger representative framework, thus overcoming the many limitations of 'general assemblies' and consensus-based deliberation.

5 Development and/or expansion of community land trusts in order to democratize decisions governing land use and to remove land from speculative real estate markets that make it vulnerable to cost inflation, predatory financial manipulation and resource extraction.

6 Nationalization of the various arms of the fossil fuel industry including the utilities industry. Doing so will provide a revamped oversight regime, reduce consumer energy prices and redirect revenue toward the research and development of a post-carbon energy economy.

7 Nationalization of the banking industry. Banking is a public utility and its model of ownership and oversight must reflect this function. No public utility of such importance should be held in private hands.

8 Establishment of a nationwide minimum wage of $15 per hour in the United States.

9 Expansion of the welfare state to include free Pre-K through Post-Doctoral education, universal single-payer health care and free childcare services.

10 Historic investment in public housing to address homelessness, and the inflationary tendencies of speculative housing markets that make housing vulnerable to market volatility and unaffordable for many.

11 The retirement of corporal punishment and the restructuring of the legal system to treat incarceration as a last resort for non-violent criminal offenses with retroactive release and counselling of current inmates fitting these criteria. Additionally, all prisons and prison-related contracts are to be returned to the public sector.

12 Extreme reductions in the budget of the United States military, the reversal of the Bush Doctrine, the end of warrantless surveillance and the closure of Guantanamo Bay, all disclosed and non-disclosed 'black sites' and the practice of 'extraordinary rendition'.

13 Restructuring of the global political economy including international trade, to reflect principles of equity, environmental sustainability and human rights. This requires, among many other things, the development of a global minimum wage weighted according to local currencies; the development of 'fair' rather than 'free' trade, the universal adoption of environmental protection standards and the enforcement of existing laws governing the protection of workers including their right to organize a union without fear of retribution.

14 Bolstering of the Kyoto Protocol in addition to developing an international progressive carbon tax that will fund adaptation and mitigation efforts in developing countries, also serving as a model for domestic environmental fiscal policy.

Conclusion

The popular discourse that portrays Occupy Wall Street's demise as a result of state repression is flawed. Of course, acts of repression in the US and abroad created challenges for OWS, but social movements are resilient, and historically they have endured much worse yet accomplished great victories. To take solace in this dominant narrative put forward by OWS supporters is to also suppress the reality that the failure of Occupy was due to the same internal flaws within the left that have constrained radical politics since the birth of the New Left.

I have great optimism that this failed experiment has presented us with an opportunity to identify and confront the ideological and tactical forms that rendered OWS impotent as a counter-hegemonic movement. This chapter is an attempt at critiquing those internal failures and presenting an alternative political strategy that might serve to inform future praxis. My hope is that this contribution gives rise to a larger discussion about how to build a more influential political left that can address the dual crises of climate change and global capitalism.

Notes

1 I use the word *catastrophe* intentionally here, as it is the language used by the IPCC to describe the consequential outcome of maintaining 'business as usual' greenhouse gas emissions output rather than making GHG reductions through mitigation practices.
2 Although the conference shall remain nameless, this anecdote draws from my previous employment as its outreach coordinator.

Part V

Socialism in the twenty-first century

15 Building a twenty-first-century socialism

Cliff DuRand

Some of the most exciting progressive developments today are taking place in Latin America. Neoliberal corporate globalization reached a dead end by the close of the last century with the exhaustion of Milton Friedman's market fundamentalism, which had first been implemented as state policy under the Pinochet dictatorship in Chile. Popular forces looked to a left alternative. Yet, the socialist model of the former Soviet Union had also failed. This opened the way to reinvent a new socialism for the twenty-first century as an alternative to both corporate capitalism and state socialism. This is the historical task that has been taken up by the Zapatistas in southern Mexico, by Venezuela and now more recently by Cuba. It is here that efforts are under way to create a socialism truer to the original vision from the nineteenth century.

The state socialism that offered the main alternative model throughout the twentieth century arose under certain historical conditions. Briefly summarized, insurrections brought revolutionaries to state power in Russia, China and elsewhere. With popular support a revolutionary state undertook to build socialism. This was conceived as state ownership of the means of production in the name of the working class. This was to make possible the rational planning of the economy in the interest of the working class. These revolutions did not occur in advanced capitalist societies that had reached the limits of what is possible under capitalist relations. That was where Marx thought the conditions would exist for socialism. Rather they occurred in underdeveloped societies. And so the socialist state focused on developing the forces of production. A socialist state sought to perform the historical role capitalism had failed to perform for them. The result was a state socialism concerned with economic development over political democracy and that ended up with vertically organized, bureaucratic and paternalistic structures. Rather than the state withering away, civil society withered away.

The experiments now under way to build an alternative socialism seek to apply the lessons learned from the failures of the past century. Twenty-first-century socialism seeks to build socialism from the bottom up by developing socialist relations within civil society – contra economism. This requires an empowerment of popular classes in daily life in their communities. The Zapatista model is based on participatory democratic development within communities – what John Holloway called changing the world without taking (state) power. Constituent power is prioritized for development. In effect, this is also what is being done in Venezuela and in Cuba as they undertake to reinvent socialism – only the constituted power of a revolutionary state is nurturing the development of constituent power. We are seeing a rejuvenation of civil society, only it is a socialist civil society based on cooperative relations among the associated producers and socialist values of responsibility, democratic decision-making and social solidarity. The aim is the full development of the human being rather than just a development of forces of production. The new socialist human being is to be built through protagonistic democracy at the local level. At the same time the local institutions such as cooperatives and communal councils are little schools of socialism operating within a national context governed by a socialist state.

There are certain core principles that inform twenty-first-century socialism. These are subsidiarity (or localism), participation, cooperation and democracy – all of which empower people and nurture human development. One of these is *subsidiarity*: decisions should be made at the lowest level feasible, with higher levels supporting the lower. This is to put power in the hands of ordinary people. State or corporate bureaucracies are to serve the people, not substitute for them in a paternalistic way. This is not quite horizontalism, but it does represent a considerable flattening of hierarchies. The resulting expansion of *participation* promotes human development. Rather than turning one's powers over to representatives, engage directly in making the decisions that affect one's life and in implementing those decisions, foster the development of human capacities – such capacities as a sense of agency, instrumental knowledge and wisdom, values clarification and social consciousness. Participation in social decision-making is *cooperative*. It involves dialogue with others in furtherance of a common project aiming toward shared values. The individual is part of a larger social whole, not an isolated atom, and thus is enriched as a social being.

These principles define a democracy. Democracy involves more than periodic voting for representatives who are then legitimated to act in your name. Democracy rooted in popular sovereignty must involve direct participation in shared decision-making for collective action for the common good. Only then can it be what the original Greek word denotes: *demos* (the people) + *cracy* (rule) = rule by the people. Such a democratic society must extend that rule to all aspects of our life together as a society. That means it must overcome the division between the political and the economic in bourgeois society where workplaces are governed by the dictatorship of owners and managers. It means that investment must be democratically directed toward the social good rather than private enrichment. What this means is the democratization of capital.

North–South convergence

In previous chapters we have looked at efforts in capitalist societies to build a degree of independence from corporate capitalism. These also point toward a society that is more participatory, more cooperative, more democratic at a local level. This is the same direction that twenty-first-century socialism points in the global South. In both cases, institutions that move beyond capitalism point toward a kind of socialism, a society in which associated producers are empowered to democratically found anew a society that is more equal and in which all may flourish. Whether this is called socialism, it is an alternative that is more humane and nurturing of our human capacities. As capitalism collapses around us, we will invent that new future. Indeed, we must in order to survive.

16 Out of the abyss, the new world

Gustavo Esteva

We are not on the edge of the abyss. We have fallen into it. It looks bottomless. We should avoid apocalyptic rapture, but we must not close our eyes before the severity of our condition. The scale of the natural and social devastation we are suffering has no precedent. The survival of the human race and even the planet we live on is in danger.

There is widespread agreement that a historical cycle is winding down. But identifying what is dying, what is coming to an end, generates intense controversy. Neoliberalism, the development enterprise and the American empire supporting it, the postwar agreements, the economic society (capitalist or socialist), the nation-state, modernity and postmodernity, the patriarchal mentality, are among the candidates. It is a fascinating and important debate, but I cannot engage in it here.

This chapter is based in the hypothesis that a new world is emerging from the womb of the old. Everywhere, social movements are transforming our neoliberal discontent into transformative action. Instead of centralization and unification, as the corporations and the bureaucrats desire, the people are organizing localization, an alternative to both localism and globalization. Instead of privatizing state functions, like the neoliberals, the people are socializing them, reclaiming them. Instead of an individualistic and statistical democracy run by political parties and media, the people are constructing radical democracy; for them, democracy should be where the people are.

Breaking out of the prison of conventional thought and its capitalist crust, the people are constructing a world beyond capitalism, beyond patriarchy, beyond representative democracy, beyond exploitation and oppression, in order to resist the current horror.

The Zapatista hope

Enough!

At midnight of 1 January 1994, NAFTA – the North American Free Trade Agreement between Mexico, the US and Canada – came into force. Barely two hours later, thousands of Indians armed with machetes, clubs and a few guns occupied seven of the main towns in Chiapas, a Mexican province bordering Guatemala, and declared war on the Mexican government. In the attack 12 police and an unknown number of rebels died.

The next day, President Carlos Salinas sneered at the rebellion as the work of 'professionals of violence, probably foreigners', and launched a massive attack against them with tanks, Swiss airplanes, US helicopters and 15,000 soldiers. Explosive violence followed, nobody knows exactly how much. But we know that many civilians were illegally arrested, tortured and killed. Rebel prisoners were shot.

The rebels revealed that they were Indians of different ethnic groups calling themselves Ejército Zapatista de Liberación Nacional (EZLN). They were rebelling not only against the president and the army, but also against 500 years of oppression and disdain. They expressed the hope that they would be able to reclaim their commons and to regenerate their own forms of governance and their art of living and dying. It was time to say '¡Basta! Enough!'

The Zapatistas received immediate national and international support. Many people could perceive that the Zapatistas incarnated new aspirations. That support plus their courage and surprising behaviour led to the following:

- After a failed ambush and enormous public pressure, the *Law of Peace and Concord* (*Ley para el Diálogo, la Conciliación y la Paz Digna en Chiapas*) was proclaimed in 1995, protecting the Zapatistas and their dialogue with the government. The law declared that as long as the Zapatistas did not abandon the dialogue no one could arrest them – not even with a court order. The law declared that the Zapatistas could occupy an area of half a million acres where the government could not intervene.
- A dialogue between the government and the Zapatistas yielded the San Andrés Accords in February 1996. These included a constitutional reform that won massive public support. But the government did not honour its commitment and the Congress approved a counter-reform. So the Zapatistas decided to apply the Accords in their communities without a legal framework.
- In 1996, the Zapatistas called all the Indian peoples of Mexico to a forum that created the National Indigenous Congress. It coordinates the action of most indigenous peoples.
- The Zapatistas launched many efforts to articulate their civil society – with mixed results.
- For 20 years the Zapatistas have refused all government funds and services. They live on their own, with a bit of solidarity from people inside and outside Mexico.

There are some who claim that the Zapatista Army of National Liberation and Subcomandante Marcos are already history. Others ignore the Zapatistas or forget them. But important thinkers like Noam Chomsky, Immanuel Wallerstein and Pablo González Casanova say that the Zapatistas have launched the most radical, and probably the most important, political initiative in the world. Millions of people find in the Zapatistas inspiration and hope in the middle of the current, overwhelming crisis, when we are experiencing the moment of danger defining the end of an historical cycle, and we are suffering the consequences of the collapse of the truths and the institutions that led the world until recently.

One of the reasons why so many seem to want to forget Zapatism, to leave it in the past or to reduce it to a few municipalities in Chiapas, is the shallowness of their radicalism. The Zapatistas challenge – in words and deeds – every aspect of contemporary society. In revealing the root cause of the current predicaments, they contribute to dismantling the dominant discourse. They undermine capitalism, the nation-state, formal democracy and all modern institutions, by challenging the concepts sustaining them. They also render obsolete conventional ways and practices of social and political movements and initiatives. In reconstructing the world from the bottom up, by the people themselves, they reveal the illusory or counterproductive nature of changes conceived or implemented from the top down. Their path encourages everywhere resistance to globalization and neoliberalism, and inspires struggles for emancipation. They also contribute to articulate those struggles.

There is nothing about the Zapatistas more important than their contribution to hope, the very essence of popular movements. Hope is the sheet anchor of every man and is at the beginning of all time, states the *Mahabharata*, the sacred book of India; if it is destroyed, grief is like your own death. For Ivan Illich, 'The Promethean ethos has now eclipsed hope. Survival of the human race depends on its rediscovery as a social force' (Illich 1973: 105). That is exactly what the Zapatistas have done.

Pan-Dora, the All-Giver, closed the lid of her amphora before Hope could escape. It is time to reclaim it, in the era in which the Promethean ethos threatens to destroy the world and the expectations it generated vanish one after the other. In liberating hope from their intellectual and political prison, the Zapatistas created the possibility of a renaissance, which is now emerging in the net of plural paths they discovered or is daily invented by the imagination they awakened. They are still a source of inspiration for those walking along those paths. But they do not pretend to administer or control such a net, which has its own impulses, strength and orientation. We all are, or can be, Zapatistas.

To accompany the Zapatistas on the twentieth anniversary of their uprising means that we should seriously ask ourselves if the impact of what they are doing now will or will not be even bigger than the impact they had in 1994, as many of us are beginning to think.

The awakening

The Zapatistas were the first to challenge the intellectual climate that until 1993 surrendered to neoliberal globalization. Their call was heard around the world. Since then, all anti-systemic social movements have recognized that the uprising was an awakening, a call to react, an opening later expressed in the World Social Forum.

There is a reason for that reaction. Years ago, Teodor Shanin pointed out the situation producing it:

> Our belief is that there are no alternatives, and that when you have no alternatives you should create them. Socialism was a magnificent guide, even for those who were not socialists .... There was an alternative. But we are no longer there. Some people still believe in finding an alternative in capitalism. They will soon be disappointed ....
>
> But perhaps that is not the question. Perhaps we must consider that we are already seeing the end of state socialism (and there is no other socialism in the real world), but also the end of real capitalism in a very concrete sense: capitalism can no longer govern a country .... Real socie-ties, that still have the form of nation-states, can no longer be governed through capitalism.
>
> (Esteva and Shanin 2005)

That was the dominant conviction. There were no alternatives. What was needed was to create them. That is what the Zapatistas did. The rumour circulating today is that they can do it again by marking out new roads. Everyone caught in a blind alley looks for a way out. The crisis has created threats and new openings.

In 1993 the dominant opinion was that nothing could stop Mexico from climbing out of the swamp of underdevelopment. The rich countries had just welcomed Mexico into their club. In the middle classes you heard optimistic rumours, such as, 'We will live better that the *gringos*. We will get everything they have: malls, cars, gadgets, all the services ... and servants at home'. This cynical formula expressed the immoral attitude of enjoying an ideal based on inequality, oppression and environmental destruction, and ignoring the view of the servants.

On the last day of 1993, in the tourist resort of Huatulco, President Carlos Salinas was celebrating his triumphs. He was nearing the end of his presi-dency. Like the fascist Francisco Franco he thought that he had everything 'tied down'. A year later, his brother Raul was in prison, he was forced into a kind of exile in Ireland and his legacy started to crumble. The Zapatista upris-ing was the main cause of this scenario. By the end of January 1994, Salinas' Institutional Revolutionary Party (PRI) had made more concessions to the opposition than it had in 50 years. He could not continue his triumphant tour.

The Zapatista uprising changed the political balance of forces in Mexico and opened a door to hope which has been crossed by millions of people in the last 20 years.

No sociopolitical movement of our time has attracted as much attention as the Zapatistas. The number of books (tens of thousands), articles (millions) or the countless Internet references are proof of their public presence. The transition of the thousands of 1994 to the millions of 1996 or 2001 are proof of their increasing convening power. But neither the Web nor the texts fully illustrate the importance and vitality of Zapatism. The only way to fully appreciate it would be to go directly to communities and *barrios*, in Mexico and the rest of the world. Wherever one tries to look, Zapatismo emerges, even in the most unexpected places, to open spaces of radical dignity.

Who are they?

Right from the first moment there were attempts to pin a label on the Zapatistas. Salinas called them 'professionals of violence'. Arturo Warman, a respected anthropologist and high officer in Salinas' government, made a pathetic effort to prove that the Zapatistas were not indigenous people. From left to right this confusion spread out like an oil spill. Nobel laureate Octavio Paz simpered that the Zapatistas were not revolutionaries. He claimed that they had no doctrine. He said that they lacked a project for the nation.

A few even suggested that the Zapatistas were narco-guerrillas. One by one the labels failed. No, the movement was not fundamentalist or messianic. The majority of them were indigenous, but their initiative was not an indigenous movement – they were not reducing its initiative to the rights of a minority. No, the Zapatistas were not separatists. No, they were not guerrillas, Che Guevara's 'fish swimming through the sea of the people' – a revolutionary group trying to stir up peasant support in order to seize state power. They were the collective decision of hundreds of communities with no interest in seizing state power. They were not fish. They were the sea.

It is well known what the Zapatistas are not. Then what are they? How to describe and characterize their radical political initiative?

The Zapatistas say, 'The first fundamental act of the Zapatista Army of National Liberation was to listen and talk' (Subcomandante Marcos 2003: Segunda parte: Una muerte). On 17 November 1983, the first group of professional revolutionaries that arrived in the jungle began to listen and talk. The intercultural dialogue that gave birth to Zapatism has continued with its unusual ability to listen. The usual political and ideological discussion groups are dialogues of the deaf. But the Zapatistas know how to listen. That is why they startled everyone by abandoning armed struggle. Civil society demanded it.

The Zapatistas created some specific spaces to meet with other people. They said, 'we wanted a space for dialogue with civil society. And dialogue means learning to listen to the other as well as learning to talk to him'

(Subcomandante Marcos 2003: Segunda parte: Una muerte). On 8 August 2003 they renamed those spaces *caracoles* (snails, spiral shells). They said one reason for the name was that

> the 'shell' helps the hearers listen to a word faraway. The *caracoles* will be like doors for entering the communities and for the communities to come out; they will be windows to see us inside and for us to look out; they will be like loudspeakers to carry our word far and to listen to the one who is faraway.
>
> (Subcomandante Marcos 2003: Tercera parte: Un nombre)

The Zapatistas don't wear an ideological shroud, they don't swear by a doctrine. They know that these begin as guides to action and end as straightjackets. Changing circumstances and dialogues with others are always enriching Zapatista proposals and styles of work. They listen, learn from others and practise self-criticism with every step. But it is not merely working by trial and error. They stick to principles of behaviour; they follow theoretical, political and cultural traditions. They have the moral rightness that comes with dignity. The dignity has deep roots. It is hospitable and open.

The Zapatistas say that Zapatismo means that the communities make their decisions against the dominant regime. 'Ours is not a liberated territory nor a utopian commune. Neither is it the experimental laboratory of an absurdity or a paradise for an orphaned left. This is a rebellious territory in resistance ...' (Subcomandante Marcos 2004a). The Lacandona Commune, observed Luis Hernández,

> is not a regime, but a practice ... a laboratory of new social relations ... [that] recovers old aspirations of the movements for self-emancipation: liberation should be the work of those it benefits, there oughtn't be authorities over the people, the subjects of the social order must have full decision-making capacity over their destinies. Their existence isn't the expression of a moral nostalgia, but the living expression of a new politics.
>
> (Hernández Navarro 2004)

There is nothing better to express who the Zapatistas are than the words of Major Ana María. In 1996 she welcomed the participants to the First Intercontinental Encounter for Humanity and against Neoliberalism:

> Behind our black mask,
> behind our armed voice,
> behind our unnamable name,
> behind what you see of us,
> behind this, we are you.
> Behind this,

we are the same simple and ordinary men and women who are
repeated in all races,
painted in all colors,
speak in all languages,
and live in all places.
Behind this, we are the same forgotten men and women,
the same excluded,
the same intolerated,
the same persecuted,
the same as you.
Behind this, we are you.

(EZLN 1996: 25)

Perhaps the most radical statement of the Zapatistas is that they are just ordinary men and women, therefore non-conformist, rebels, dreamers.

It is time to stop locking them up in one of the usual categories. The question, 'Who are they?' tries to place them in a current, in a style, in a brand name. It's time to acknowledge without reservations their political and sociological innovations. They are Zapatistas. And if you want more precision, they are Neozapatistas. Period.

The redefinition of politics

The Zapatistas rose up against a dictatorial regime that accelerated the breaking up and surrender of the country. On the day of the uprising, the *First Declaration of the Lacandon Jungle* appealed to the Constitution and to the established powers to restore the rule of law and to meet their legal demands. Over the following years they chose paths demanded by civil society to test those powers' ability to build a free and democratic country. What happened instead was 'the relentless and frenzied dismantling of the nation state, driven by a political class lacking professional capacities and decency' (Subcomandante Marcos 2004c). The Zapatistas foresaw the coming chaos – our life in the present nightmare. They had to create an alternative.

As the nation falls apart, the Zapatistas continue their construction. The Boards of 'Good Government' (*buen gobierno*) are proof that Zapatism wants neither to hegemonize nor to homogenize the world in which we live in either its ideas or methods. What they have been doing is proof that 'in the Zapatista land there is no aim to pulverize the Mexican nation. On the contrary, it is here that the possibility of its reconstruction is being born' (Subcomandante Marcos 2004b).

The government betrayed the San Andrés Accords. By putting them into practice, the Zapatistas demonstrated that they don't generate the negative impacts that were used as pretext for the constitutional counter-reform. Although it is those same powers-that-be that have not fulfilled their commitments, civil society is also at fault for not putting enough pressure on them.

The Zapatistas, with their autonomous practice, anticipated a universal disillusionment with formal democracy, when it became evident that the ruling powers don't represent the people and learned how to ignore their will. Subordinated to capital, they serve what Occupy Wall Street called the upper one per cent. They are not only aggravating the dispossession and exploitation of the majorities, but endanger the survival of the whole human race.

The Zapatista call is now a general alert. In 2001 the Argentine people roared at the politicians: '*!Que se vaya todos!*' ('Away with all of you!'). In Greece, the demonstrators roared: 'We'll leave only when you leave'. The Spanish *indignados* roared, 'My dreams don't fit into a ballot box'. In the US, Occupy Wall Street had a liberating 'Aha!' effect. It allowed millions to say out loud what they had always suspected but dared not say, because it seemed a crazy challenge to the conventional wisdom.

The initiatives taken by the Zapatistas from 1994 to 2005 to articulate the civil society reflect what they learned on the way, and the results of their action. Every day there are more people who realize how useless it is to change their leaders. The apparatuses the leaders lead are obsolete and rusting. Every day people join the ranks of those who want to build an alternative from the bottom up. Like the Zapatistas.

Anticapitalism

The Zapatistas displayed the character of their struggle from the first day of the uprising. Ten years later they perfected their analysis. *The Sixth Declaration of the Lacandon Jungle* synthesizes the years of Zapatista struggle, its systematic reflection and learning and its intention to articulate the general discontent in order to transform it into a struggle for liberation.

The political parties made cowardly compromises with the neoliberals. These sell-outs were locking up the people's hope. The Zapatistas freed it. People began to accompany the Zapatistas along unknown roads. Many people, for example, accepted the invitation of *The Fourth Declaration of the Lacandon Jungle*, in 1996. They began to walk their own path, without the government and the political parties. Time and again the Zapatistas not only tried to open themselves to others, but to cede the initiative to civil society – both national and international. The *Sixth Declaration* took another step. It completed the diagnosis of what is happening in Mexico and the world. It spelled out its anticapitalist road signs. It announced support for similar resistance and anticapitalist struggles across the planet.

Many governments and parties pretend to be somewhere on the left but they keep their association with capital. For Zapatism, today's struggle for survival must be anticapitalist. That is the only way to end the horror swirling around us.

Capital is plundering the planet. The indigenous peoples are on the front line of the fight back against this pillage of the world. In Mexico the

Zapatistas put the 'Indian Question' on the front page of the national agenda. Today they are contributing to reactivate the Indigenous National Congress.

Dignity

In their own way the *Zapatistas* go on testing the speed of dreams with their libertarian breeze. In the last two years people have come from all parts of Mexico and 50 countries to learn from them and to work with them.

Their radical promise is not an ideological construction of possible futures. It realizes itself in deeds. It redefines hope. It does not express it as expectation, as the conviction that something will happen in a certain way. It expresses the conviction that something makes sense, no matter what happens. 'Hope is that rebellion that rejects conformism and defeat' (EZLN 1996: 126). It is also known as *dignity*: 'Dignity is that nation without nationality, that rainbow that is also a bridge, that murmur of the heart no matter what blood lives it, that rebel irreverence that mocks borders, customs, and wars' (EZLN 1996: 126).

The Zapatistas know that widening the dignity of every human and human relation challenges the existing systems. Their radically democratic localization is an alternative to both localism and globalization. They regenerate their commons with an autonomy that marginalizes the economy and resists capitalist and modern individualization fostered by internal and external colonialisms.

Rooted in their dignity, the Zapatistas have been erecting some landmarks and signposts in what looks like a net of plural paths. Whoever walks these paths can see, with the diffuse and intense quality of a rainbow, a large range of political perspectives that herald a new social order, beyond the economic society (capitalist or socialist), and beyond formal democracy and the nation-state. *Más allá* (beyond) the current conditions of the world and their intellectual, ideological and institutional underpinnings.

The Zapatistas are one of a kind, and at the same time typical. They come from an old tradition, yet they are immersed in today's ideas and technologies. They are ordinary men and women with extraordinary behaviour. They are still a mystery and a paradox, as the grassroots epic now running around the world.

The Zapatistas are no longer the Zapatism circulating through the world. Today's Zapatism is no longer in their hands. And those daily reinventing it may ignore that the Zapatista initiatives are their original or current source of inspiration.

Escuelitas: learning freedom

On 21 December 2012, some 40,000 Zapatistas marched in silence in a disciplined and peaceful way in the same towns they had occupied during their uprising on 1 January 1994. They left a brief communiqué: 'Did you listen? It is the sound of your world falling apart. It is the sound of our world re-emerging. The day that was the day was night. And night will be the day that will be the day' (Subcomandante Marcos 2012).

A little later a flood of communiqués announced the course 'Freedom according to the Zapatistas', to be held on 11–16 August 2013 and repeated in December 2013 and January 2014. Almost 6,000 people from 50 countries attended the invitation. The communiqués explained that the teachers of this course would not be certified professionals and no expert pedagogue would be around. None of the formal requirements of a classroom or an academic space would be met. The idea would be to learn not about the world but from the world, and to learn from those constructing a new world. The teachers in the course would be those constructing a world without exploitation or social classes, without oppression or hierarchies, a world in which the patriarchal and sexist mentality has been profoundly broken, a space which is no longer utopian because it exists in the real world.

This bold initiative opened to the outside world the daily reality of the Zapatista communities and displayed the current status of their astonishing sociological and political construction. I was one of those attending the course and I am sharing here not only my own impression but also those of several dozens of people of my organization also attending the course. What we saw, smelled, tasted and experienced was a new world, with a new kind of human being: the Zapatista world, constructed in the course of the last 30 years. The people starting the movement in 1983 and organizing the uprising in 1994 had been totally dispossessed. In the 1970s and the 1980s they were dying like flies from hunger and curable diseases, oppressed by a very violent and barbaric structure of power. Many of them were working as semi-slaves on private ranches or as servants in the cities. A refrain heard in the oral tradition of the Zapatista communities states: 'In the villages, there were very few children; most of them were dying'. Since 1994, they have been continually exposed to harassment, physical and psychological aggression, paramilitary assaults and encirclement stricter than the Cuban embargo, and so on. They constructed their new world from scratch, against all odds, with no funds, works or social services from the government, starting with their bare hands. They have been on their own, accepting, on their own terms, some irregular solidarity with people around the world. These folks were the teachers of the course.

Freedom, law, social order

The word freedom produces an association with those who have lost it and generates solidarity with those in jail. But the course would not be about that kind of freedom. A few years ago the poet John Berger observed that, if he were forced to use only one word to express the current condition of the world, he would use the word 'prison'. We are in it, even those of us who pretend we are free. The *Escuelita*, as the Zapatistas called the pedagogical experience, would attempt to show what freedom is for them. In that way, we may perhaps learn to see the bars of our own prisons.

> The structures of political and legal procedures are integral to one another. Both shape and express the structure of freedom in history. If this is recognized, the framework of due procedure can be used as the most dramatic, symbolic and convivial tool in the political area. The appeal to law remains powerful even where society makes access to legal machinery a privilege, or where it systematically denies justice, or where it cloaks despotism in the mantle of show tribunals .... Only the word in its weakness can associate the majority of the people in the revolutionary inversion of inevitable violence into convivial reconstruction.
>
> (Illich 1973: 109–110)

The word reigns in Zapatista territory and it is openly used for the convivial reconstruction of society.

We observed a well-enforced state of law and a solid, peaceful social order in which all forms of violence have basically vanished (except, of course, the violence of paramilitaries and other people surrounding the Zapatistas).

If we consider a state of law to exist only for those societies in which all members of the social body know and accept the norms ruling their lives and those norms are universally enforced with fairness and justice, then we must acknowledge that no society lives today under a state of law. Except Zapatista society and probably many other indigenous societies around the world. In modern society:

- only the experts, as a group, know the norms ruling society;
- the law itself, as well as all the rules produced by different levels of government and by corporations, are conceived and formulated by a small minority that does not represent the interests of the people;
- those norms are increasingly formulated in such a way that a small group can violate them with impunity, while the majority is forced to obey and respect them (Foucault 2006);
- the norms are not universally enforced and respected.

Zapatista norms are in clear contrast with such a regime. They are produced at three levels: the community, the municipality (a group of communities) and the *caracol* (a group of municipalities). Each of these bodies varies in size. A community can be a settlement of a few families; the bigger communities can have 600 or 700 families.

All members of a community participate in the decisions about the *norms* and the *accords* governing life in the community. The norms are general rules of behaviour and include the consequences for violating them. The accords establish the conditions to implement specific decisions concerning communal activities for the common good.

Norms and accords at the level of municipalities and *caracoles* are conceived and formulated by the common folk of the communities temporarily serving in positions of authority at the level of the municipality or *caracol*. The norms and most accords cannot be enforced unless and until they are accepted at the level of the communities – a bottom-up and universally shared (rather than top-down and elite) structuring of decision-making and power relations.

There are norms for all Zapatistas:

1   the seven principles of commanding by obeying, applied to all Zapatistas when they are in a position of authority; and
2   the revolutionary laws.

The seven principles are:

*   to serve, not to serve yourself (*servir y no servirse*);
*   to represent and not to supplant;
*   to construct and not to destroy;
*   to obey and not to command;
*   to propose and not to impose;
*   to convince and not to win;
*   to go down and not to go up.

These principles were conceived and formulated by common folk, widely discussed for a long time, and finally adopted consensually by all Zapatistas.

The revolutionary laws (about the land and about women) were formulated clandestinely, before the uprising on 1 January 1994, and published that day. It is well known that many people participated in their formulation and all Zapatistas know them pretty well, but it is not known how they were enacted. They are very simple and operate as general principles that are in continual revision. For example, the communities are currently discussing a proposal of 33 points about women, which will be a substitute for the ten points of the law of women if and when everyone agrees on them.

Given these conditions, the real norms and forms of enforcement vary widely in different communities, municipalities and *caracoles*.

All the decisions on important matters require consensus in order to take effect, but for minor decisions voting procedures can be used.

There are no police ... and no need for them. The Zapatista communities, in spite of the external aggression they experience, are the safest place in Mexico and one of the safest in the world.

Common folk participate in different kinds of commissions to watch and control all functions of government and the implementation of communal projects. Transparency and accountability are totally ensured. A few cases of corruption have been discovered and their perpetrators required to engage in redemptive work for the communities.

Domestic violence has been basically eliminated, whereas, prior to the uprising, beating women and children had been a daily event. As a result of these community-led transformations, children are showered with love and enjoy amazing freedom – a reality that is a palpable experience when you visit a Zapatista village.

Social functions

Eating

Most Zapatista families produce their own food and complement what they produce through some exchange with neighbours or through purchases in Zapatista shops, sometimes to procure what they are not able to produce (such as salt, oil and so on) and sometimes to fill in a shortfall on occasions in which they were not able to produce quite enough. As a group, they have a high level of self-sufficiency.

Learning

Everyone is learning all the time, basically from each other. The Zapatistas can be seen as a learning community. There is no compulsory education. Children participate in family activities but they are basically free until they decide to go to 'school'. Schools have no teachers. Young men and women are 'promoters of learning' and they organize the learning process with the children. There are no standard curricula, syllabi or grades. There are some general themes, like history (of the community, the region, the ethnic group, the Zapatistas, Mexico, etc.), approached in different ways in different areas. What dominates is learning by doing, but some folks like to read. 'Mathematics' is a recurrent theme. One participant said: 'At some point we will have our own mathematics, but for the time being we are using their mathematics'. The word often alludes to knowing how to count.

Healing

Most Zapatistas live a healthy life. There are a lot of activities associated with what is usually called preventive medicine, implemented by young men and women serving as 'promoters of health'. Many women serve as *yerberas*, *hueseras* and *parteras* – using herbs or massages or as midwives, without professionalization. They have clinics in the hands of trained, local folks. They may use traditional remedies or modern equipment and medicines – X-rays, ultrasound, blood tests, antibiotics, etc. All *caracoles* have ambulances for the transportation of patients to non-Zapatista hospitals, when their health problems cannot be solved in their clinics. Non-Zapatistas, of nearby communities, often come to Zapatista clinics, given the poor attention they get in the government hospitals.

Settling

Zapatistas build their own houses, mostly with local materials. They use a wide variety of styles, sizes, materials, etc. They have good access to potable water or means of making their water drinkable. Some of them use conventional latrines; many of them use ecological dry toilets. There are no homeless people or overcrowding.

Exchanging

They have a variety of forms of exchange among themselves, including barter. They also buy and sell in the open market, most of the time in groups – a community buys for the local shop, a group of coffee-producers exports coffee, a *caracol* buys medical equipment for a clinic, etc. With the permission of the corresponding authorities, a man or a woman may leave the community for some time to work in other parts of Mexico or the US.

Moving

They use their feet, horses, *burros*, boats or bicycles to perform most of their daily activities. They have some communal vehicles for transportation of people and goods and they may use public transportation. The main movements out of the community are for fiestas, political activities, serving as an authority and visiting friends or family.

Owning

The land recuperated by the uprising (250,000 hectares)[1] has been allocated to the communities as communal land.

There is no private ownership of the land or the means of production. All families have access to a piece of common land, of similar size and conditions (a new couple will have access to another piece). (The availability of land for the families varies greatly in different *caracoles*.)

Most families have some chickens or cattle, for direct consumption, for exchange (to get some income to satisfy daily needs), or as a saving for special needs.

In many cases, a group of families may have in common some chickens, cattle, a shop and equipment to produce something. More complex activities, such as a factory making boots, facilities to process coffee, etc., are owned collectively at the level of the community, the municipality or the *caracol*. The workers in these activities, organized in a very horizontal structure, get a salary and the surplus goes to a social fund.

There are several communal banks, providing credit at a very low rate of interest, for the special needs of some families or for productive projects.

Doing

The Zapatistas perform many activities during the day:

- activities for the sustenance of the family;
- activities for a communal project created by a collective or other group within a community, in which the participants get a portion of the outcome (in products or cash), and the rest is designated to recipients chosen in advance by the group, which could be: the group itself, a social fund, the community. The members of the group agree upon the proportions before starting the activity or project;
- activities for the common good of the community, in which all the fruits of the work support the specific purpose decided by the community (for example, a public work such as a bridge or a road, a communal bank or a clinic and its equipment).

Other activities include attending meetings, serving in a commission or position of authority, serving in some social services, etc.

The pedagogical experiment

The amazing organization was the first surprise of the *Escuelita*. They were waiting for us in *Unitierra Chiapas*. With great efficiency they gave us our credentials, by which we could be identified as a student of the *Escuelita*, and put every one of us in the appropriate means of transportation to go to one of the five *caracoles*: more than ten hours of transportation from San Cristóbal de Las Casas, in some cases. In every *caracol* long lines of Zapatistas clapped as we arrived. After a warm and spirited reception, every one of us was given a *votán*: a guardian, a man or a woman, who would take care of us 24 hours a day, would be the interpreter (our hosts spoke in their own indigenous languages) and would support our studies (guiding us in the reading of the textbooks, for example) and answer questions. They guided us to the homes that were going to host us, sometimes after a long walk, a boat ride or whatever was needed to reach the communities in which we were to stay for our learning.

The whole experience was very intense, convivial and joyful. We shared in the activities of the family, including their daily work – in which our lack of the pertinent skills and physical condition was often very evident and produced a lot of laughter. We had time to read our textbooks, which are a collection of interviews with members of the five *caracoles*. We could ask any question and usually received enlightening answers. And of course we participated in many joyful activities, particularly the long, final fiesta.

The textbooks are a good illustration of the nature of the experience. There is frequent interaction and sharing in communities and municipalities, where they speak the same language and share the same culture. When the *caracoles* were created, they needed a *lingua franca*: Spanish (which is not mastered by everyone), because in each *caracol* there are people of different cultures. Since the people of the communities orient the *caracoles* from below, differences between them started to emerge. They needed to share the experiences of the different *caracoles* and learn from each other. In an effort that lasted several years, folks that had been authorities or had fulfilled different functions in the communities, the municipalities or the *caracoles*, began to openly discuss the experience, without fear or inhibitions, without reservations, examining mistakes or difficulties, in order to share with others their experience. There was a moment in which they had accumulated a lot of materials and someone imagined that it could be good to share those materials with other people, in order to sow outside their territory the seed of autonomy. That is how the *Escuelita* was born.

In this course we completed only the first level (there will be more), but we learned a lot. We learned new categories created in the struggle for freedom. We learned that resistance, for example, was not something that started with the Zapatistas: their *abuelos* and *abuelas* (grandfathers and grandmothers) had been for centuries resisting and they kept that experience in their hearts. We learned that there is a Zapatista way, entirely transparent but difficult to understand or define, because it is a very *other* way, which cannot fit well in our mentality or our common way of understanding. We learned how autonomy is constructed, how the works are done, how authentic resistance is not only to endure things but to construct something new, what it is to organize.

But we lacked words, because we were before radical novelties that did not come from books or ideologies, but from practice, and they are clearly enterprises of imagination. I believe there is no historical precedent, for example, for the process of orderly and coherent transfer of power from what the Zapatistas call *mandos político-militares* – those in political and military command before the uprising. The power the politico-military group had accumulated in that period, given to them by their 'support bases' to organize and lead the uprising in 1994, had been gradually given back to the communities, as the people themselves, ordinary folk of the communities, step by step assumed all of the functions of government and of sociopolitical organization, such that currently it is the ordinary people who together control the decision-making and norm-setting processes at all levels of autonomy and government. A way of living and governing was constructed from below: political power and radical democracy are located where the people are, not above them. The *mandos* are still around, ready to offer support if it is required and occasionally consulting with the people on some initiatives.

Some of the students of the *Escuelita* have already felt the temptation of translating what we learned into a formal course, transforming the experience into a package of knowledge and skills to transfer to others. But such an exercise would imply a betrayal of the meaning, style and intention of the *Escuelita*. We were not invited to be educated in a doctrine, and even less to be taught what to do. The Zapatistas shared with us a living experience whose substance can only exist in diversity, in a variety of forms. Every community, every municipality, every *caracol*, had evident differences, because they had been created in freedom by different communities of people. They have many things in common, but the specific shape of those 'principles' or 'forms' corresponds not only to the natural and cultural diversity of the places in which people's lives have been organized, but also to the differential imagination of those participating in the process. The challenge is not to reduce the whole thing to a formal discourse, more or less technical, with some abstract categories, but to reproduce the experience in the personal style of every student through contagion. This requires, however, time to process the experience and prepare fertile soil in which the seed of autonomy can prosper.

On Saturday, 17 August, when we were still bewildered by the emotions of the *Escuelita*, we observed the arrival of hundreds of delegates of the National Indian Congress for an encounter convened by the Zapatistas. For many hours, during the weekend, we heard the voices of indigenous peoples from the whole country, in what was called the Chair Tata Juan Chávez, in homage to one brilliant indigenous leader, one of the founders of the Congress, who had died two years earlier. The chair is intended to be a kind of nomadic chair, which can be organized in any place, to hear the voices of the indigenous peoples.

It was overwhelming to listen to the never-ending enumeration of plunder and aggression. The name of the protagonists and the matter of the plunder changed from one place to the other. But it was always the same crime: a war against subsistence waged by capitalist corporations, sometimes behind the façade of a local boss or a landowner but always with the active participation and the open complicity of the government and the political parties.

Even more impressive was to observe the common denominator of most presentations: a combative, articulated and vigorous resistance, waged with spirit and dignity; a battle in which they are not only defending their territories, ways of life, forms of self-government and traditions, but also struggling for the survival of all of us.

In sum, exhausted after this intense, convivial and joyful week that at times seemed interminable, overwhelmed by the weight of a learning that brings with it the moral obligation of sharing it, we came back to our places full of hope. We drank until slaked in this fountain of inspiration. We also learned that every one of us, in his or her own way, can do what we need to do, which will be as diverse as our worlds. We can construct a world in which everyone will be embraced. Inertias, paralysis and fears will be dismantled. We are on our way.

Epilogue

I read and re-read what I have written. I can see that I said nothing about the hard or exhausting work involved in constructing and defending autonomy and self-sufficiency, nor about the tensions and contradictions that still exist.

As the Zapatistas recognize, reconstructing their lives after centuries of oppression is a long and hard process. It is sometimes possible to encounter residues of the old system, such as occasional instances of *machismos* or violence.

This is not a balanced account. But the fact is that these amazing folks, ordinary men and women, living in a 'rebellious territory in resistance', have been able to transform one of the most unjust and miserable social conditions of the world into the materialization of their dreams of a decent society. I have produced a quick report in order to share with others the good news. Yes, it seems possible to find a way out of our current dead-ends, to create a valid alternative in the midst of one of the worst crises in human history. Perhaps others engaged in the search for such alternatives may find in this story some inspiration.

Note

1 The law of 1995 acknowledges the Zapatista occupation of the land. However, since the legal procedures to certify the property of the land have not been followed, non-Zapatista communities, with the support of the government, are continually trying to invade Zapatista territory.

17 The communal state (Venezuela)

Communal councils and workplace democracy

Dario Azzellini

The particular character of the process of change in Venezuela identified with president Hugo Chávez that became known as the Bolivarian process lies in the understanding that social transformation can be constructed from two directions, 'from above' and 'from below'. Bolivarianism – or Chavismo – includes among its participants both traditional organizations and old and new autonomous groups; it encompasses both state-centric and anti-systemic currents. The process thus differs from traditional Leninist or social democratic approaches, both of which see the state as the central agent of change; it differs as well from movement-based approaches that conceive of no role for the state in a process of revolutionary change. The current transformation in Venezuela is thus the product of a tension between constituent and constituted power, with the principal agent of change being the constituent.

Constituent power is the legitimate collective creative capacity of human beings expressed in movements and in the organized social base to create something new without having to derive it from something previously existing. In the Bolivarian process, the constituted power – the state and its institutions – accompany the organized population; it must be the facilitator of bottom-up processes, so that the constituent power can bring forward the steps needed to transform society.

This approach was elaborated on various occasions by former president Hugo Chávez, and has been confirmed by his successor Nicolás Maduro during the recent electoral campaign. It is shared by sectors of the administration and by the majority of the organized movements. Both from the government and from the rank and file of the Bolivarian process, there is a declared commitment to redefine state and society on the basis of an interrelation between top and bottom, and thereby to move toward transcending capitalist relations. Although not free of contradictions and conflicts, this two-track approach has been able to uphold and deepen the process of social transformation in Venezuela.

Constituent power, being comprehensive and expansive, has been the fundament for every revolution, democracy and republic; it is the greatest motor of history, the most powerful, innovative social force. Historically, however, we have seen constituent powers silenced and weakened after barely carrying out their role of legitimating the constituted power. In a genuine revolutionary process, then, the constituent power must maintain its capacity to intervene and to shape the present, to create something new that does not derive from the old. This is what defines revolution: not the act of taking power, but rather a broad process of constructing the new, an act of creation and invention (Negri 1992: 382). This is the global legacy of the Bolivarian process.

In Venezuela, the concept of constituent power arose at the end of the 1980s as the defining trait of a continuous process of social transformation. The main slogan of the neighbourhood assemblies was 'We don't want to be a government, we want to govern'. This idea, understood in increasingly radical terms, came to orient the revolutionary transformation, acquiring a hegemonic status in the political-ideological debate of the 1990s (Denis 2001: 65).

The Bolivarian process began by calling for a strengthening of civil and human rights and for the building of a 'participatory and protagonistic democracy' in search of a 'third way' beyond capitalism and socialism. Starting in late 2005, however, President Hugo Chávez described socialism as the only alternative for bringing about the necessary transcendence of capitalism. The presidential election of 2006 was defined by Chávez as a choice between capitalism and a path towards socialism. The onset of the era of Chávez's presidency expanded and reinforced participatory possibilities and council structures and created new ones. The idea of participation was officially defined in terms of popular power, revolutionary democracy and socialism. Because of the obvious difficulties of defining a clear path to socialism or a clear concept of what socialism can be today, the goal was defined as 'socialism of the twenty-first century', which is an ongoing project. The name also serves to distinguish it from the 'real socialisms' of the twentieth century. The process of seeking and building is guided above all by values such as collectivity, equality, solidarity, freedom and sovereignty (MinCI 2007: 30). It is embodied in the construction of councils.

In January 2007, Chávez proposed to go beyond the bourgeois state by building the communal state. He thus picked up and applied more widely a concern originating with anti-systemic forces. The main idea was to form council structures of all kinds (communal councils, communes and communal cities, for example), as bottom-up structures of self-administration. Councils of workers, students, peasants and women, among others, would then have to cooperate and coordinate on a higher level in order to gradually replace the bourgeois state with a communal state. According to the *National Plan for Economic and Social Development 2007–2013*, 'since sovereignty resides absolutely in the people, the people can itself direct the state, without needing to delegate its sovereignty as it does in indirect or representative democracy' (MinCI 2007).

The notion of a separation between 'civil society' and 'political society' or the state – as expressed, for example, by NGOs – is thus rejected. The focus is rather upon fostering the potential and the direct capacity of the popular base to analyse, decide, implement and evaluate what is relevant to its life. The constituent power is embodied in councils, in the institutions of popular power, and in the basic concept of the communal state. As was proposed in the constitutional reform that was rejected in the 2007 referendum, the future communal state must be subordinated to popular power, which replaces bourgeois civil society (AN-DGIDL 2007). This would overcome the rift between the economic, the social and the political – between civil society and political society – which underlies capitalism and the bourgeois state. It would also prevent, at the same time, the over-centralization that characterized the countries of 'real socialism' (Chávez 2008: 38).

Communal councils

The communal councils are a non-representative structure of direct democracy and the most advanced mechanism of self-organization at the local level in Venezuela. In 2013, approximately 44,000 communal councils had been established in Venezuela. Since the new constitution of 1999 defined Venezuela as a 'participatory and protagonistic democracy' a variety of mechanisms for the participation of the population in local administration and decision-making have been experimented with. In the beginning they were connected to local representative authorities and integrated into the institutional framework of representative democracy. Competing on the same territory as local authorities and depending on the finances authorized by those bodies, the different initiatives showed little success.

Communal councils began forming in 2005 as an initiative 'from below'. In different parts of Venezuela rank-and-file organizations, on their own, promoted forms of local self-administration named 'local governments' or 'communitarian governments'. During 2005, one department of the city administration of Caracas focused on promoting this proposal in the poor neighbourhoods of the city. In January 2006, Chávez adopted this initiative and began to spread it. On his weekly TV show, 'Aló Presidente', Chávez presented the communal councils – *consejos comunales* – as a kind of 'good practice'. At this point some 5,000 communal councils already existed. In April 2006, the National Assembly approved the Law of Communal Councils, which was reformed in 2009 following a broad consulting process of councils' spokespeople. The communal councils in urban areas encompass 150 to 400 families; in rural zones, a minimum of 20 families; and in indigenous zones, at least ten families. The councils build a non-representative structure of direct participation that exists parallel to the elected representative bodies of constituted power.

The communal councils are financed directly by national state institutions, thus avoiding interference from municipal organs. The law does not give any entity the authority to accept or reject proposals presented by the councils. The relationship between the councils and established institutions, however, is not always harmonious; conflicts arise principally from the slowness of constituted power to respond to demands made by the councils and from attempts at interference. The communal councils tend to transcend the division between political and civil society (between those who govern and those who are governed). Hence, liberal analysts who support that division view the communal councils in a negative light, arguing that they are not independent civil society organizations, but rather are linked to the state. In fact, however, they constitute a parallel structure through which power and control is gradually drawn away from the state in order to govern on their own (Azzellini 2010).

At a higher level of self-government there is the possibility of creating socialist communes, which can be formed by combining various communal councils in a specific territory. The councils decide themselves about the geography of these communes. These communes can develop medium- and long-term projects of greater impact while decisions continue to be made in assemblies of the communal councils. As of the end of 2014 there were more than 900 officially constituted communes.

In the context of the creation of communes and communal cities it is important to analytically distinguish between (absolute) political-administrative space and socio-cultural-economic (relational) space (Harvey 2006: 270–293). Communes reflect the latter; their boundaries do not necessarily correspond to existing political-administrative spaces. As these continue to exist, the institutionalization of the communal councils, communes and communal cities develops and shapes the socio-cultural-economic space. Thus, the idea of council-based non-representative local self-organization creates a 'new power-geometry'. The concept of power in human geography, as elaborated by Doreen Massey, has been put 'to positive political use' following the 'recognition of the existence and significance, within Venezuela, of highly unequal, and thus undemocratic, power-geometries' (Massey 2009: 20).

Various communes can form communal cities, with administration and planning 'from below' if the entire territory is organized in communal councils and communes. The mechanism of the construction of communes and communal cities is flexible; they themselves define their tasks. Thus the construction of self-government begins with what the population itself considers most important, necessary or opportune. The communal cities that have begun to form so far, for example, are rural and are structured around agriculture, such as the Ciudad Comunal Campesina Socialista Simón Bolívar in the southern state of Apure or the Ciudad Comunal Laberinto in the northwestern state of Zulia. Organizing and the construction of communes and communal cities has been easier in suburban and rural areas than in metropolitan areas, since there is less distraction and less presence of opposition, while at the same time common interests are easier to define.

Democracy at work

Regarding the democratization of ownership, and administration of the means of production, Venezuela has experimented with a series of different models. Between 2001 and 2006 the Venezuelan government – in addition to asserting state control over the core of the oil industry – focused on promoting cooperatives for any type of company, including models of cooperatives co-administered with the state or private entrepreneurs. The 1999 constitution assigned the cooperatives a special weight. They were conceived as contributing to a new social and economic balance, and thus received massive state assistance. The favourable conditions led to a boom in the number of cooperatives founded.

In mid-2010, according to the national cooperative supervisory institute Sunacoop, 73,968 cooperatives were certified as operative, with an estimated total of two million members, although some people participated in more than one cooperative.[1] The initial idea that cooperatives would automatically produce for the satisfaction of social needs and that their internal solidarity based on collective property would extend to their local communities proved to be an error. Most cooperatives still followed the logic of capital; concentrating on the maximization of net revenue without supporting the surrounding communities, many failed to integrate new members (Azzellini 2012a: 259–278; 2012b: 147–160). In the light of these experiences the government's focus in supporting the creation of cooperatives switched to cooperatives controlled and owned by the communities.

In response to the employers' lockout of 2002–2003, the 'entrepreneurs strike', with the stated intention of toppling the Chávez government, workers began the process of taking over workplaces abandoned by their owners. At first, the government relegated the cases to the labour courts, and then in January 2005 began expropriations. Beginning in July 2005, the government began to pay special attention to the situation of closed businesses, and since then hundreds of such companies have been expropriated. But a systematic policy for expropriations in the productive sector did not exist until 2007. The expropriated enterprises are officially supposed to be turned into 'direct social property', under the direct control of workers and communities. In reality most of them are not administered by workers and communities but by state institutions. Working conditions have not fundamentally changed, and expropriations have not automatically produced co-management or workers' control.

The concept of 'direct social property' is also supposed to apply to hundreds of new 'socialist factories' built by the government in the context of an overarching strategy of industrialization. The workers are selected by local communal councils, and the required professionals are drawn from state and government institutions. The aim is to gradually transfer the administration of the factories into the hands of organized workers and communities. But most state institutions involved do little to organize this process, or prepare the employees, which has generated growing conflicts between workers and institutions.

In 2007, Chávez picked up the idea of 'socialist workers councils', which was already being discussed by many rank-and-file workers, existing councils and workers' initiatives in favour of workers councils. In fact, there was a network with the same name: Socialist Workers Councils (CST). Chávez presented CST as a good practice and called on workers to form CST at their workplaces. Nevertheless since most institutions were opposed to workers councils, only a few councils were formed at the beginning, mainly in recovered factories like the valve factory, Inveval, or the water pipe factory, Inefa.

Growing pressure from below led several government institutions to start to accept or even promote the creation of workers councils in institutionally administered workplaces, even without the benefit of an enacted law on workers councils. But while on the one hand the majority of institutions tried to prevent the constitution of workers councils in their workplaces, in others, and in state administered enterprises, the institutions often tried to assume the lead and constitute the CST themselves. This move represents the attempt to distort the councils' purpose and reduce them to a representative authority dealing with work- and salary-related questions within the government bureaucracy. As a consequence, the CST turned into another site of struggle for workers control (Azzellini 2012c: 183–196).

The most successful attempt at a democratization of ownership and administration of means of production is the model of Enterprises of Communal Social Property (EPSC), promoted to create local production units and community services enterprises. The EPSC are collective property of the communities that decide on the organizational structure of enterprises, the workers incorporated and the eventual use of profits. Government enterprises and institutions have promoted the communal enterprises since 2009, and since 2013 several thousand EPSC have been constituted. Most belong to the sectors of community services like public transport, or are engaged in food production and food processing. The state-owned oil company PDSVA set up a local liquid gas distribution administered by communities called Gas Comunal (Gil Beróes 2010).

Challenges

Since 2007, the government's ability to reform has increasingly clashed with the limitations inherent in the bourgeois state and the capitalist system. The movements and initiatives for self-management and self-government geared toward overcoming the bourgeois state and its institutions, with the goal of replacing it with a communal state based on popular power, have grown. The broadening of direct grassroots participation brings an increase in the conflicts between the state and its popular base (especially in the sphere of production) as well as within the state, which itself becomes a site of class conflict. Not surprisingly, the deepening of social transformation multiplies the points of confrontation between top-down and bottom-up strategies. But simultaneously, because of the expansion of state institutions' work, the consolidation of the Bolivarian process and growing resources, state institutions have been generally strengthened and have become more bureaucratized. Institutions of constituted power aim at controlling social processes and reproducing themselves. Since the institutions of constituted power are at the same time strengthening and limiting constituent power, the transformation process is very complex and contradictory.

Institutions, as well as many individuals in charge in institutions, follow an inherent logic of perpetuating and expanding their institutional power and control to guarantee the institution's survival. Or as Thamara Esis, a *consejo comunal* activist from Caracas explains in a personal interview, 'These nice people who already made themselves comfortable in their offices, are not willing to renounce their benefits, they live on the needs of the people. It is like a little enterprise, you understand?' This tendency is strengthened in times of profound structural changes when the purpose and existence of any institution is questioned in the context of transformation.

In fact, the Ministry of Communes turned out to be one of the biggest obstacles to the construction of communes until April 2013 when a new minister was appointed. Before that, only the growing organization 'from below', especially the self-organized National Network of Communards, could bring enough pressure on the Ministry of Communes to start changing its politics at the end of 2011. They forced the ministry to register some 20 communes. In return, the communes had to set up the registration sheet since the Ministry of Communes not only did not register any communes in the first three years of its existence, but one year after the law on communes had been enacted, it had not even created an official procedure for the registration of communes.

In his government plan for 2013–2019, presented during the electoral campaign for the 2012 presidential elections, Chávez clearly stated that 'We should not betray ourselves: the still dominant socioeconomic formation in Venezuela is of capitalist and rentist character' (Chávez 2012: 2). In order to move further towards socialism, Chávez underlined the necessity to advance in the construction of communal councils, communes and communal cities and the 'development of social property on the basic and strategic factors and means of production' (Chávez 2012: 7). His successor Nicolás Maduro committed to the programme and one of the central slogans of the movements supporting his electoral campaign was '*Comuna o nada*'.

After Chávez's death in March 2013, Venezuela's opposition politicians saw an opportunity to win presidential elections, perhaps assuming the public merely cared about Chávez's famous charisma. However, the opposition's leading candidate, Miranda state governor Henrique Capriles Radonski, lost to Chávez's successor, Nicolás Maduro. Having been defeated in 18 of 19 elections since 1998, part of the opposition decided not to hold out hope for electoral victory any longer, but instead, to destabilize the country and violently oust its elected government. From February 2014 onwards the country was struck for several months by a wave of violent upper-class protests and terrorist attacks. Most often the municipalities where the riots were taking place were governed by anti-Chavista mayors who support the violent actions, either by participating themselves or by ignoring the barricades defended with petrol bombs and firearms, instead of sending in municipal police, and neglecting to collect trash so that material for barricades was provided. Some 40 people lost their lives during three months of opposition 'protests'. Most of them were government supporters, policemen or bystanders killed by opposition gunmen and bombs, some even beheaded by barbed wire traps set up by opposition supporters. On 1 April a group of rioters set the Ministry of Housing on fire with Molotov cocktails while 1,200 workers were inside the building. The fire was set close to the ministry's nursery school, and 89 toddlers had to be evacuated by firemen. This lethal act is no exception. During the 'protests' a university has been burned down, as well as nurseries, subway stations, buses, medical centres, food distribution centres, tourist information sites and other civic spaces. In Merida, the drinking water reservoir was deliberately contaminated with fuel, and in Caracas, the nature reserve on the north side of the city was set on fire to destroy the power lines that supply the city with electricity. Other natural reserves in other parts of the country followed. The more the violence lost support inside Venezuela the more terrorist commando actions were carried out, and they partly continued even after the destabilization attempt proved unsuccessful. At the end of September 2014, government party PSUV MP Robert Sierra and his partner were murdered in their house in Caracas.

The protests were said to be against the high inflation and the government's economic policies. There is no doubt that Venezuela is now going through a difficult economic situation; it has suffered high inflation and acute shortages of food and electricity during 2013 and 2014. While mismanagement and corruption are problems, as the government itself has admitted, the shortages were mainly caused by speculation, smuggling and intentional reduction of production and hoarding by the private sector, just as before the US-backed coup in Chile in 1973.

Confronted with falling oil prices, the Maduro government has taken a hard stand to counter the economic and financial attacks on the country as well as to make up for widespread corruption and inefficiency. Economic and financial politics as well as the question of how to deal with the opposition and private entrepreneurs have raised serious criticisms and strong disagreements among Chavistas. But even in this adverse situation Chavismo did not lose mass identification and the Maduro government could not be destabilized. Regarding the communes, Maduro appointed Reinaldo Iturriza as the new Minister for Communes in April 2013. Since then, the ministry has massively supported the constitution of communes. Together with the fast-growing communards movement, this resulted in more than 900 self-constituted communes by the end of 2014. At the same time, the autonomous 'National Network of Communards' has also been growing from 70 communes at the end of 2011 to more than 350 communes at the end of 2014. The communes and the new politics of the Ministry of Communes face strong resistance from many mayors and governors of the PSUV. Nevertheless, strategies 'from above' and 'from below' have maintained themselves in the same process of transformation for 15 years and the conflictive relationship between constituent and constituted power has been the motor of the Bolivarian process.

Note

1 'Interview of Juan Carlos Baute, Presidente de Sunacoop', accessed 16 January 2009, www.sunacoop.gob.ve/noticias_detalle.php?id=1361.

18 The necessary renovation of socialist hegemony in Cuba

Contradictions and challenges[1]

Olga Fernández Ríos

Fifty-five years after the triumph of the Cuban Revolution, the country has begun a process of socioeconomic changes that signifies a rupture in the patterns associated with what is called real socialism. This implies a new stage of the socialist transition that will transform development in order to achieve what has officially been defined as prosperous and sustainable socialism.

The main economic changes were approved by the VI Congress of the PCC in April 2011. The Congress reaffirmed socialism and the socialist state enterprise as the main economic actor, at the same time broadening the terms of social ownership associated with the development of more cooperatives and self-employment, and encouraging the decentralization that promotes local development. In other words, Cuba is redesigning the state's function in socioeconomic life. All of this introduces changes to the way socialism is constructed, to the relationship between the individual and the state and civil society. It is a move away from a state that dominates the economic framework to a state that must balance diverse forms of ownership and protect the interests of a changing society. The changes impact sociopolitical life; when the state stops being the sole economic actor, when new economic actors start to participate, introducing social differences and creating a more heterogeneous society.

It must be recognized, now more than ever, that within the context of a new model of economic and social development, the construction of socialism is an integrated process that must concurrently provide socialist hegemony and the conditions for human and social emancipation within an integrated and varied system, something not achieved merely through economic development.

Issues under debate

There has been much analysis and research in Cuba about transformations that have a place in economic and social development. The success of these transformations depends, in large measure, on the capacity they generate for achieving the continuity of the socialist transition, which requires the predominance of production relations that reproduce socialism. For the socialist hegemony to be maintained beyond economic advances, there are three crucial sociopolitical factors: the reinforcement of a democracy whose core must be popular empowerment, at the very least broadening popular participation and improving institutions; the ratification of social justice policies within a context of even greater social class diversity and complexity; and the reconstruction of political consensus under conditions that create a new model of socialist development.

Our main thesis deals with these three areas in an integrated way recognizing that economic development is fundamental for guaranteeing socialist hegemony, but that it takes time.[2] In the short term, political relationships and social work must become a top priority and must even more clearly express the reaffirmation of power achieved by the Cuban people in 1959. It is therefore necessary to create new forms of popular empowerment that balance citizen representation with public participation in decision-making and in the control of resources and management, which means a broadening of socialist democracy that takes into account the complexity of changes and their sociopolitical, cultural and ethical-axiological impacts.

It means 'governing' the changes, evaluating and measuring their impacts, evaluating in each moment the correlation between political consensus, governability and legitimacy of those that carry out management functions, including the reconstruction of political consensus achieved through the previous model in which state ownership predominates over means of production. At the same time, in contrast to what was proposed by the subversive USAID Democracy Program in Cuba, the reinforcement of democracy does not mean assimilating neoliberal mechanisms used by the United States, but achieving a greater popular empowerment.

The civil society connection

This is a strategic issue at the centre of the analysis and debate taking place in Cuba at present and that, one way or another, confirms the importance of achieving greater interconnectedness between political power and democracy that requires greater proximity between the state and civil society, breaking down barriers between them.

In the socialist transition the state must generate communication channels with civil society, that in each instance tip the balance a bit more towards the development of political potentialities of civil society as expressed by Marx in his 'Critique of the Gotha Programme', when he declared that true liberty consists in 'converting the state from an organism that rules over society to one that is completely subordinate to it'.

The strength of the state in the socialist transition is tested in two ways: (a) its willingness to represent the interests that occupy political power, which in Cuba's case is the people; and (b) its capacity to interact with all the society, to represent the socio-class reality, and to blur the lines between the individual and the state and the state and civil society.

One of the most complex issues in the history of socialism is how to promote the connection between the individual and society, expressed here in terms of the interconnection between human beings seeking individual interests and human beings with political possibilities as citizens. In other words, in the socialist transition it is necessary to improve civil society to develop political functions by networks of grassroots and social organizations. It deals with eliminating the alienation that exists within capitalism when common citizens are separated from political understanding by political professionals and elites that are predetermined to make decisions in the name of all society. It is to eliminate the liberal concept of the state as an 'intermediary' between citizens and decisions. These are issues that are taken up in any authentic socialist project.

Cuba is re-imagining the state to create a more logical and balanced interaction between what could be called the 'guarantor state' that guarantees everything, and a state capable of governing with varied economic forms that separate it from economic heads of state, but that at the same time favour social justice policies inherent to a socialist process. It is in this context that the state must modernize in terms of structure, functions and ownership and management relations. At the same time civil society is made more heterogeneous and is characterized as a space for the development of new forms of ownership with impact on subjectivities and production relations. This also introduces changes in the interconnectedness in both spheres and, therefore, in relationships between individual–state and individual–society, different from previous stages.

Popular empowerment must not simply be abstract or declarative. It must be demonstrated in increasingly quantitative and qualitative popular participation in all forms. It is founded on the understanding that within the socialist transition politics has noble work to do: achieving interaction between different social sectors that embraces the wishes and complaints, anxieties and doubts of the people, and at the same time that incorporates their experiences into the public discourse.

Community work as an avenue for citizen participation

There are many formulas for promoting popular empowerment. In all, an important role is played by persons, social organizations and groups that have existed in Cuba as unions, organizations of women, small farmers and students, together with the neighbourhood committees along with many other social and professional organizations. But these organizations have also been called on to improve the way they work and to promote efforts that coincide with the new socioeconomic realities of the country. They must revolutionize their offerings in order to motivate a wide spectrum of society, most importantly young people.

The formulas needed to strengthen all the popular organizations so that they can actually call themselves participatory channels are varied. Here we highlight the work that has begun to unfold at a local level: the community projects. Even if some of these experiences are still in their organizational phase, in some places they have begun to show viability and positive results such as in the municipality of Central Havana in the country's capital and Holguin province, for example.

The community projects and programmes have been called on to perform an active role in local politics, and can influence in the new ways in which they are implemented. Among the common features of these programmes the following stand out:[3] they all came about through popular initiative according to the conditions and needs of each location and coordination groups have been formed including representatives of the general population, social organizations and local entities. They receive help from the Social Sciences Councils that exist in each province and are formed by specialists from different disciplines such as sociologists, psychologists, anthropologists, economists and teachers. They also receive help from research centres and universities, along with doctors, nurses and architects, among other professionals.

These projects have channels that allow them to interact with authorities in the system of Popular Power and the Communist Party at the local and provincial level. In the community projects objectives and plans are outlined in accordance with the conditions, needs and interests of each location. They also develop participatory research with the objective of directly consulting with the population about the main problems that they face and the criticisms they provide in the search for solutions. They work to identify concrete forms of popular participation that can be implemented and they also promote what we could call citizen participation education – in a participatory environment – that has an impact on those in charge of decision-making.

We stress that this type of participatory project is still in development and there are differences from one province to another and also obstacles to overcome, such as developing a greater level of integration between the participants and projects or programmes and overcoming the centralist culture that is still present among members, welfare models and institutional fragmentation. To sum up, these are formulas for community work that are not organized using pre-conceived moulds, but emerge from the needs, conditions and interests of the community and that at the same time have the responsibility to develop participatory subjects and channels. In our opinion, the community projects are called on to fulfil an important role in managing Cuba's social justice policies when it is necessary to apply state subsidies based on personal and family needs instead of universal subsidies for all citizens in the areas of health, education and social security. So Cuba will combine the two types of state subsidies: universal and differentiated. In both cases the state must be the main guarantor, but with differentiated subsidies the local community must play a defining role.

Final comments

Cuba's current political system is perfectible and from this assumption, it is possible to reinforce the two most visible dimensions of popular empowerment: representation in state organisms and popular political participation. Both require education and political culture, a participative environment and the development of personal and social motivations. This entails developing a concept that broadens both sides of political power in the socialist transition: the authority to represent interests and the authority to convince, to commit to a wide spectrum of society, to generate consensus from the base. It means a concept of hegemony that goes beyond its political character and is expressed as a cultural hegemony within which the state increases its capacity to demonstrate superiority in the values it defends.

The success of the new model of socialism that is consolidated in Cuba depends a great deal on its capability to generate greater empowerment and popular involvement in decision-making and in the control of resources, management and the environment. Popular empowerment is an objective condition and a subjective factor for the conceptual and practical framework of the work entailed in the renovation of the social and economic development model in Cuba taking into account (1) the people hold political power and are not merely a participant in it and (2) in the socialist transition it is necessary to vindicate a new type of interrelations between those who call themselves 'followers' and 'leaders', in favour of the followers and merging the culture of those that govern and those that are governed.

Notes

1 Translation by Lydia Carey.
2 If the difficult conditions within which Cuba's socialist transition has unfolded are taken into account: its beginnings in an underdeveloped and neocolonialist country that has had to confront a very adverse geopolitical environment because of the continued hostility of the US government, the reinforcing of the blockade and terrorist and media attacks. In addition there is the influence of so-called real socialism and the dramatic impact of the fall of the USSR and Eastern Europe.
3 For more information about this topic see Acea Terry (2013) and Bellido Aguilera and González Calzadilla (2010).

19 Cuba's cooperatives

Their contribution to Cuba's new socialism

Camila Piñeiro Harnecker

One of the changes that emerged as part of the process of 'updating' or renovating Cuban socialism is the promotion of cooperatives. Beginning in 2012 a series of measures have been taken – even if rushed and insufficient – to overcome existing agricultural cooperatives' problems and simultaneously promote cooperative creation in other economic sectors through the establishment of a legal framework called 'non-agricultural cooperatives' approved in December of that same year. The objective of this chapter is to analyse the development of (these new) cooperatives in Cuba, highlighting the impact they can have on new Cuban socialism.

Promotion of non-agricultural cooperatives

> '*The Economic and Social Policy Guidelines of the Party and the Revolution*' and official statements suggest that cooperatives play an important role in Cuba's new economic model. The promotion of cooperatives seeks to transfer jobs, *in the most socialized way possible*, from the state to the non-state sector, redundant workers as well as some activities that under the state's management have been ineffective (personal and technical services, gastronomy, marketing). Another objective is generating employment and increasing the availability of consumer goods and services.
>
> (Piñeiro Harnecker 2011b: 48–57)

President Raúl Castro, Vice President Marino Murillo and other officials have said, and it is reflected in approved regulations, that cooperatives as a business model are prioritized and preferred over private business (what in Cuba is known as 'self-employment'), because they are more 'socialized'. That means they are recognized as socioeconomic organizations that generate and distribute wealth in a more equitable and just way: all cooperative members are also owners and have the same right to participate in decision-making, management and control, and distributed profits are divided according to work contribution, not capital contribution.

Due to the financial restrictions of the Cuban economy and the high cost to the budget of guaranteeing public services, Cuban cooperatives must be profitable, paying taxes into the national and local budget. It is understood that these socioeconomic organizations are better prepared than private enterprises for economic management that satisfies social needs and promotes socialist social relations, which one would hope means their economic management would be successful. As has been argued in other work (Piñeiro Harnecker 2012a: 84–87), thanks to democratic management that allows for the articulation of all individual interests along with members' collective interest and the potential social interests of the community and social organizations, cooperatives have the following advantages over private enterprises:

- They have their own sources of motivation to increase productivity, quality and innovation, based mostly on 'positive' incentives (not based on the fear of failure or dismissal).
- They allow an increase in work productivity with a smaller concentration of means of production, a minimum use of contracted work, greater income equality and a more just distribution of wealth.
- They provide more stable and dignified employment.
- They facilitate the fulfilment of their members' material and spiritual needs, their full human development.
- They are better prepared to contribute to local development.
- Within them, they allow for socialist social relations based in equality, solidarity, democracy and justice.

So, the expansion and consolidation of cooperatives in Cuba's economy and society seeks to achieve the aforementioned objectives and, at the same time, promote ethical values and practices congruent to the building of socialism, as we will see below.

The legal framework that allows the creation of non-agricultural cooperatives establishes the possibility of creating associated work cooperatives (also known as 'worker cooperatives', where members must work and are only allowed to contract labour temporarily) and producer cooperatives (independent producers that maintain individual ownership of their means of production and only use the cooperative to obtain supplies and market or obtain other support services for their collective production). This means that consumer cooperatives and other forms of cooperatives are still not legislated, nor are second tier cooperatives. As has happened with other measures taken, this stage is considered experimental and the idea is that from these pilot experiences problems can be identified in the legal or institutional framework so that when these measures are more broadly applied they will have the best conditions possible for success. Different from the previous experiments such as the leasing of the state shops to Self-employed Workers (TCPs) and what was regulated for the TCPs, it does not establish limitations in regard to activities as long as they have a social interest, nor does it limit them in regard to the geographical areas in which they can be created.

The intention to approve the *General Cooperative Law* that exists in a majority of countries worldwide has been publicly announced for 2016 (Castro 2012a, 2012b).

The following are a list of the most relevant aspects of the legal framework for non-agricultural cooperatives:

- Only producer and worker cooperatives are permitted.
- The minimum number of members (the term used in the legislation is 'partners') is three.
- All associates must work.
- The contracting of workers is limited to temporary terms (no more than three consecutive months) and the work they provide must not exceed ten per cent of the associates' total hours.
- No subordination, only 'methodological' supervision by the corresponding ministry of their principal activity.
- They register in the commercial registry, acquiring a legal standing like a business.
- They are not limited to any specific activities, as long as what they are doing has a social interest.
- Profits must be distributed according to work, but a reserve emergency fund is obligatory.
- They set their prices, except for goods or services that have a 'social impact' (until recently only personal transportation, cigarettes, tobacco, rum and a few other products were included in this classification).
- They can buy supplies from state enterprises; some will be assigned by the state.
- They can import and export through state agencies.
- They can rent state establishments for periods of ten years, with the option to renew such contracts.
- They will receive preferential treatment in comparison to other forms of non-state businesses:
  - They will have priority in bidding for state establishment.
  - They can carry out activities prohibited to TCPs.
  - Their taxation is approximately 50 per cent less than that of TCPs:
    - They contribute 5 per cent less to Social Security (5 per cent less than TCPs).
    - The scale for calculating income tax is 5 per cent less in each range (10–45 per cent instead of the 15–50 per cent for TCPs).
    - They can deduct all expenses, except cash advances (TCPs can only deduct up to 60 per cent).
    - They deduct the average provincial salary, multiplied by the number of members.
    - They enjoy a grace period of three months from the start of operations.

- They can purchase supplies from state enterprises at retail prices minus 20 per cent.
- They can receive soft loans from state banks.

The legal and institutional framework of the new cooperatives has come with some deficiencies and questions that will hopefully be resolved with the implementation of these approved experiences and at the very least before their general application in 2016. Just to mention the most crucial, this new framework does not give cooperative education the importance it deserves: the only International Cooperative Alliance (ICA)-defined universal principle not explicitly recognized is this one; neither does it establish that persons should educate themselves in cooperativism before joining a cooperative. Another important issue with the new legal framework is that, in those cases where cooperatives emerge from state-owned businesses, it does not encourage the workers to initiate the shift nor respect the principle of voluntary membership. The way that the cooperative creation process is designed is that any initiative must come from the business and worker collectives only have the option to join the cooperative or become 'available' (lose their jobs).

As has been recognized by the very institutions involved in its creation, the procedure of establishing cooperatives is too complicated, slow and subordinate to the whim of the administration because the approval criteria have not been made explicit. Even if cooperatives should be formed in accordance with the interests of the regions and sectors where they are created, and they should coordinate their activities with the appropriate local and municipal government departments, these objectives could be achieved without the cooperatives' plans held hostage by the will of provincial governments, ministries or the Implementation Council. At the same time as the procedures for forming cooperatives are streamlined, procedures and areas for coordination (each different for the different needs of each territory or sector) must be established that fulfil the aforementioned objectives and ensure that the cooperatives created fulfil, as much as possible, the needs of the territories and contribute to the national economy through the creation or consolidation of productivity networks, development and the diffusion of technology. Included in each cooperative proposal should be a social impact study. In order to avoid the abuse of public officials' discretionary power, the criteria for whether an activity is considered a social good or not should be defined and decided by the public studies.

As far as the institutional environment of new cooperatives goes, the absence of an institution that supervises their internal functioning is noteworthy, especially in their observance of democratic governance principles and the rights and responsibilities of members. This supervision has been entrusted to the organisms that authorize their constitutions (Provincial Administration Councils or corresponding ministries) but they have shown no ability to perform that task. It would be wise to create an organization that represents the interests of new cooperatives from the municipal to national level and that, among other tasks, could carry out similar functions to that of the Asociación Nacional de Agricultores Pequeños (ANAP) in relation to agricultural cooperatives. These two institutions could complement each other by offering support to the cooperative sector in the form of training, consulting, accompaniment and even intervention into cooperatives with serious problems in order to avoid their failure and dissolution.

The current state of non-agricultural cooperatives

After the new legal framework was approved in December 2012, the first cooperatives weren't formed until the beginning of July 2014. This delay was the result of the creation of the procedure's characteristics outlined above. Today, 498 cooperatives have been authorized. These have been approved in four groups, as part of the measures taken by the Council of Ministers in their monthly meetings. The majority (77 per cent) originated from the state, which means they were created by state-owned enterprises. The rest were proposed by groups of people.

By October 2014, according to the non-agricultural cooperative registry of the National Office of Statistics and Information (ONEI), of the total cooperatives approved only 315 had formed. The difference between the number approved and the number formed is mostly related to communication delays about their approval from the corresponding ministries and Provincial Administration Councils. Until they know they are approved they cannot begin the process of constitution.

As shown in Table 19.1, the cooperatives cover diverse activities, with a special focus on gastronomy (43 per cent), retail sale of agricultural products (20 per cent), construction and the production of construction materials (14 per cent) and personal and technical services (6 per cent). Figure 19.1 shows the geographic concentration of the cooperatives in Havana (63 per cent), Artemisa (14 per cent), Matanzas (4 per cent), Mayabeque (3 per cent) and Pinar del Río (2 per cent).

Between February and May 2014, colleagues at the Center for the Study of the Cuban Economy of the University of Havana (CEEC) and the National Association of Cuba Economists (ANEC) diagnosed some 40 non-agricultural cooperatives; all except one were located in Havana. The sample was sufficiently representative of the country's cooperatives formed at the moment, and its results can therefore be, to a large extent, generalized to all cooperatives, especially those in Havana, considering the majority of those studied were located there (Piñeiro Harnecker 2014).

In the study we found that non-agricultural cooperatives, despite their relatively short time in existence (when we did the study the longest-running were nine months old and the shortest had been operating for a month) were experiencing positive changes. The most noteworthy is that in general workers were satisfied with the decision to start a cooperative, especially because in the majority of cases their wages had risen considerably, tripling on average. Also not to be disregarded is the effect autonomy and democratic management or, 'the power to make the most important decisions', as one member put

Table 19.1 Areas of cooperative activities, Cuba, 2014

#	Area	No.	%
1	Gastronomy	213	42.9
2	Retail sales of agricultural products	101	20.3
3	Construction and production of construction materials	68	13.7
4	Personal and technical services	32	6.4
5	Poultry sales	17	3.4
6	Trash collection	15	3.0
7	Shipping and transportation services	11	2.2
8	Production and repair of furniture, ceramics, textiles, blacksmithing nails, shoe repair materials, leather products and plastics	11	2.2
9	Passenger transportation	6	1.2
10	Accounting services	6	1.2
11	Decorative manufacturing and services	5	1.0
12	Energy services	5	1.0
13	Food and drink production	3	0.6
14	Technical maintenance and equipment repair services	3	0.6
15	Graphic printing, decoration and interior design	1	0.2
16	Wholesale marketing of agricultural products	1	0.2
	Total	**498**	

Source: Created by the author with information from Comisión para la Implementación y Desarrollo de los Lineamientos (CIDEL), May 2014.

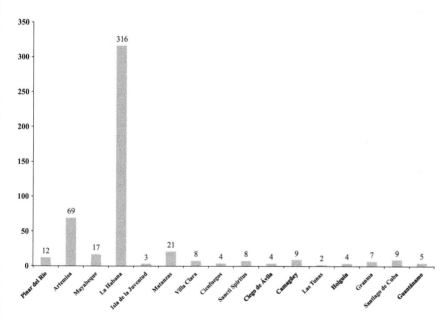

Figure 19.1 Authorized cooperatives, distribution by province, March 2014
Source: Created by the author with information from Comisión para la Implementación y Desarrollo de los Lineamientos (CIDEL), May 2014.

it, have on an overall sense of satisfaction and belonging. Even if a broader study is needed to determine the reach and depth of the democratization of decision-making, and the time required for a cultural change to result from participating in decision-making, in general cooperative members understand and are happy with their power to make the most important decisions in the general assembly.

The interviewees perceived greater unity, collaboration and teamwork. They said that tasks were distributed regardless of responsibilities or titles, allowing for multitasking and a reduction in the division between direct (manual) work and indirect (administrative or intellectual) work. They said that work discipline had improved: people were fulfilling time commitments and technical standards, and working with greater intensity. Likewise, they were conserving more resources like electricity, water and the telephone and taking better care of work tools, performing maintenance on them when needed.

Even if cooperativism training in terms of administration is far from sufficient, and in general – a reflection of the insufficient legal framework in this regard – there are no existing training plans, most managers seem interested in improving accounting, management and strategy, in order to improve management; and some have already taken advantage of the available courses in cooperative accounting offered by ANEC.

Some cooperatives had assimilated the values of solidarity and mutual help and had given loans to members with problems or visited sick members helping them with food shopping and picking up medicines. A few have even made donations to old people's homes, daycare centres and schools in their communities.

On the other hand, the new cooperatives are confronting issues in the creation process, as well as in training and in constitution, storage of supplies and other situations that have resulted from a rise in their operational costs and taxes. The problems seen in the cooperative creation process as well as those involved in training and in formation, have important repercussions not only in the quality of the cooperatives but also in their social sustainability (in particular, the relationships between members have been affected by conflicts that have resulted from a process designed from above and a lack of preparation) as well as an economic one (the feasibility studies were carried out by external sources and just as a formality). The economic sustainability of these cooperative businesses is also affected by other problems related to supplies and operational costs as well as training and information. And the problems related to taxes challenge their ability to carry out this important component of social responsibility that can serve as an example for self-employed workers (Piñeiro Harnecker 2014: 313–323).

The promotion of non-agricultural cooperatives in Cuba has, in addition to the challenges that come with the creation of this kind of economic and social organization, in particular when there are public policies that give them preferential treatment (for example, effective supervision to avoid false cooperatives or the distortion of honest cooperatives), a large challenge in the fact that the majority of cooperatives created – at least at the beginning – will originate from the state, from state-owned enterprises. This experience is almost unprecedented worldwide, and therefore requires constant critical evaluation and for political decisions to advance slowly and carefully instead of the forming of lots of cooperatives that are not really cooperatives and that fail because they don't have the minimum requirements needed for success.

In these cases it is fundamental that the persons forming the cooperatives do not see them as an imposition but as a positive change in their work lives. That's why it's essential to provide training to all members during the induction process, to respect the necessary time needed for workers to make informed and conscientious decisions, and to promote the initiative of collectives themselves. Even though these cooperatives emerge from groups of people that already know and in great part will continue with the same activities that they have been doing, an effective integrated accompaniment – that attends to the social dimension of the cooperative as well as the economic one – is vital for their current and future success.

As is well known, cooperatives are organizations with a social as well as an economic component, with ethical principles and organizational particularities like democratic management that the members of a cooperative are not going to adopt or understand and are even less likely to carry out, if they are unaware of them. Making sure that all members – founders and those that join later – know these principles, and with practice, adopt the values and behaviours that they imply, is a complex task but advantageous because precisely from these behaviours emerge the 'added value' of the cooperative expansion. Because of this, it is vitally important that all cooperatives – those that originate from the state as well as those that emerge from collective initiatives – receive support not only through training and consulting services (legal, accounting, administrative and management in general) but also through accompaniment for those who need it most.

For all of the aforementioned, the success of this experiment with non-agricultural cooperatives requires, in addition to the kind of business environment necessary for any enterprise, the creation of an 'institutional infrastructure' that supervises them from a pedagogical standpoint, supports them and integrates them:

1   a supervisory and developmental institution;
2   a federation that brings them together and supports development work; and
3   a network of organizations (ideally, but not necessarily organized as cooperatives) prepared to offer training and accompaniment, certified and coordinated by the supervisory and developmental institution. It also requires a wholesale market and the possibility of establishing productive linkages with the state sector, among other measures (Piñeiro Harnecker 2014: 326–329).

Cuban cooperatives and socialism in Cuba

As it is laid out in official regulations and statements, the cooperative – considered a 'socialist form of collective property' (*Regulation 25*) – will play an important role in Cuba's new economic model and complement the socialist state enterprise. The formation of cooperatives will allow state-sector businesses to focus on fundamental activities and its companies to dedicate themselves to principal activities, counting on cooperatives to carry out support and secondary activities.

As evidenced by the identifying and organizational principles of cooperatives (Piñeiro Harnecker 2012a: 33–42) and keeping in mind the flexibility inherent in these organizations that make it possible to internalize social interests in an institutional way, the cooperative model seems much more appropriate for the transfer of economic activities to small and medium-sized businesses in a society committed to socialism. The advantages of the cooperative management model – previously discussed – is even more evident in the sense that it seeks to promote relationships and cooperation among people and recognizes salaried work as unjust and inappropriate for the socialist goal of full human development.

A correct expansion of cooperatives in Cuba would bring benefits that would contribute to the consolidation and advancement of socialism. It would allow the necessary transfer of economic activities from the state sector to the non-state sector in the most socialist way possible: without having to revert to privatization, firings and the establishment of subordinate relationships between workers. It would institutionalize the self-management practices already present in some state enterprises. It would promote the formalization of cooperative relationships that are already happening among self-employed workers. It would facilitate supervision and guidance and the coordination of these autonomous businesses in a way that responds to social interests. Through their operation *vis-à-vis* already existent private enterprises, they could contribute to improving work conditions for those hired by self-employed workers, lower prices and increase contributions to local development. In addition, they could demonstrate the possibilities and strengths of collective solutions, democratic management and the exercise of socialist relations in production.

These benefits are fundamentally obtained through the possibility that these socioeconomic organizations offer in regard to a change in the motivations and conditions required for effective work performance along with what is necessary to exercise and consolidate socialist values and behaviours. That means, that they allow us to satisfy our material needs without giving up our spiritual ones, which, in reality, are very tightly interwoven. So, these kinds of organizations allow us to break the low productivity/low income cycle and generate a high productivity/greater human development (material and spiritual) cycle that, as it is expanded into ever more workplaces, brings us ever closer to the socialist horizon.

Without a doubt, cooperative management is not a panacea applicable to all economic activities (it is not recommended for strategic activities and even some regarding basic necessities) or groups of people (you must have certain communication skills and trust, without which they function much the same as a regular business), nor can it resolve all problems on its own. Promoting cooperatives entails risks, such as private enterprises taking advantage of the legal framework only for the benefits they can glean from it, cooperatives formed by well-intentioned people that cannot achieve democratic management and distort the cooperative concept, as well as other antisocial behaviours that any non-state entity could display (Piñeiro Harnecker 2012b: 87–89).

For the cooperative model to bear fruit it requires 'cooperativists', people willing to put the cooperative principles into practice. They must fulfil their responsibilities and exercise their rights collectively, with common goals and not only out of individual interest; they must actively participate in decision-making, and democratic decision-making, which requires abilities and attitudes that are underdeveloped in our society: critical thinking, tolerance for different ideas, consensus building. Nevertheless, these abilities and attitudes are achieved through practice, meaning that cooperatives could be 'schools' of democratic participation, teamwork, solidarity and justice. If cooperatives function in accordance with identifying and organizational principles, they will build spaces where Cubans can develop those abilities and attitudes without which socialism cannot advance.

Regardless of all of the risks in promoting cooperatives, all of the requirements and the effort necessary for correct promotion, the cooperative is a useful tool and crucially important to solving numerous problems that exist in Cuba, not only economically, but culturally and socially as well. Many of these challenges can be overcome with the correct policies and the creation of institutions that support and guide without imposition (Piñeiro Harnecker 2011a).

Either way, in my opinion, the management model of Cuban cooperatives must be revised in light of the experiences of revolutionary cooperativism, multiple cooperatives and the solidarity economy, and more emphasis must be placed on the social contract and the need for guidance and in some cases control by the societal interests they impact.

Final thoughts

In order for the current process of cooperative promotion and consolidation in Cuba to be successful, the correct institutional conditions, both economically and culturally, must be created so that the formation of new cooperatives happens holistically and not in an improvised manner. We must make sure that new cooperatives have the minimum conditions needed for success, business-wise as well as socially (in particular cooperative education and supervision) and that they are allowed the time required to develop organizational culture. The push to form cooperatives from state enterprises must avoid the mistakes made in the formation of the UBPCs (above all related to training and voluntary will), as well as avoid becoming a way to leave workers unprotected that could be more productive if the enterprises simply improved, nor should consumers or the general public be affected by any antisocial behaviours of the new cooperatives (Piñeiro Harnecker 2012b, 2011a).

Cooperatives are a business model that is better prepared to simultaneously achieve goals that seem irreconcilable but – with effort and consistency – are possible to balance effectively: economic requirements with social aspirations, and business autonomy with social responsibility. In this way, cooperatives can contribute in the long run to the main goal of Cuba's current changes: to maintain achieved socialist gains while making them economically sustainable. In this way they can also bring the revolutionary process one step closer to a more socialist society.

20 The dialectic of constituent power and constituted power

Cliff DuRand

One of the persistent issues for the left has been whether we make fundamental change from below or from the top, by building the new society in small communities or from the state down, by changing our social relations and ourselves or by taking political power. This has been a longstanding debate between anarchists and Marxists, between advocates of social movements and advocates of political parties as the instrument of change, between horizontalism and verticalism.

In our times the first position was expressed by John Holloway in his 2002 book *Change the World without Taking Power* and is represented in the political practice of the Zapatistas. The second position is advanced by Gregory Wilpert in his 2007 book *Changing Venezuela by Taking Power* about Venezuela's Bolivarian Revolution. These two views look at power as coming from the people vs power as residing in the institutions of the state; constituent power vs constituted power. How you change society depends on where you see power lying.

As I reflect on current processes of social change in Venezuela, in Cuba and in Zapatista territory I have a sense that both sides of this classic debate are correct and a synthesis of them is emerging as the key to building a democratic socialism. Let me try to explain.

A rejuvenation of civil society has been key to democratic empowerment in the Zapatista areas of the Mexican state of Chiapas. There the constituent power of indigenous communities has recovered a traditional economy and constituted a new kind of state as an alternative to the surrounding nation-state. Participatory democratic institutions of good governance, *buen gobierno*, have been built in inward oriented *caracoles* (snails), with their own educational and health care systems, production cooperatives, credit unions, media and legal system. It is within these small autonomous territories that a cooperative alternative has been created that nurtures the human development of men and women. They have changed their world and themselves by taking back their own powers as communities.

This has been possible within the protected enclaves the Zapatistas have been able to create. They have been able to hold at bay the hostile power of the Mexican state that surrounds them. Based on their own model of social change they have refused to participate in the electoral politics of that larger society (cf. *Sixth Declaration of the Lacandon*). In the 2006 national elections they refused to participate, knowing that playing that corrupt game would only corrupt them. Instead they announced the Other Campaign, going throughout the country offering their podium to ordinary people to voice their grievances and ideas. Change must come from within civil society. The nation must be rebuilt from a rejuvenated civil society. That is their strategy for social change.

In the twentieth century the dominant model took the form of *state socialism*. An insurrection brought revolutionaries into state power. This made possible a rupture from the capitalist social formations in Russia, China and Cuba. With popular support, that state power was used to build socialism from the top down in the name of the working class. Institutions of central planning undertook the development of the material forces of production. What we saw was the historical emergence of what might be called developmental socialism that undertook to do what capitalism had failed to do. Its material accomplishments were remarkable – up to a point.

However, the accomplishments of state socialism in building new socialist relations of production were much more limited. In the case of the Soviet Union, Stalinism enforced a passive compliance on the population. In the case of the People's Republic of China, the revolutionary leadership had to create its own industrial working class who were dependent on the state and as a result lacked a revolutionary consciousness.

In the case of Cuba, four decades of mass mobilizations under a charismatic leader and a half-century of resistance to the siege by a powerful imperialist neighbour fostered a strong sense of national solidarity among the people. Institutions of mass participation in the state gave the Cuban model a democratic character so that it could truly claim to represent the interests of the working class. But it was still essentially a form of state socialism with its vertical structure that tended to turn popular participation into a passive participation. The state guaranteed people the basics for their livelihood, secure employment, health care, education, culture, etc. and in return the people gave it their loyalty. There were ample avenues for popular participation, but little space for initiative. The paternalistic state undertook to do everything. And as a result, rather than the state withering away, it was civil society that withered away. These are the harsh assessments of state socialism that one hears in Cuba today. A common saying is 'whatever is not regulated is prohibited'.

The renovation of socialism now under way in Cuba is an effort to reinvigorate civil society, opening up spaces for initiative outside of the state. A nonstate sector of the economy consisting of private businesses and cooperatives is being created. And in a few years it is projected to provide 35 per cent of employment and along with foreign and joint enterprises 45 per cent of the gross domestic product. Addressing the problem of the lack of worker incentives under state socialism, these reforms are unleashing new productive energies that will lift the economy. But beyond that they stand to replace the passive participation of state socialism with the protagonistic participation better suited to a democratic socialism. This implies a new relation between the state and civil society.

In a way this relation can be seen in the Bolivarian Revolution in Venezuela. With the popular election of Hugo Chávez, progressive forces had come into possession of a bourgeois state. What can be done under such decidedly non-revolutionary circumstances? It was not possible to expropriate the capitalist class and establish state socialism. What the Bolivarian Revolution evolved was a gradual empowerment of popular classes by directing state resources to them. Rather than acting for society in a paternalistic way, the state plays a more facilitating role to develop the capacities of civil society to direct the common affairs of the people. In Venezuela, the state provides resources to local levels to facilitate cooperatives and communal councils, thereby building constituent power. As the constituted power of society, the state is planting the seeds of an alternative economy and an alternative government along-side capitalist society and its representative institutions. In effect the state is creating a situation of dual power. Following the principle of subsidiarity, it empowers ordinary people collectively in their daily lives through partici-patory and protagonistic institutions of direct democracy. In so doing it is nurturing the seeds of a non-capitalist society within what is still a capitalist one. But equally important, it is developing non-capitalist sensibilities within civil society.

Something of the same thing can be seen in Cuba's renovation of its state socialism. This is particularly so with the promotion of urban cooperatives. Camila Piñeiro Harnecker reports in Chapter 19 that in the first 12 months, 498 new cooperatives have been formed, 77 per cent of them from former state enterprises, mostly in the food services area. State restaurants are notorious for their lackadaisical service by unmotivated workers, low quality of food and limited menu ('You can have anything you want on the menu as long as it is pizza or ham and cheese sandwich'). But now those former state workers who were on a fixed salary are cooperative members, they have an incentive to work better. In fact, in the 29 new cooperatives Camila has studied, incomes have increased an average of threefold and as much as sevenfold.

One of the new cooperatives I visited was a small bar/restaurant in a poor section of Central Havana. A former state enterprise, the Okinawa bar coop-erative has five members. It had been a cooperative for eight months before I visited it in June 2014 and the president told me that being able to make their own decisions is one of the greatest benefits they find. His fellow work-ers elected him. Interestingly, the former state manager, who is also a member, was not selected to lead the new cooperative.

The motivation engendered by this empowerment was dramatically dem-onstrated by a self-organized construction cooperative we met at the Institute of Philosophy. They were repairing the Institute building that had been badly damaged two years ago when the ceiling of the main first-floor room collapsed, rendering most of the building unusable. A state construction company had made little progress on the repairs for the past two years. But now the Institute has been able to engage this newly formed cooperative and in a short time they have made major progress. Our group was scheduled to have a meeting at the Institute on a Monday morning. And between the previous Thursday and that morning the ceiling had been rewired and plastered. And by the following week the Institute staff were moving back into their offices on the second floor. The 20 co-op members are motivated by the fact that for the first time they control their work. They make the decisions. This is a powerful demonstration of the strength of cooperatives.

What we are seeing with the promotion of new cooperatives in Cuba is the constituted power of the state nurturing constituent power in civil society. Cooperatives are a socialist form of property under democratic management. As such, cooperatives have the virtue of nurturing socialist values, responsibility, democratic decision-making, cooperation and social solidarity. They are *little schools of socialism.* They embed socialism into the daily life of working people, engendering a socialist civil society.

In this respect they contrast with the new petty bourgeois small and medium-sized private businesses now also being opened by the self-employed. A petty bourgeoisie is seen as compatible with socialism – compatible as long as it is regulated and taxed so it doesn't become a big bourgeoisie. Great inequalities of income and accumulation of wealth are to be avoided – a cautionary note made in the Guidelines. But it is clear a petty bourgeoisie is not socialist, it does not nurture a socialist consciousness, but the narrow mentality of the petty shopkeeper. It does not nurture socialist social relations but individualism. A petty bourgeoisie is compatible with socialism when kept within limits. But it is not socialist.

But cooperatives are socialist. They represent associated producers coming together on a small scale to govern their worklife in a democratic way. It is this relation that the socialist transition needs to point toward. With the current opening to cooperatives, Cuba's state socialism is finding a new road forward. Socialism cannot be built top down by state power alone. It has to be rooted at the base of society among ordinary people. Its values, its practices and its social relations have to be built into daily life where people live and work. This is the virtue of cooperatives. Cooperatives thus can help make socialism irreversible.

As Gramsci pointed out, the state penetrates down into civil society. Foucault takes this a step further with his notion of governmentality. This refers to those systems of control that extend even into the subjectivity of the human, into the self. This is what makes a social system self-governing and self-replicating. Cooperatives educate their members to the values and practices of a participatory socialism. This is more than an invigoration of civil society; it is also construction of a socialist governmentality in Foucault's deeper sense. It is a resocialization of workers away from their passivity under a paternalistic state socialism to protagonistic participants able to found society anew. Some Marxists see cooperatives as a step back from what they consider a more advanced state socialism, perhaps even a step toward capitalism. But my view is that it is a step forward toward a society ruled by the associated producers.[1]

If a social order is to be sustainable over the long run, it needs to be rooted in the character of the people. Their values, their sensibilities, their taken-for-granted understandings, their very subjectivity needs to be consonant with its institutions. The socialist transition is a process that needs a people with a socialist character if it is to continue. Socialism needs a socialist state, to be sure. But a socialist state needs a socialist people. The social relations of cooperatives help build such a character among the people.

That's why it is of the utmost importance that cooperatives be widely promoted. The benefits of cooperatives need to be publicized and training in cooperative practices needs to be available. There needs to be a network of *promotoras* who go out into society like the literacy workers in the early 1960s and teach the co-op way. Camila Piñeiro Harnecker's study of the first experimental urban cooperatives points to the need for cooperative education. She also calls for a supervising and support organization to assist cooperatives, ensuring their democratic character and mediating internal conflicts, as well as an organization that represents the cooperative sector to the state. A regulatory regime for the cooperative sector needs to be constructed. The socialist state is moving along this new road with caution, inventing it as they go. Hopefully as they learn from these initial steps and begin to realize the immense creative power of their socialist constituency, they too will be emboldened.

I am optimistic that Cuba is poised to become the first country with cooperatives as a major sector of its economy. Therein lies its world historical importance, as it invents a new socialist path, as it builds a socialism for the twenty-first century. In the midst of the present crisis of global capitalism, humanity needs the example of its success.

Note

1 In one of his rare characterizations of a future communist society, Marx said it would arise on the basis of 'an association of free men, working with the means of production held in common, and expending their many different forms of labor-power in full self-awareness as one single labor force'. This sounds much like a cooperative (*Capital, Volume 1*, Marx 1976: 171).

Bibliography

AA.VV. (1969) *Congresos de las internacionales socialistas, selección de documentos.* Siglomundo. Buenos Aires: CEAL.

Acea Terry, S. (2013) Significados éticos y políticos de la participación popular en los gobiernos locales en Cuba. Doctoral Thesis in Philosophy. Havana: Institute of Philosophy Library.

Acosta, A. (2012) Extractivism and Neoextractivism: Two Sides of the Same Curse. In Lang, M. and Mokrani, D. (eds). *Beyond Development: Alternative Visions from Latin America.* Quito: TNI/Rosa Luxemburg Foundation. pp. 61–86.

Aguinaga, M., Lang, M., Mokrani, D. and Santillana, A. (2012) Critiques and Alternatives to Development: A Feminist Perspective. In Lang, M. and Mokrani, D. (eds). *Beyond Development: Alternative Visions from Latin America.* Quito: TNI/Rosa Luxemburg Foundation. pp. 41–60.

Alayza, A and Gudynas, E. (eds) (2011) El Perú y el modelo extractivo: Agenda para un nuevo gobierno y necesarios escenarios de transición. *RedGE.* 24 March. Available from: http://redge.org.pe/node/637. [Accessed 14 August 2015].

Algranati, C. (2012) La ofensiva extractivista en América Latina. Crisis global y alternativas. *Herramienta.* 50. July. Available from: www.herramienta.com.ar/revista-herramienta-n-50/la-ofensiva-extractivista-en-america-latina-crisis-global-y-alternativas. [Accessed 14 August 2015].

Alperovitz, G. (2006) *America Beyond Capitalism: Reclaiming Our Wealth, Our Liberty, Our Democracy.* Hoboken, NJ: Wiley.

Alperovitz, G. (2013) *What Then Must We Do?: Straight Talk about the Next American Revolution.* White River Junction, VT: Chelsea Green.

Alperovitz, G. and Daly, L. (2009) *Unjust Deserts: How the Rich Are Taking Our Common Inheritance and Why We Should Take It Back.* New York: The New Press.

Amin, A. (ed.) (2009) *The Social Economy: International Perspectives on Economic Solidarity.* London: Zed Books.

Amin, S. (2014) Popular Movements Toward Socialism: Their Unity and Diversity. *Monthly Review.* 66 (2). pp. 1–31.

AN-DGIDL – Asamblea Nacional Dirección General de Investigación y Desarrollo Legislativo. (2007) *Ejes fundamentales del Proyecto de Reforma Constitucional. Consolidación del nuevo estado.* Caracas: AN-DGIDL.

Arnstein, S.R. (1969) A Ladder of Citizen Participation. *Journal of the American Planning Association.* 35 (4). pp. 216–224.

Aronowitz, S. (2006) *Left Turn: Forging a New Political Future.* Boulder, CO and London: Paradigm Publishers.

Arrighi, G. (1994) *The Long Twentieth Century: Money, Power, and the Origins of Our Time*. London: Verso.

Azzellini, D. (2010) *Partizipation, Arbeiterkontrolle und die Commune*. Hamburg: VSA.

Azzellini, D. (2012a) From Cooperatives to Enterprises of Direct Social Property in the Venezuelan Process. In Harnecker, C.P. (ed.). *Cooperatives and Socialism: A View from Cuba*. Basingstoke, UK: Palgrave Macmillan. pp. 259–276.

Azzellini, D. (2012b) Economía solidaria en Venezuela: Del apoyo al cooperativismo tradicional a la construcción de ciclos comunales. In Lianza, S. and Chedid Henriques, F. (eds). *A economia solidária na América Latina: Realidades nacionais e políticas públicas*. Rio de Janeiro: Pró Reitoria de Extensão UFRJ. pp. 147–160.

Azzellini, D. (2012c) De la cogestión al control obrero. Lucha de clases al interior del proceso bolivariano. PhD dissertation. Puebla, Mexico: Benemérita Universidad Autónoma de Puebla.

Azzellini, D. (2013) The Communal State: Communal Councils, Communes, and Workplace Democracy. *NACLA Report on the Americas*. 46 (1). pp. 25–30.

Barber, B.R. (2003) *Strong Democracy: Participatory Politics for a New Age*. Twentieth Anniversary Edition. Berkeley, CA: University of California Press.

Barnet, M.L. (2004) Book Review: Are Globalization and Sustainability Compatible?: A Review of the Debate between the World Business Council for Sustainable Development and the International Forum on Globalization. *Organization & Environment*. 17 (4). p. 523.

Barry, B. (2005) *Why Social Justice Matters*. Cambridge: Polity Press.

Basurto, X. and Ostrom, E. (2008, 2009) Beyond the Tragedy of the Commons. *Economia delle fonti di energia e dell'ambiente*. 52 (1). pp. 35–60.

Bauwens, M. (2012) The Triune Governance of the Digital Commons. In Bollier, D. and Helfrich, S. (eds). *The Wealth of the Commons*. Amherst, MA: Levelers Press. pp. 375–378.

Bauwens, M. and Iacomella, F. (2012) Peer-to-Peer Economy and New Civilization Centered around the Sustenance of the Commons. In Bollier, D. and Helfrich, S. (eds). *The Wealth of the Commons*. Amherst, MA: Levelers Press. pp. 323–330.

Beckert, J. (2012) *Capitalism as a System of Contingent Expectations: On the Microfoundations of Economic Dynamics*. MPIfG Working Paper 12/4. Cologne: Max Planck Institute for the Study of Societies.

Bellido Aguilera, O. and González Calzadilla, C. (2010) Consideraciones teórico-metodológicas acerca de la experiencia de trabajo comunitario en el Consejo Popular de Alcides Pino, Holguín. *Revista Cubana de Ciencias Sociales*. 43. July–December. pp. 35–45.

Bjork-James, C. (2013) Claiming Space, Redefining Politics: Urban Protest and Grassroots Power in Bolivia. PhD Dissertation. New York: Anthropology Department, CUNY.

Blauwhof, F.B. (2012) Overcoming Accumulation: Is a Capitalist Steady-State Economy Possible? *Ecological Economics*. 84. pp. 254–261.

Boff, L. (2009) ¿Vivir mejor o 'el Buen Vivir'? *Revista Fusión*. 3 April. Available from: www.revistafusion.com/20090403817/Firmas/Leonardo-Boff/ivivir-mejor-o-el-buen-vivir.htm. [Accessed 27 August 2015].

Boggs Jr., C. (1977) Revolutionary Process, Political Strategy, and the Dilemma of Power. *Theory & Society*. 4 (3). pp. 359–393.

Bollier, D. (2003) *Silent Theft: The Private Plunder of Our Common Wealth*. New York: Routledge.

Bollier, D. and Helfrich, S. (2012) *The Wealth of the Commons: A World beyond Market and State*. Amherst, MA: Levelers Press.

Bookchin, M. (1990) *Remaking Society*. Montreal: Black Rose Books.

Boron, A. (2013) Mercosur, Unasur and the Indecisión of Brazil. *ALAI – Latin America in Movement*. Available from: www.alainet.org/en/active/65639. [Accessed 27 August 2015].

Borzaga, C. and Mittone, L. (1997) *The Multi-Stakeholders Versus the Nonprofit Organization*. ISSAN Working Paper. Trento, Italy: University of Trento.

Bradsher, K. (2014) Solar Rises in Malaysia during Trade Wars over Panels. *New York Times*. 11 December. Available from: www.nytimes.com/2014/12/12/business/energy-environment/solar-rises-in-malaysia-during-trade-wars-over-panels.html?_r=0. [Accessed 27 August 2015].

Broué, P. and Témine, E. (1962) *La revolución y la guerra de España*. México: Fondo de Cultura Económica.

Brown, E. (2012) *The Web of Debt: The Shocking Truth about Our Money System and How We Can Break Free*. Fifth Edition. Baton Rouge, LA: Third Millennium Press.

Brown, E. (2013) *The Public Bank Solution: From Austerity to Prosperity*. Baton Rouge, LA: Third Millennium Press.

Brown, E. (2014) Wall Street Journal Reports: Bank of North Dakota Outperforms Wall Street. *Truth-Out*. 20 November. Available from: www.truth-out.org/news/item/27560-wall-street-journal-reports-bank-of-north-dakota-outperforms-wall-street. [Accessed 14 August 2015].

Brown, R., Giszpenc, N. and Van Slyke, B. (2014) Workers in Maine Buy Out Their Jobs, Set an Example for the Nation. *Yes! Magazine*. 30 September. Available from: www.yesmagazine.org/commonomics/workers-in-maine-buy-out-their-jobs-set-an-example-for-the-nation. [Accessed 14 August 2015].

Brynjolfsson, E. and MacCaffey, A. (2011) *Race against the Machine*. LaVergne, TN: Ingram Lightning Source.

Buglione, S. and Schlüter, R. (2010) *Solidarity-based and Co-Operative Economy and Ethical Business: Trends, Innovations, and Experiences in Europe*. Background Paper. Brussels: Rosa Luxembourg Foundation.

Burawoy, M., Blum, J.A., George, S., Gille, Z., Gowan, T., Haney, L., Klawiter, M., Lopez, S.H., Ó Riain, S. and Thayer, M. (2000) *Global Ethnography: Forces, Connections, and Imaginations in a Postmodern World*. Berkeley, CA: University of California Press.

Caffentzis, G. and Federici, S. (2013) Commons against and beyond Capitalism. *Upping the Anti: A Journal of Theory and Action*. 15. pp. 83–97 and *Community Development Journal*, Special Supplement. 49 (1). pp. 92–105.

Campos, P. (2007) Ejemplo cubano de socialización: la producción cooperativa cañera 1960–62. La Habana. August. Available from: www.oocities.org/es/amigos_pedroc/EjemploSocializacionII.html. [Accessed 27 August 2015].

Cassidy, J. (2010) What Good Is Wall Street? *The New Yorker*. 29 November. Available from: www.newyorker.com/magazine/2010/11/29/what-good-is-wall-street. [Accessed 21 August 2015].

Castoriadis, C. (1993) *Political and Social Writings, Volume 3, 1961–1979. Recommencing the Revolution: From Socialism to the Autonomous Society*. Minneapolis: University of Minnesota Press.

Castro, F. (2010) Mensaje de Fidel a los estudiantes. *CubaDebate*. 17 November. Available from: www.cubadebate.cu/especiales/2010/11/17/mensaje-de-fidel-a-los-estudiantes/#.Vc5bg4uJm-I. [Accessed 14 August 2015].

Castro, R. (2012a) *Discurso pronunciado por el General de Ejército Raúl Castro Ruz, Primer Secretario del Comité Central del Partido Comunista de Cuba y Presidente de los Consejos de Estado y de Ministros, en la clausura del IX Período Ordinario de Sesiones de la Asamblea Nacional del Poder Popular. Palacio de Convenciones. La Habana.* 23 July. Available from: www.cuba.cu/gobierno/rauldiscursos/2012/esp/r230712e.html. [Accessed 27 August 2015].

Castro, R. (2012b) *Discurso pronunciado por el General de Ejército Raúl Castro Ruz, Presidente de los Consejos de Estado y de Ministros, en la clausura del Sexto Período Ordinario de Sesiones de la Séptima Legislatura de la Asamblea Nacional del Poder Popular. La Habana.* 18 December 2010.

Cattani, A.D. (ed.). (2004) *La otra economía.* Buenos Aires: Altamira.

Cavanagh, J. and Mander, J. (eds). (2004) *Alternatives to Economic Globalization.* San Francisco, CA: Berrett-Koehler Publishers.

CEPAL – Comisión Económica Para América Latina y el Caribe. (2012) *La inversión extranjera directa en América Latina y el Caribe 2011.* Santiago de Chile: CEPAL.

Cerezal, M. (2013) Dialéctica de la integración latinoamericana. In Lang, M., López, C. and Santillana, A. (eds). *Alternativas al capitalismo-colonialismo del siglo XXI.* Quito: Rosa Luxemburg Foundation. pp. 101–128.

Cesarín, S. (2013) Mirando el futuro: América del Sur, integración, partición, o convergencia? *Revista do IMEA-UNILA.* 1 (2). pp. 114–122. Available from: https://ojs.unila.edu.br/index.php/IMEA-UNILA/article/download/186/183. [Accessed 27 August 2015].

Chatterton, P. (2012) Articulating Climate Justice in Copenhagen: Antagonism, the Commons, and Solidarity. *Antipode.* 45 (3). pp. 602–620.

Chávez, H. (2008) *El poder popular.* Caracas: Ministerio de Comunicación e Información.

Chávez, H. (2012) 'Propuesta del Candidato de la Patria Comandante Hugo Chávez para la Gestión Bolivariana Socialista 2013–2019'. Available from: www.chavez.org.ve/Programa-Patria-2013–2019.pdf. [Accessed 15 September 2012].

Chenery, H., Ahluwalia, M.S., Bell, C.L.G., Duloy, J.H. and Jolly, R. (1974) *Redistribution with Growth.* Oxford: Oxford University Press.

Citizens United v. Federal Election Commission, 558 U.S. (2010). *Opinion.* Justicia – US Supreme Court. Available from: https://supreme.justia.com/cases/federal/us/558/08-205/. [Accessed 14 August 2015].

Cleaver, H. (1994) The Chiapas Uprising and the Future of Class Struggle in the New World Order. Available from: http://la.utexas.edu/users/hcleaver/kcchiapasuprising.html. [Accessed 27 August 2015].

Cole, G.D.H. (1957) *Historia del pensamiento socialista. Tomo I, Los precursores 1789–1856.* Mexico: Fondo de Cultura Económica.

Cole, G.D.H. (1959) *Historia del pensamiento socialista, Tomo 3 La Segunda Internacional 1889–1914.* Mexico: Fondo de Cultura Económica.

Colectivo de autores (1996) *UBPC. Desarrollo y participación.* La Habana: Universidad de La Habana.

Coraggio, J.L. (1999) *De la economía de los sectores populares a la economía del trabajo.* Quito: ILDIS.

Coraggio, J.L. (2004) Una alternativa socioeconómica necesaria: La economía social. In Danani, C. (ed.). *Política social y economía social. Debates fundamentales.* Buenos Aires: Universidad Nacional de General Sarmiento and Editorial Altamira.

Craig, J.G. (1993) *The Nature of Co-operation.* Montreal: Black Rose Books.

Crary, J. (2013) *24/7: Late Capitalism and the Ends of Sleep*. London and New York: Verso.

Crooks, E. (2014) Exxon Warns Global Warming Targets 'Unlikely' to Be Met. *Financial Times*. 31 March. Available from: www.ft.com/intl/cms/s/0/67f73d56-b90a-11e3-a189-00144feabdc0.html. [Accessed 23 August 2015].

Cruz, J. (1997) Uniones municipales de cooperativas. *Revista Economía y Desarrollo*. 2.

Cruz, J. (2014) Cooperativas en Cuba. Presentación en el 1er Evento de Economía, Contabilidad y Gestión de la Universidad de La Habana. 3 October.

Curl, J. (2009) *For All the People: Uncovering the Hidden History of Cooperation, Cooperative Movements and Communalism in America*. Oakland, CA: PM Press.

Dahl, R.A. (1985) *A Preface to Economic Democracy*. Berkeley, CA: University of California Press.

Daly, H. (1997) *Beyond Growth: The Economics of Sustainable Development*. Boston, MA: Beacon Press.

Daly, H. (2005) Economics in a Full World. *Scientific American*. 293. pp. 100–107.

Dávalos, P. (2008) El 'Sumak Kawsay' ('Buen vivir') y las cesuras del desarrollo. *ALAI – América Latina en movimiento*. May. Available from: www.alainet.org/es/active/23920. [Accessed 17 August 2015].

Davidson, C. (2011) *New Paths to Socialism*. Pittsburgh: Changemaker Publications.

Day, R.J.F. (2004) *Gramsci Is Dead: Anarchist Currents in the Newest Social Movements*. London: Pluto.

Dean, A.B. (2013) Why Unions Are Going into the Co-op Business. *Yes! Magazine*. 5 March. Available from: www.yesmagazine.org/issues/how-cooperatives-are-driving-the-new-economy/union-co-ops. [Accessed 14 August 2015].

De Angelis, M. (2006) *The Beginning of History: Value Struggles and Global Capital*. London: Pluto Press.

De Angelis, M. (2012) Crises, Capital and Co-optation: Does Capital Need a Commons Fix? In Bollier, D. and Helfrich, S. (eds). *The Wealth of the Commons*. Amherst, MA: Levelers Press. pp. 184–191.

De Angelis, M. and Harvie, D. (2014) The Commons. In Parker, M., Cheney, G., Fournier V., and Land, C. (eds). *The Routledge Companion to Alternative Organization*. London: Routledge. pp. 280–294.

DeFilippis, J., Fisher, R. and Shragge, E. (2010) *Contesting Community: The Limits and Potential of Local Organizing*. New Brunswick, NJ: Rutgers University Press.

DeGraw, D. (2014) *The Economics of Revolution*. Available from: www.lulu.com/shop/david-degraw/the-economics-of-revolution/paperback/product-21813472.html. [Accessed 13 August 2015].

De Leon, C., Desai, M. and Tuğal, C. (2009) Political Articulation: Parties and the Constitution of Cleavages in the United States, India, and Turkey. *American Sociological Association*. 27 (3). pp. 193–219.

Delgado Guerra, S. and Leyva, A.I. (2012) Medidas para mejorar el funcionamiento de las UBPC. Autonomía básica para la producción cooperativa. *Granma*. 11 September. Available from: www.granma.cubaweb.cu/2012/09/11/nacional/artic02.html. [Accessed 27 August 2015].

Denis, R. (2001) *Los fabricantes de la rebelión*. Caracas: Primera Línea and Nuevo Sur.

De Pasquale, J. (2009) Personal interview. [Recorded and transcribed by Marcelo Vieta in July 2009].

De Peuter, G. and Dyer-Witheford, N. (2010) Commons and Cooperatives. *Affinities: A Journal of Radical Theory, Culture and Action*. 4 (1). pp. 30–56.

Diamond, J. (2012) *The World until Yesterday: What Can We Learn from Traditional Societies?* New York: Viking Press.

Diaz, B. (forthcoming) Cooperatives in the Enhancement of the Cuban Economic Model: The Challenge of Cooperative Education. *Latin American Perspectives*.

El Kilombo Intergalactica. (2007) *Beyond Resistance: Everything. An Interview with Subcomandante Insurgente Marcos*. Durham, NC: Paper Boat Press.

Escobar, A. (2010) Latin America at a Crossroads. *Cultural Studies*. 24 (1). pp. 1–65.

Esteva, G. (2013) *The Future of Development: A Radical Manifesto*. Bristol, UK: Policy Press.

Esteva, G. and Shanin, T. (2005) *Pensar todo de nuevo*. Oaxaca, Mexico: Ediciones ¡Basta!.

Evergreen Cooperative. (2014) About. Available from: http://evergreencooperatives.com/about/. [Accessed 13 August 2015].

EZLN – Ejército Zapatista de Liberación Nacional. (1996) *Crónicas intergalácticas EZLN*. Chiapas, Mexico: Planeta Tierra.

Farmer, P. (1979) Enjoying Language: An Adventure with Words. *The English Journal*. 68 (5). pp. 58–61.

Federici, S. (2004) *Caliban and the Witch: Women, the Body and Primitive Accumulation*. Brooklyn, NY: Autonomedia.

Federici, S. (2012) *Revolution at Point Zero: Housework, Reproduction and Feminist Struggle*. New York and Oakland, CA: Common Notions and PM Press.

Feenberg, A. (2002) *Transforming Technology*. Oxford: Oxford University Press.

Fernández, P. (2011) El sector agropecuario en el contexto de la economía cubana. Presentación del equipo de ACTAF. La Habana. 15 December.

Fernández Lorenzo, A. (2011) Metodología para el perfeccionamiento del sistema de gestión empresarial de las cooperativas de producción agropecuaria tabacaleras. Tesis presentada en opción al grado científico de Doctor en Ciencias Económicas. Pinar del Río, Cuba: Universidad de Pinar del Río.

Fernández Peiso, A. (2011) Notas características del marco legal del ambiente cooperativo cubano. In Piñeiro Harnecker, C. (ed.). *Cooperativas y socialismo: Una mirada desde Cuba*. La Habana: Ed. Caminos. pp. 366–396.

Fernández Ríos, O. (2014) Socialist Transition in Cuba: Economic Adjustments and Socio-political Challenges. *Latin American Perspectives*. 41 (4). pp. 48–63.

Flanders, L. (2014) How America's Largest Worker Owned Co-Op Lifts People Out of Poverty. *Yes! Magazine*. 14 August. Available from: www.yesmagazine.org/issues/the-end-of-poverty/how-america-s-largest-worker-owned-co-op-lifts-people-out-of-poverty. [Accessed 14 August 2015].

Folke, C., Carpenter, S.R., Walker, B., Scheffer, M., Chapin, T. and Rockström, J. (2010) Resilience Thinking: Integrating Resilience, Adaptability and Transformability. *Ecology and Society*. 15 (4). pp. 20–28.

Foster, J.B. (2015) Chávez and the Communal State: On the Transition to Socialism in Venezuela. *Monthly Review*. 66 (11).

Foster, J.B. and Clark, B. (2012) The Planetary Emergency. *Monthly Review*. 64 (7). pp. 1–25.

Foster, J.B. and Magdoff, F. (2009) *The Great Financial Crisis: Causes and Consequences*. New York: Monthly Review Press. pp. 111–141.

Foucault, M. (2006) *Los anormales*. México: FCE.

Francis, Pope (2015) Encyclical Letter 'Praised Be' ('Laudato Si') of The Holy Father Francis On Care for Our Common Home. Available from: http://w2.vatican.va/content/dam/francesco/pdf/encyclicals/documents/papa-francesco_20150524_enciclica-laudato-si_en.pdf. [Accessed 14 August 2015].

Franks, B. (2006) *Rebel Alliances: The Means and Ends of Contemporary British Anarchisms.* Oakland, CA: AK Press.

Franks, B. (2010) Vanguards and Paternalism. In Nun, J. and Wahl, S. (eds). *New Perspectives on Anarchism.* Plymouth, UK: Lexington Books. pp. 99–120.

Gaiger, L.I. and Dos Anjos, E. (2011) Economía solidaria en Brasil: La actualidad de las cooperativas para la emancipación histórica de los trabajadores. In Piñeiro Harnecker, C. (ed.). *Cooperativas y socialismo: Una mirada desde Cuba.* La Habana: Editores Caminos. pp. 245–271.

Gallagher, K.P., Irwin, A. and Koleski, K. (2012) *The New Banks in Town: Chinese Finance in Latin America.* Inter-American Dialogue Report. February. Available from: http://ase.tufts.edu/gdae/Pubs/rp/GallagherChineseFinanceLatinAmerica.pdf. [Accessed 4 January 2015].

Gibson-Graham, J.K. (2003) Enabling Ethical Economies: Cooperativism and Class. *Critical Sociology.* 29 (2). pp. 123–161.

Gibson-Graham, J.K. (2006) *A Postcapitalist Politics.* Minneapolis: University of Minnesota Press.

Gil Beróes, A. (2010) Los Consejos Comunales deberán funcionar como bujías de la economía socialista. *Rebelión.* Available from: www.rebelion.org/noticia. php?id=98094. [Accessed 4 January 2015].

Gillis, J. (2014) UN Climate Panel Warns Speedier Action Is Needed to Avert Disaster. *New York Times.* 13 April. p. A1. Available from: www.nytimes.com/2014/04/14/science/earth/un-climate-panel-warns-speedier-action-is-needed-to-avert-disaster. html. [Accessed 17 August 2015].

Gindin, S. (2014) Unmaking Global Capitalism. *Jacobin.* 14. June. Available from: www.jacobinmag.com/2014/06/unmaking-global-capitalism. [Accessed 20 August 2015].

Golinger, E. (2006) *The Chávez Code: Cracking U.S. Intervention in Venezuela.* Northampton, MA: Olive Branch Press.

González, C. (2005) Radio interview. In Vieta, M. (ed.). *There's No Stopping the Workers: Crisis,* Autogestión, *and Argentina's Worker-recuperated Enterprises.* Leiden and Chicago: Brill and Haymarket Books.

Gordon, J.R. (2012) *Is U.S. Economic Growth Over? Faltering Innovation Confronts the Six Headwinds.* NBER Working Paper Series. No. 18315. Cambridge, MA: National Bureau of Economic Research.

Graeber, D. (2009) *Direct Action: An Ethnography.* Oakland, CA: AK Press.

Gramsci, A. (1971) *Selections from the Prison Notebooks.* New York: International Publishers.

Gray, R. (2013) Ecuador Rebrands Itself as the Home of Internet Freedom. *BuzzFeed News.* 6 December. Available from: www.buzzfeed.com/rosiegray/ecuador-bids-to-be-seen-as-the-home-of-internet-freedom. [Accessed 24 August 2015].

Gudynas, E. (2012) Transitions to Post-extractivism: Directions, Options, Areas of Action. In Lang, M. and Mokrani, D. (eds). *Beyond Development: Alternative Visions from Latin America.* Quito: TNI/Rosa Luxemburg Foundation. pp. 165–188.

Gudynas, E. (2013) Transiciones hacia un nuevo regionalism autonomo. In Lang, M., López, C. and Santillana, A. (eds). *Alternativas al capitalismo-colonialismo del siglo XXI.* Quito: Rosa Luxemburg Foundation. pp. 129–160.

Gudynas, E. (2014) Integración regional y materias primas. *La Primera.* 9 January. Available from: www.laprimeraperu.pe/online/columnistas-y-colabouradores/integracion-regional-y-materias-primas_159394.html. [Accessed 28 August 2015].

Gudynas, E. and Acosta, A. (2012) La renovación de la crítica al desarrollo y el buen vivir como alternativa. *Journal of Sustainable Education*. March. Available from: www.jsedimensions.org/wordpress/content/la-renovacion-de-la-critica-al-desarrollo-y-el-buen-vivir-como-alternativa_2012_03. [Accessed 24 August 2015].

Gustafson, R. (2013) Close the NGOs: Asserting Sovereignty or Eroding Democracy? *NACLA Online Column: Extractives in Latin America*. 31 December. Available from: https://nacla.org/blog/2013/12/31/close-ngos-asserting-sovereignty-or-eroding-democracy. [Accessed 24 August 2015].

Haiven, M. (2014) *Crises of Imagination, Crises of Power: Capitalism, Creativity and the Commons*. London: Zed Books.

Hanauer, N. (2014) The Pitchforks Are Coming... For Us Plutocrats. *Politico Magazine*. 26 June. Available from: www.politico.com/magazine/story/2014/06/the-pitchforks-are-coming-for-us-plutocrats-108014.html#.VOItmVJ0zcs. [Accessed 23 August 2015].

Hansen, J., Kharecha, P., Sato, M., Masson-Delmotte, V., Ackerman, F., Beerling, D.J., Hearty, P.J., Hoegh-Guldberg, O., Hsu, S.-L., Parmesan, C., Rockstrom, J., Rohling, E.J., Sachs, J., Smith, P., Steffen, K., Van Susteren, L., von Schuckmann, K. and Zachos, J.C. (2013) Assessing 'Dangerous Climate Change: Required Reduction of Carbon Emissions to Protect Young People, Future Generations and Nature'. *PLOS One*. 8 (12). pp. 1–26.

Hardin, G. (1968) The Tragedy of the Commons. *Science*. 162. pp. 1243–1248.

Harnecker, M. (2010) Twenty-First Century Socialism. *Monthly Review*. 62 (3). Available from: http://monthlyreview.org/2010/07/01/ii-twenty-first-century-socialism. [Accessed 18 August 2015].

Harnecker, M. (2015) *A World to Build: New Paths toward Twenty-First Century Socialism*. New York: Monthly Review Press.

Harvey, D. (2003) *The New Imperialism*. Oxford: Oxford University Press.

Harvey, D. (2005) *A Brief History of Neoliberalism*. Oxford: Oxford University Press.

Harvey, D. (2006) Space as a Keyword. In Castree, N. and Gregory, D. (eds). *David Harvey: A Critical Reader*. Malden, MA: Blackwell. pp. 270–294.

Harvey, D. (2008) The Right to the City. *New Left Review*. 53. September/October. pp. 23–40. Available from: http://newleftreview.org/II/53/david-harvey-the-right-to-the-city. [Accessed 23 August 2015].

Harvey, D. (2012) *Rebel Cities*. London and New York: Verso.

Havel, V. (2011) Never Hope against Hope. *Esquire*. 19 December. Available from: www.esquire.com/news-politics/news/a12135/vaclav-havel-hope-6619552/. [Accessed 14 August 2015].

Hawken, P. (1993) *The Ecology of Commerce*. New York: Harper.

Hayden, T. (2014) Environmentalists, Capitalists Should Broker Green New Deal. *San Francisco Chronicle*. 8 July. Available from: www.sfgate.com/opinion/article/Environmentalists-capitalists-should-broker-5599215.php. [Accessed 13 August 2015].

Hedges, C. (2014) The Myth of Human Progress and the Collapse of Complex Societies. *Truthdig*. 26 January. Available from: www.truthdig.com/report/item/chris_hedges_jan_27_column_transcript_collapse_of_complex_societies_2014012. [Accessed 14 August 2015].

Heilbroner, R.L. and Milberg, W.S. (1998) *The Making of Economic Society*. Upper Saddle River, NJ: Prentice Hall.

Heinberg, R. (2011) *The End of Growth: Adapting to Our New Economic Reality*. Gabriola Island, British Columbia: New Society Publishers.

Helman, C. (2014) The Billionaire Oilman Fueling America's Recovery. *Forbes*. 5 May (print) / 16 April (web). Available from: www.forbes.com/sites/christopherhelman/2014/04/16/harold-hamm-billionaire-fueling-americas-recovery/. [Accessed 26 August 2015].

Hernández Navarro, L. (2004) Autonomía sin pedir permiso. *La Jornada*. 7 September. Available from: www.jornada.unam.mx/2004/09/07/023a1pol.php?origen=opinion. php&fly=1. [Accessed 14 August 2015].

Hinkelammert, F.J. and Mora Jiménez, H. (2005) *Hacia una economía para la vida: Preludio a una reconstrucción de la economía*. San José, Costa Rica: DEI.

Hobsbawm, E. (1964). *Labouring Men: Studies in the History of Labour*. London: Basic Books.

Hodgson, G.M., Itoh, M. and Yokokawa, N. (eds) (2001) *Capitalism in Evolution: Global Contentions, East and West*. Cheltenham, UK: Edward Elgar.

Hollender, R. and Shultz, J. (2010) *Bolivia and Its Lithium: Can the 'Gold of the 20th Century' Help Lift a Nation out of Poverty?* Cochabamba, Bolivia: The Democracy Center. Available from: http://democracyctr.org/pdf/DClithiumfullreportenglish. pdf. [Accessed 27 August 2015].

Holloway, J. (2002) *Change the World without Taking Power*. Ann Arbor, MI: Pluto Press.

Horvat, B. (1982) *The Political Economy of Socialism: A Marxist Social Theory*. Armonk, NY: M.E. Sharpe.

Ibáñez, A. (2012) Un acercamiento al 'buen vivir'. *Xipe Totek*. 22. (2). May. Available from: http://xipetotek.iteso.mx/contenido/un-acercamiento-al-buen-vivir. [Accessed 22 August 2015].

Illich, I. (1973) *Tools for Conviviality*. New York: Harper and Row.

Jackson, T. (2009) *Prosperity without Growth: Economics for a Finite Planet*. London: Earthscan.

Jasper, W. (2014) Risky Business: Billionaires Hype Climate for Power and Profit. *The New American*. 12 August. Available from: www.thenewamerican.com/tech/environment/item/18899-risky-business-billionaires-hype-climate-for-power-and-profit. [Accessed 15 August 2015].

Jiménez, R. (2002) Diagnostico del estado actual de la educación cooperativa en el sector de las Unidades Básicas de Producción Cooperativa: desarrollo y expectativas. In *Documento de trabajo*. La Habana: Programa FLACSO-Cuba.

Jiménez, R. (2003) El cooperativismo cubano: Historia, presente y perspectiva. *Revista UniR coop. Red Universitaria de las Américas en estudios Cooperativos y Asociativismo*. 1 (2). pp. 178–200.

Jones, V. (2008) *The Green Collar Economy*. New York: Harper One.

Kaufman, C. (2012) *Getting Past Capitalism: History, Vision, Hope*. New York: Lexington Books.

Khasnabish, A. (2008) *Zapatismo beyond Borders: New Imaginations of Political Possibility*. Toronto: University of Toronto Press.

Kropotkin, P. (1989) *Mutual Aid: A Factor of Evolution*. Montreal: Black Rose Books.

Krugman, P. (2008) *The Return of Depression Economics and the Crisis of 2008*. New York: Norton.

Krugman, P. (2009) The Jobs Imperative. *New York Times*. 29 November. Available from: www.nytimes.com/2009/11/30/opinion/30krugman.html?_r=0. [Accessed 18 August 2015].

Kurzweil, R. (1999) *The Age of Spiritual Machines: When Computers Exceed Human Intelligence*. New York: Viking Press.

Lang, M. (2013) Por qué buscar alternativas? In Lang, M., López, C. and Santillana, A. (eds). *Alternativas al Capitalismo del Siglo XXI*. Quito: Grupo Permanente de Trabajo sobre Alternativas al Desarrollo. pp. 7–24.

Langer, E. (2011) *The Green Economy: The Wolf in Sheep's Clothing*. Amsterdam: Transnational Institute. Available from: www.tni.org/files/download/green-economy.pdf. [Accessed 27 August 2015].

Larrabure, M., Vieta, M. and Schugurensky, D. (2011) The 'New Cooperativism' in Latin America: Worker-recuperated Enterprises and Socialist Production Units. *Studies in the Education of Adults*. 43 (2). pp. 81–196.

Laville, J.L. (2011) *What Is the Third Sector? From the Non-Profit Sector to the Social and Solidarity Economy: Theoretical Debate and European Reality*. EMES European Research Network Working Paper. 11 (01). Available from: http://emes. net/publications/working-papers/what-is-the-third-sector-from-the-non-profit-sector-to-the-social-and-solidarity-economy-theoretical-debate-and-european-reality/. [Accessed 28 August 2015].

Lebowitz, M.A. (2005) Constructing Co-management in Venezuela: Contradictions along the Path. Talk delivered at El Encuentro Nacional de Trabajadores Hacia la Recuperación de Empresas (the National Meeting of Workers for the Recovery of Enterprises). 22 October. Unión Nacional de Trabajadores. Caracas, Venezuela / *Monthly Review*. Available from: http://mrzine.monthlyreview.org/lebowitz241005. html. [Accessed 23 August 2015].

Lebowitz, M.A. (2006) *Build It Now: Socialism for the Twenty-First Century*. New York: Monthly Review Press.

Lebowitz, M.A. (2010) *The Socialist Alternative: Real Human Development*. New York: Monthly Review Press.

Lebowitz, M.A. (2012) *The Contradictions of Real Socialism: The Conductor and the Conducted*. New York: Monthly Review Press.

Lebowitz, M.A. (2014) Proposing a Path to Socialism: Two Papers for Hugo Chávez. *Monthly Review*. 65 (10). Available from: http://monthlyreview.org/2014/03/01/proposing-path-socialism-two-papers-hugo-chavez/. [Accessed 25 August 2015].

Lebowitz, M.A. (2015) *The Socialist Imperative: From Gotha to Now*. New York: Monthly Review Press.

Leff, E. (2006) La ecología política en América Latina. Un campo en construcción. In Alimonda, H. (ed.). *Los tormentos de la materia. Aportes para una ecología política latinoamericana*. Buenos Aires: CLACSO. pp. 21–39.

Lester, R.A. (1938) Currency Issues to Overcome Depressions in Pennsylvania, 1723 and 1729. *Journal of Political Economy*. 46 (3). pp. 324–375. Available from: www. jstor.org/stable/1824000. [Accessed 14 August 2015].

Linebaugh, P. (2008) *The Magna Carta Manifesto: Liberties and Commons for All*. Berkeley, CA: University of California Press.

López, E. and Vértiz, F. (2012) Capital transnacional y proyectos nacionales de desarrollo en América Latina: Las nuevas lógicas del extractivismo neodesarrollista. *Herramienta*. 50. July. Available from: www.herramienta.com.ar/revista-herramienta-n-50/capital-transnacional-y-proyectos-nacionales-de-desarrollo-en-america-latin. [Accessed 23 August 2015].

Lovins, A. and Lovins, L.H. (1997) *Factor Four: Doubling Wealth – Halving Resource Use*. London: Earthscan.

Luxemburg, R. (2004) Social Reform or Revolution? In Hudis, P. and Anderson, K.B. (eds). *The Rosa Luxemburg Reader*. New York: Monthly Review Press. pp. 128–167.

McManus, D. (2008) Americans Reluctant to Bail Out Wall Street. *Los Angeles Times*. 24 September. Available from: http://articles.latimes.com/2008/sep/24/nation/na-econpoll24. [Accessed 27 August 2015].

McMurtry, J. (1999) *The Cancer Stage of Capitalism*. London: Pluto.

Magdoff, F. (2013) Global Resource Depletion: Is Population the Problem? *Monthly Review*. 64 (8). pp. 13–28.

Magnani, E. and Semenzin, M. (2013) Fabbriche Recuperate. *Pagina 12*. 26 May. Available from: www.pagina12.com.ar/diario/suplementos/cash/17-6846-2013-05-26.html. [Accessed 17 October 2014].

Malleson, T. (2010) Cooperatives and the 'Bolivarian Revolution' in Venezuela. *Affinities: A Journal of Racial Theory, Culture, and Action*. 4 (1). pp. 155–175. Available from: http://journals.sfu.ca/affinities/index.php/affinities/article/view/28/125. [Accessed 22 August 2015].

Mance, E.A. (2007) Solidarity Economics. *Turbulence: Ideas for Movement*. Available from: http://turbulence.org.uk/turbulence-1/solidarity-economics/. [Accessed 16 August 2015].

Mandel, E. (1973) *Control obrero, consejos obreros, autogestión. Antología*. Buenos Aires: Ediciones La Ciudad Futura.

Marcuse, H. (1964) *One-dimensional Man: Studies in the Ideology of Advanced Industrial Society*. Boston, MA: Beacon Press.

Marcuse, H. (1969) *An Essay on Liberation*. Boston, MA: Beacon Press.

Marshall, P. (1992). *Demanding the Impossible: A History of Anarchism*. London: HarperCollins.

Martínez, L. and Puig, Y. (2014) Sesionó reunión del Consejo de Ministros. Fueron aprobadas varias políticas y medidas para la actualización del modelo económico cubano. *Granma*. 26 October. Available from: www.granma.cu/cuba/2014-10-26/sesiono-reunion-del-consejo-de-ministros. [Accessed 28 August 2015].

Martínez-Alier, J. (2002) *The Environmentalism of the Poor: A Study of Ecological Conflicts and Valuation*. Cheltenham, UK: Edward Elgar.

Marx, K. (1976) *Capital, Volume 1*. London: Penguin.

Marx, K. (1994) Private Property and Communism. In Simon, L. (ed.). *Karl Marx: Selected Writings*. Indianapolis, IN: Hackett. pp. 68–78.

Marx, K. and Engels, F. (1848) Manifesto of the Communist Party. In Tucker, R. (ed.). *The Marx-Engels Reader*. (1972). New York: Norton. pp. 331–362.

Marx, K. and Engels, F. (1988) *The Communist Manifesto*. New York: Norton.

Massey, D. (2009) Concepts of Space and Power in Theory and in Political Practice. *Documents d'Anàlisi Geogràfica*. 55, pp. 15–26. Available from: www.raco.cat/index.php/DocumentsAnalisi/article/view/171747/224065. [Accessed 29 August 2015].

Max-Neef, M. (1993) *Desarrollo a escala humana: Conceptos, reflexiones y algunas aplicaciones*. Barcelona: ICARIA.

Melville, H. (1961) Bartleby, the Scrivener: A Story of Wall Street. In *Billy Budd and The Piazza Tales*. Garden City, NY: Doubleday & Company.

Mendizábal, A. and Errasti, A. (2008) Premisas teóricas de la autogestión. Paper presented at the EcoCri 2008: XI Jornadas de Economía Crítica conference. Bilbao, Basque Country.

Mészáros, I. (1995) *Beyond Capital: Toward a Theory of Transition*. London: Merlin Press.

Midnight Notes Collective. (1992) *Midnight Oil: Work, Energy, War, 1973–1992*. Brooklyn, NY: Autonomedia.

Midnight Notes Collective. (2001) *Auroras of the Zapatistas: Local and Global Struggles in the Fourth World War*. Brooklyn, NY: Autonomedia.

Midnight Notes Collective and Friends. (2009) *Promissory Notes: From Crisis to Commons*. Available from: www.midnightnotes.org/Promissory%20Notes.pdf. [Accessed 14 August 2015].

Miller, A. and Hopkins, R. (2013) *Climate after Growth: Why Environmentalists Must Embrace Post-Growth Economics and Community Resilience*. Santa Rosa, CA: Post Carbon Institute and Transition Network. Available from: www.postcarbon.org/publications/climate-after-growth/. [Accessed 13 August 2015].

Miller, E. and Albert, M. (2009) Post-capitalist Alternatives: New Perspectives on Economic Democracy. *Socialist Renewal Publishing Project*. (GEO) Collective. Available from: www.readingfromtheleft.com/PDF/SRPP/PostCapAlternatives. pdf. [Accessed 12 August 2015].

MinCI – Ministerio del Poder Popular para la Comunicación y la Información (2007) *Líneas generales del Plan de Desarrollo Económico y Social de la Nación 2007–2013*. Caracas: MinCI.

Monge, C. (2011) Entre Río y Río: El apogee y la crisis del extractivismo neoliberal y los retos del postextractivismo en el Perú. In Alayza, A. and Gudynas, E. (eds). *Transiciones y alternativas al extractivismo en la región andina: Una mirada desde Bolivia, Ecuador y Perú*. Red Peruana por una Globalización con Equidad. pp. 75–100. Available from: www.redge.org.pe/sites/default/files/PDF%20FINAL%20 VB%202013%20TEXTO%20COMPLETO.pdf. [Accessed 22 August 2015].

Monzón, R. (2012) El movimiento cooperativo en el sistema agropecuario cubano. Presented at the XIth Convención Internacional COOPERAT. La Habana, Cuba. 7 March.

Mookerjea, S. (2010) The Sangham Strategy: Lessons for a Cooperative Mode of Production. *Affinities: A Journal of Radical Theory, Culture and Action*. 4 (1). pp. 110–132. Available from: http://journals.sfu.ca/affinities/index.php/affinities/ article/view/46/155. [Accessed 28 August 2015].

Moreno, C. (2012) Las ropas verdes del rey: La economía verde: una nueva fuente de acumulación primitiva. In Lang, M., López, C. and Santillana, A. (eds). *Alternativas al capitalismo-colonialismo del siglo XXI*. Quito: Rosa Luxemburg Foundation. pp. 63–100.

Mosca, G. (1960) *The Ruling Class Elementi di Scienze Politica*. New York: McGraw-Hill.

Negri, A. (1992) *Il potere costituente*. Carnago, Italy: Sugarco Edizioni.

Neill, M. (2001) Rethinking Class Composition Analysis in Light of the Zapatistas. In Midnight Notes Collective (ed.). *Auroras of the Zapatistas: Local and Global Struggles in the Fourth World War*. Brooklyn, NY: Autonomedia. pp. 119–143.

Ness, I. and Azzellini, D. (2011) *Ours to Master and to Own: Workers' Control from the Commune to the Present*. Chicago: Haymarket Books.

Neuman, W. (2014) Turnabout in Bolivia as Economy Rises from Instability. *New York Times*. 16 February. Available from: www.nytimes.com/2014/02/17/world/ americas/turnabout-in-bolivia-as-economy-rises-from-instability.html?_r=0. [Accessed 17 August 2015].

New York Times (Editorial Board). (2014) Running Out of Time. *New York Times*. 21 April (print) / 20 April (online). p. A20. Available from: www.nytimes.com/2014/04/ 21/opinion/running-out-of-time.html. [Accessed 14 August 2015].

Ngai Pun Cham, J. and Selden, M. (2013) The Politics of Global Production: Apple, Foxconn and China's New Working Class. *The Asia-Pacific Journal.* 11 (32). No. 2. 12 August. Available from: www.japanfocus.org/-Pun-Ngai/3981/article.html. [Accessed 12 August 2015].

Noble, D. (1993) *Progress without People: In Defence of Luddism.* Chicago: Charles H. Kerr.

Nova, A. (2011) Las cooperativas agropecuarias en Cuba: 1959-presente. In Piñeiro Harnecker, C. (ed.). *Cooperativas y Socialismo: Una mirada desde Cuba.* Habana: Ediciones Caminos. pp. 321–336.

Nova, A. (2012) La economía cubana a las puertas de un nuevo cooperativismo. *IPS.* 5 March. Available from: www.ipscuba.net/espacios/por-su-propio-peso/con-lupa/la-economia-cubana-a-las-puertas-de-un-nuevo-cooperativismo/. [Accessed 18 August 2015].

Novaes, H.T. (2011) *O retorno do caracol a sua concha: alienaçao e desalienaçao em associacioes de trabalhadores.* Sao Paulo: Editora Expressao Popular.

Obama, B. (2006) *The Audacity of Hope: Thoughts on Reclaiming the American Dream.* New York: Crown Publishers.

O'Connor, J. (2014) James O'Connor: Selling Nature. Online supplement to Allan, K.D. (ed.). *Contemporary Social and Sociological Theory: Visualizing Social Worlds.* Thousand Oaks, CA: Sage Publications. Available from: www.sagepub.com/upmdata/13298_Chapter_9_Web_Byte_James_O'Connor.pdf. [Accessed 20 August 2015].

Omi, M. and Winant, H. (2014) *Racial Formation in the United States.* Third edition. New York: Routledge.

Ortiz, I., Burke, S.L., Berrada, M. and Cortes, H. (2013) *World Protests 2006–2013.* Working Paper No. 2013. Initiative for Policy Dialogue and Friedrich-Ebert-Stiftung New York. Available from: http://ssrn.com/abstract=2374098. [Accessed 22 August 2015].

Ostrom, E. (1990) *Governing the Commons: The Evolution of Institutions for Collective Action.* New York: Cambridge University Press.

Panitch, L. (2008) *Renewing Socialism: Transforming Democracy, Strategy and Imagination.* Pontypool, UK: The Merlin Press.

Panitch, L. and Gindin, S. (2012) *The Making of Global Capitalism: The Political Economy of American Empire.* London and New York: Verso.

Parker, M., Cheney, G., Fournier, V. and Land, C. (eds). (2014) *The Routledge Companion to Alternative Organization.* London: Routledge.

Parramore, L. (2014) How Piketty's Bombshell Book Blows Up Libertarian Fantasies. *Alternet.* 28 April. Available from: www.alternet.org/economy/how-pikettys-bombshell-book-blows-libertarian-fantasies. [Accessed 21 August 2015].

Pastore, R.E. (2010) Un panorama del resurgimiento de la economía social y solidaria en la Argentina. *SocioEco.* Available from: www.socioeco.org/bdf_fiche-document-834_en.html. [Accessed 22 August 2015].

Peixoto de Albuquerque, P. (2004) Autogestión. In Cattani, A.D. (ed.). *La otra economía.* Buenos Aires: Editorial Altamira. pp. 39–46.

Perkins, P.E. (2003) Social Diversity, Globalization and Sustainability in Community-Based Economics. *Canadian Woman Studies.* 23 (1). pp. 38–45. Available from: http://cws.journals.yorku.ca/index.php/cws/article/view/6356/5544. [Accessed 27 August 2015].

Perkins, P.E. (2007) Feminist Ecological Economics and Sustainability. *Journal of Bioeconomics.* 9 (3). pp. 227–244.

Peters, P. (2012) The New Cooperatives Law (summary). 12 December. Available from: http://cubantriangle.blogspot.ca/2012/12/the-new-cooperatives-law.html. [Accessed 14 August 2015]. Full text published in the *Gaceta Oficial de la República de Cuba*. 11 December. Available from: www.fgr.cu/sites/default/files/Decreto%20 Ley%20305%20y%20306.pdf. [Accessed 14 August 2015].

Picketty, T. (2013) *Capital in the Twenty-First Century*. Cambridge, MA: The Belknap Press of Harvard University Press.

Pieterse, J.N. (1996) *My Paradigm or Yours? Alternative Development, Post-development, Reflexive Development*. ISS Working Paper 229.

Piñeiro Harnecker, C. (ed.) (2011a) *Cooperativas y socialismo: una mirada desde Cuba*. Havana: Editorial Caminos.

Piñeiro Harnecker, C. (2011b) Empresas no estatales en la economía cubana: potencialidades, requerimientos y riesgos. *Revista Universidad de La Habana*. 272. pp. 45–65.

Piñeiro Harnecker, C. (2012a) Las cooperativas en el nuevo modelo económico. In Vidal, P. and Pérez, O.E. (eds). *Miradas a la economía cubana: El proceso de actualización*. Habana: Ed. Camino. pp. 75–96.

Piñeiro Harnecker, C. (2012b) An Introduction to Cooperatives. In Piñeiro Harnecker, C. (ed.). *Cooperatives and Socialism: A View from Cuba*. London, Palgrave Macmillan. pp. 25–45.

Piñeiro Harnecker, C. (ed.). (2013a) *Cooperatives and Socialism: A View from Cuba*. New York: Palgrave Macmillan.

Piñeiro Harnecker, C. (2013b) *Repensando el socialismo Cubano: Propuestas para una economia democratica y cooperativa*. La Habana: Ruth Casa Editorial.

Piñeiro Harnecker, C. (2014) Cooperativas no agropecuarias en La Habana. Diagnóstico preliminary. In Centro de Estudios de la Economía Cubana (CEEC) (ed.). *Economia Cubana: Transformaciones y desafios*. La Habana: Editorial Ciencias Sociales. pp. 291–334.

Piven, F.F. (2006) *Challenging Authority: How Ordinary People Change America*. Lanham, MD: Rowman and Littlefield.

Polanyi, K. (1957 [1944]) *The Great Transformation: The Political and Economic Origins of Our Time*. Boston, MA: Beacon Press.

Porcaro, M. (2013a) Occupy Lenin. In Panitch, L., Albo, G. and Chibber, V. (eds). *Socialist Register 2013: The Question of Strategy*. New York: Monthly Review Press. pp. 84–97.

Porcaro, M. (2013b) A New Type of Art: From Connective to Strategic Party. *Rosa Luxemburg Stiftung: Gesellschaftsanalyse und Linke Praxis*. Berlin. Available from: www.socialistproject.ca/bullet/868.php. [Accessed 22 August 2015].

Posner, R.A. (2010) *The Crisis of Capitalist Democracy*. Cambridge, MA: Harvard University Press.

Przeworski, A. (1993) *Capitalism and Social Democracy*. Cambridge: Cambridge University Press.

Purcell, M. (2006) Urban Democracy and the Local Trap. *Urban Studies*. 43 (11). pp. 1921–1940.

Rama, C.M. (1962) *Revolución social en el siglo veinte*. Montevideo: Nuestro Tiempo.

Ratner, C. (2015) Neoliberal Co-optation of Leading Co-op Organizations, and a Socialist Counter-Politics of Cooperation. *Monthly Review*. 66 (9). Available from: http://monthlyreview.org/2015/02/01/neoliberal-co-optation-of-leading-co-op-organizations-and-a-socialist-counter-politics-of-cooperation/. [Accessed 24 August 2015].

Rebick, J. (2014) Long Live Occupy: Occupy Three Years Later. *InterOccupy*. 16 October. Available from: http://interoccupy.net/blog/long-live-occupy-occupy-three-years-later/. [Accessed 14 August 2015].

Reed Jr., A. (2014) Nothing Left: The Long, Slow Surrender of American Liberals. *Harper's Magazine*. March. Available from: http://harpers.org/archive/2014/03/nothing-left-2/. [Accessed 28 August 2015].

Reich, R.B. (2007). *Supercapitalism*. New York: Alfred A. Knopf.

Ridley-Duff, R.J. (2009) Cooperative Social Enterprises: Company Rules, Access to Finance and Management Practice. *Social Enterprise Journal*. 5 (1). pp. 50–68.

RIPESS. (2013) Intercontinental Network for the Promotion of Social Solidarity Economy. www.ripess.org/about-us/. [Accessed 22 August 2015].

Rivarola Puntigliano, A. (2013) Brasil, America Latina y la integracion regional, Mirando el futuro: América del Sur, integración, partición, o convergencia? *Revista do IMEA-UNILA*. 1 (2). pp. 73–87. Available from: https://revistas.unila.edu.br/index.php/IMEA-UNILA/article/view/183/165. [Accessed 24 August 2015].

Rodríguez, A. (2013) Para la defensa de la vida, la paz y el desarrollo de la región – UNASUR: una estrategia integral. *América latina en movimiento*. 488: 'Recursos y desarrollo: Estrategias en la unión suramericana'. September. pp. 2–6.

Rodríguez, E. and López, A. (2011) La UBPC: forma de rediseñar la propiedad estatal con gestión cooperative. In Piñeiro Harnecker, C. (ed.). *Cooperativas y socialismo: Una mirada desde Cuba*. La Habana: Ed. Caminos. pp. 337–365.

Rogers, H. (2010) *Green Gone Wrong: How Our Economy Is Undermining the Environmental Revolution*. New York: Scribner.

Rowe, J. (2013) *Our Common Wealth: The Hidden Economy That Makes Everything Else Work*. San Francisco, CA: Berrett-Koehler.

Rubin, R. (2014) How Ignoring Climate Change Could Sink the US Economy. *Washington Post*. 24 July. Available from: www.washingtonpost.com/opinions/robert-rubin-how-ignoring-climate-change-could-sink-the-us-economy/2014/07/24/b7b4c00c-0df6-11e4-8341-b8072b1e7348_story.html. [Accessed 28 August 2015].

Ruggeri, A. (2005) *Las empresas recuperadas en la Argentina. Informe del segundo relevamiento del Programa Facultad Abierta*. Buenos Aires: Facultad de Filosofía y Letras de la Universidad de Buenos Aires.

Ruggeri, A. (2009a) *Las empresas recuperadas: autogestión obrera en Argentina y América Latina*. Buenos Aires: Editorial de la Facultad de Filosofía y Letras.

Ruggeri, A. (2009b) *La economía de los trabajadores: autogestión y distribución de la riqueza*. Buenos Aires: Ediciones de la cooperativa Chilavert.

Ruggeri, A. (2011) *Las empresas recuperadas en la Argentina. Informe del tercer relevamiento de empresas recuperadas*. Buenos Aires: Ediciones de la Cooperativa Chilavert.

Ruggeri, A. (2012) Historia de la autogestión. Los comienzos. *Revista Autogestión*. 21 (1). October.

Ruggeri, A. (2013) Historia de la autogestión. Los pioneros de Rochdale. *Revista Autogestión*. 21 (2). January.

Ruggeri, A. (ed.). (2014) *Nuevas empresas recuperadas, 2010–2013. IV relevamiento*. Biblioteca Economia de los Trabajadores. Buenos Aires: Ediciones Continente/Peña Lillo.

Ruggeri, A., Martínez, C. and Trinchero, H. (2005) *Las empresas recuperadas en la Argentina. Informe del segundo relevamiento de empresas recuperadas por los trabajadores*. Buenos Aires: Facultad de Filosofía y Letras-UBA.

Sacchetto, D. and Semenzin, M. (2013) Workers' Cooperatives in Italy between Solidarity and Autocratic Centralism. International Forum Rethinking Economy: Social/Solidarity Economy in China and the World. U-PolyU China Social Work Research Centre, Beijing. 27–28 April 2013.

Sale, K. (1996) *Rebels against the Future: The Luddites and Their War on the Industrial Revolution: Lessons for the Computer Age*. Reading, MA: Basic Books.

Sardá de Faria, M. (2011) *Autogestão, cooperativa, economia solidária: avatares do trabalho e do capital*. Florianópolis, Brazil: Editora Em Debate, Universidade Federal de Santa Catarina.

Sarria Icaza, A.M. and Tiribia, L. (2004) Economía popular. In Cattani, A.D. (ed.). *La otra economía*. Buenos Aires: Editorial Altamira. pp. 173–186.

Schwartz, J. (2014) Rockefellers, Heirs to an Oil Fortune Will Divest Charity from Fossil Fuels. *New York Times*. 21 September. Available from: www.nytimes.com/2014/09/22/us/heirs-to-an-oil-fortune-join-the-divestment-drive.html. [Accessed 12 August 2015].

Schweickart, D. (2011) *After Capitalism*. 2nd edition. Lanham, MD: Rowman and Littlefield.

Scott, J. (1998) *Seeing Like a State: How Certain Schemes to Improve the Human Condition Have Failed*. New Haven, CT and London: Yale University Press.

Sen, A. (1999) *Development as Freedom*. New York: Knopf.

Sen, A. (2009) *The Idea of Justice*. Cambridge, MA: Harvard University Press.

Sharzer, G. (2012) *No Local: Why Small-Scale Alternatives Won't Change the World*. Winchester, UK and Washington, DC: Zero Books.

Shukaitis, S. (2010) Sisyphus and the Labour of Imagination: Autonomy, Cultural Production, and the Antinomies of Worker Self-management. *Affinities: A Journal of Radical Theory, Culture and Action*. 4 (1). pp. 57–82. Available from: http://journals.sfu.ca/affinities/index.php/affinities/article/view/52/156. [Accessed 18 August 2015].

Shutt, H. (1998) *The Trouble with Capitalism: An Inquiry into the Causes of Global Economic Failure*. London: Zed Books.

Singer, P. and Souza, A.R. (eds). (2000) *A economia solidária no Brasil: A autogestão como resposta ao desemprego*. São Paulo: Contexto.

Solomon, J. (2014) These Young People Are Pioneering Appalachia's Post-Coal Economy. *Yes! Magazine*. 17 July. Available from: www.yesmagazine.org/commonomics/these-young-people-are-pioneering-a-post-coal-economy-in-appalachia. [Accessed 14 August 2015].

Sotelo, V. and Francke, P. (2011) Es economicamente viable una economia postextractivista en el Peru? In Alayza, A. and Gudynas, E. (eds). *Transiciones. Post extractivismo y alternativas al extractivismo en el Peru*. Lima: Ediciones del CEPES. pp. 115–142. Available from: www.redge.org.pe/sites/default/files/tema_5_Vicente%20Sotelo%20y%20Pedro%20Francke.pdf. [Accessed 22 August 2015].

Sousa Santos, B. (2007) Más allá de la gobernanza neoliberal: El Foro Social Mundial como legalidad y politica cosmopolitas subalternas. In Sousa Santos, B. and Rodriguez Garavito, C.A. (eds). *El derecho y la globalizacion desde abajo. Hacia una legalidad cosmopolita*. Mexico: Anthropos. pp. 31–60.

Spannos, C. (ed.) (2008) *Real Utopia: Participatory Society for the 21st Century*. Oakland, CA: AK Press.

Stevens, L. (2002) *Zapata Lives! Histories and Cultural Politics in Southern Mexico*. Berkeley, CA: University of California Press.

Streeck, W. (2011) The Crises of Democratic Capitalism. *New Left Review.* 71. September/October. pp. 5–29.

Subcomandante Marcos. (2003) Chiapas: La treceava estela. EZLN Press Release, February. Available from: http://komanilel.org/BIBLIOTECA_VIRTUAL/treceava_estela.pdf [Accessed 4 April 2016].

Subcomandante Marcos. (2004a) *The Speed of Dreams Part Two: Shoes, Sneakers, Flip-Flops, Sandals and Heels.* Translated by irlandesa. Available from: http://caminarpreguntando.pbworks.com/w/page/13443404/Speed%20of%20Dreams. [Accessed 14 August 2015].

Subcomandante Marcos. (2004b) Leer un video. Cuarta parte: Cuatro falacias. *La Jornada.* 23 August. pp. 7–9.

Subcomandante Marcos. (2004c) Leer un video. Primera parte: Un islote. EZLN Press Release. 20 August. Available from: http://enlacezapatista.ezln.org.mx/2004/08/20/leer-un-video-primera-parte-un-islote/ [Accessed 4 April 2016].

Subcomandante Marcos. (2012) EZLN Press Release. 21 December. Available from: www.enlacezapatista.ezln.org.mx [Accessed 4 April 2016].

Svampa, M. (2012) Resource Extractivism and Alternatives: Latin American Perspectives on Development. In Lang, M. and Mokrani, D. (eds). *Beyond Development: Alternative Visions from Latin America.* Quito: TNI/Rosa Luxemburg Foundation. pp. 117–144.

The Editorial Collective. (1994) *¡Zapatistas! Documents of the New Mexican Revolution.* Brooklyn, NY: Autonomedia.

The Working World. (n.d.) *WORCs – Worker-Owned Rockaway Cooperatives.* Available from: www.theworkingworld.org/us/341–2/worker-owned-rockaway-cooperatives/. [Accessed 14 August 2015].

Thompson, E.P. (1991) *Customs in Common.* New York: New Press.

Thompson, M.J. (2011) The Limits of Liberalism: A Republican Theory of Social Justice. *International Journal of Ethics.* 71 (3–4). pp. 1–21.

Trinchero, H.H. (2009) De la exclusión a la autogestión: innovación social desde las empresas recuperadas por sus trabajadores (ERT). In Ruggeri, A. (ed.). *La economía de los trabajadores: autogestión y distribución de la riqueza.* Selection of works presented to the First International Meeting. Open Faculty Program. Buenos Aires: Ediciones de la Cooperativa Chilavert. pp. 19–48.

Valdés Paz, J. (2009) *Los procesos de organización agraria en Cuba. 1959–2006.* La Habana: Fundación Antonio Núñez Jiménez de la Naturaleza y el Hombre.

Van Arsdale, D. and McCabe, M.P. (2012) Manifesto For Economic Democracy and Ecological Sanity. In Wolf, R. and Barsamian, D. (eds). *Occupy the Economy: Challenging Capitalism.* San Francisco, CA: City Lights. pp. 177–186.

Veltmeyer, H. (ed.) (2011) *21st Century Socialism: Reinventing the Project.* Halifax and Winnipeg: Fernwood Publishing.

Vieta, M. (ed.). (2010) The New Cooperativism. *Affinities: A Journal of Radical Theory, Culture and Action,* 4 (1). pp. 1–11. Available from: http://journals.sfu.ca/affinities/index.php/affinities/issue/view/4/showToc. [Accessed 13 August 2015].

Vieta, M. (2014) Learning in Struggle: Argentina's New Worker Cooperatives as Transformative Learning Organizations. *Relations Industrielles/Industrial Relations.* 69 (1). pp. 186–218.

Vieta, M. (2015) The Stream of Self-Determination and *Autogestión*: Prefiguring Alternative Economic Realities. *Ephemera: Theory and Politics in Organization.* 14 (4). pp. 779–806.

Vieta, M. (2016) *There's No Stopping the Workers: Crisis, Autogestión, and Argentina's Worker-Recuperated Enterprises.* Leiden and Chicago: Brill and Haymarket Books.

Villegas, P. (2013) Geopolítica de las carreteras y el saqueo de los recursos naturales. *Centro de Documentación e Información Bolivia – CEDIB.* Available from: www.cedib.org/publicaciones/descarga-geopolitica-de-las-carreteras-y-el-saqueo-de-los-recursos-naturales/. [Accessed 18 August 2015].

Vonnegut, K. (2005) *A Man without a Country.* New York: Seven Stories Press.

Webber, J. (2012a) Revolution against Progress: The TIPNIS Struggle and Class Contradictions in Bolivia. *International Socialism.* 133. Spring. Available from: www.isj.org.uk/?id=780. [Accessed 23 August 2015].

Webber, J. (2012b) Emancipation by Dispossession? A Rejoinder to Federico Fuentes. *International Socialism.* 136. Fall. Available from: www.isj.org.uk/index.php4?id=856&issue=136. [Accessed 12 August 2015].

Wilpert, G. (2007) *Changing Venezuela by Taking Power: The History and Policies of the Chavez Government.* London and New York: Verso.

Wolff, R. (2012a) *Occupy the Economy: Challenging Capitalism.* San Francisco: City Lights Books.

Wolff, R. (2012b) *Democracy at Work: A Cure for Capitalism.* Chicago: Haymarket Books.

Wolin, S. (2010) *Democracy Incorporated: Managed Democracy and the Specter of Inverted Totalitarianism.* Princeton, NJ: Princeton University Press.

Wright, E.O. (2010) *Envisioning Real Utopias.* London and New York: Verso.

Zamagni, S. and Zamagni, V. (2010) *Cooperative Enterprise: Facing the Challenge of Globalization.* Cheltenham, UK: Edward Elgar.

Zapatistas (2013) *Autonomous Resistance. First Grade Textbook for the Course 'Freedom According to the Zapatistas'.* Translated by the El Kilombo Collective. Available from: http://schoolsforchiapas.org/wp-content/uploads/2014/03/EZLN-2013-AutonomousResistance.pdf. [Accessed 14 August 2015].

Zibechi, R. (2012) *Territories in Resistance: A Cartography of Latin American Social Movements.* Oakland, CA: AK Press.

Zibechi, R. (2013) The Challenges of the Pacific Alliance: Regional Sovereignty or a Pampered Periphery. Available from: http://alainet.org/en/active/65035. [Accessed 12 August 2015].

Zibechi, R. (2014) *Until the Rulers Obey: Voices from Latin American Social Movements.* Oakland, CA: PM Press.

Žižek, S. (2012) *The Year of Dreaming Dangerously.* London and New York: Verso.

Žižek, S. (2014) Rotherham Child Sex Abuse: It Is Our Duty to Ask Difficult Questions. *The Guardian – Opinion.* Available from: www.theguardian.com/commentisfree/2014/sep/01/rotherham-child-sex-abuse-difficult-questions. [Accessed 14 August 2015].

Žižek, S. (2015) Greece: The Courage of Hopefulness. *The New Statesman.* 22 July. Available from: www.newstatesman.com/world-affairs/2015/07/slavoj-i-ek-greece-courage-hopelessness. [Accessed 14 August 2015].

Index

For Product Safety Concerns and Information please contact our EU
representative GPSR@taylorandfrancis.com
Taylor & Francis Verlag GmbH, Kaufingerstraße 24, 80331 München, Germany

www.ingramcontent.com/pod-product-compliance
Ingram Content Group UK Ltd.
Pitfield, Milton Keynes, MK11 3LW, UK
UKHW021850240425
457818UK00020B/790